DRAGONFLY

BALIDOVA AND THE DRAGON

LISA MK LING

This is a work of fiction. Names, characters, places, events, and incidents are products of the author's imagination or used fictitiously.

Copyright © 2022 Lisa M.K. Ling
DragonFly: Balidova and the dragon
Published by Universal Dynamic FLoW

The moral right of the author has been asserted.

All rights reserved. No part of this publication may be reproduced, distributed or transmitted in any form or by any means, including photocopying, recording, or other electronic or mechanical methods, without the prior written permission of the publisher, except in the case of brief quotations embodied in critical reviews and certain other noncommercial uses permitted by copyright law.

Although the author and publisher have made every effort to ensure that the information in this book was correct at press time, the author and publisher do not assume and hereby disclaim any liability to any party for any loss, damage, or disruption caused by errors or omissions, whether such errors or omissions result from negligence, accident, or any other cause.

Adherence to all applicable laws and regulations, including international, federal, state and local governing professional licensing, business practices, advertising, and all other aspects of doing business in the US, Canada or any other jurisdiction is the sole responsibility of the reader and consumer.

Neither the author nor the publisher assumes any responsibility or liability whatsoever on behalf of the consumer or reader of this material. Any perceived slight of any individual or organization is purely unintentional.

The resources in this book are provided for informational purposes only and should not be used to replace the specialized training and professional judgment of a health care or mental health care professional.

Neither the author nor the publisher can be held responsible for the use of the information provided within this book. Please always consult a trained professional before making any decision regarding treatment of yourself or others.

ISBN: 978-1-956669-00-8

For all those who want to connect with and feel loved by the most important person in the world
— yourself.

∽

And for all the young people of the world.
May you come to know —
what lovingly powerful
creators you are.

A new story is born — Balidova prepares to enter the dragon doorway into another world.

The idea for this book came to me at the time of my daughter's 10th birthday. I thought of a girl, learning the ancient wisdom—the *dragon magic*— through the 7 steps of the dragon tail breath. I ran upstairs and told Meijin. She immediately drew this picture on the white board in our kitchen—two trees guarding the entrance to the dragon kingdom, symbolized by the door handle in the shape of a dragon's tail. She added the girl, whose name I already knew, and an evil king who tried to stop the girl from realizing her powers.

Seven years later, the first copy of this book is in my daughter's hands on her 17th birthday. The story has come alive within me, and now, for you. What if this story of the dragon magic were true? What if *you* could enter the dragon kingdom too?

Based on a true story.
Told from the perspective of the standing people.

Don't think. Feel...

*What if the tiniest bee
could affect the workings of the universe?*

*And you, being human
could too.*

KEY WORDS

Dragons of Light — dragons of fire, water, earth and air who want to free all of creation by spreading love

Dark Dragons — dragons who want to control all of creation by spreading fear

Drakoban - leading group of dark dragons

Cloak of Fear - 9 forms of fear blended together in various combinations: anger (and its close allies rage & frustration), hatred, revenge, jealousy, shame, (and it's younger cousin guilt), sadness, helplessness (and its sibling, depression), worry, doubt

Dragon Tail Breath - breathing the seven colors of light through the seven energy centers of the human body

Dragon Magic - ability to transform energy from fear to love

Balidova Forester — girl martial artist of mixed blood, who must learn the 7 steps of the dragon tail breath

April — Balidova's oldest sister

May — Balidova's second sister

June — Balidova's youngest sister

Gypsy — Balidova's mom's horse, mother of Melody

Melody — Balidova's horse, bay mare with white diamond

Nutmeg — the family dog (Akita)

Boots — the family barn cat (Calico)

Luminora — leader of the dragons of light

Gus Polter — school bully

Mr. Winston — Balidova's science teacher

Angel — Balidova's best friend

A.R.M. — **A**ccept, **R**elease, **M**ove on

S.D.R.W. — **S**top, **D**etach, **R**emove your commitment to the emotion, **W**rap it with love and let it go

G.R.C.H. — **G**ood, **R**elaxed, **C**alm, **H**appy

Karate words:
    sensei - karate teacher
    seiza - kneeling position, back straight, eyes forward
    mokso - eyes closed
    shomani rei - forward-facing bow
    octogani rei - partner-facing bow
    hajime / yame - start / stop a karate match
    bunkai - application of kata moves with a live partner
    kata - pre-arranged sequence of moves on your own
    kumite - free-sparring with an opponent
    gi - karate uniform
    dojo - the place where martial arts training occurs

ocean

Wolf Mountain

home

M.E.S.S.

K.G.H.

Road to town

the place where it all began

KITIMAT VALLEY

crystal cave

lagoon

river

meadow

barn

Riding ring

water tower

oldest cedar

Giant Sitka Spruce

CONTENTS

Message from the Trees	xvii
In the Beginning	1
1. Twelfth Birthday	5
2. The Butcher Knife	17
3. Fight for Approval	27
4. Trapped in Her Head	41
5. Unexpected Encounters	57
6. Chopping Wood	67
7. The Emerald Green Light	81
8. A Weight Lifted	101
9. Karate Confusion	115
10. The Riddle	121
11. Golden Light Stream	131
12. Balidova Ostracized	143
13. The Forester Sisters	153
14. Blue Light Breath	165
15. The Horse Barn	183
16. A Powerful Decision	191
17. Family Dinner	203
18. The Four Elements	219
19. ARMed with Orange Light	231
20. Sisters Jealous	247
21. Teacher Trust	257
22. Bully Brewing	271
23. Not Enough	283
24. Indigo Light Vision	293
25. The Knowing	307
26. Elimination Rounds	319
27. All Tied Up	327
28. Red Light Root	337

29. The Finals	357
30. Potions	365
31. Purple Light Crown	381
32. The Oldest Cedar	397
33. Transformation Circle	411
34. The Giant Sitka Spruce	419
35. Dangerous Doubts	435
36. Dragon Flight	447
37. I am ME	459
38. The Secret	467
Message from the Trees	479
Message from the Author	480
Dragon Magic	487
Feel	488
Breathe	489
Listen	490
The DragonFly Oath	491
Dear Reader	492
Coming soon	493
Acknowledgments	495
About the Author	496
Connect	497

MESSAGE FROM THE TREES

This is a story that has been told
amongst the oldest trees on earth...
the aspen and cedar,
the oak and pine,
the sequoia and cypress,
the yew, frankincense, and myrrh,
and the giant Sitka spruce.

We are the standing people.
The historians of the planet.
With the longest memory
of what happened...
in the beginning.

IN THE BEGINNING

L ong, long ago, when there was only darkness all around, dragons were born. And they, in turn, created the heavens and the earth.

Fire dragons created warmth and light. Water dragons created liquid and flow. Earth dragons created the solidity of sand, soil, and stone, as well as trees, minerals, and metals. Air dragons created the winds and the open sky. Together, these dragons of creation were known as the *Dragons of Light*. Dragon magic formed the basis of all things... an energetic current running through everything in the universe.

After the earth was formed, creatures who lived on the planet were also formed to tend to it. Animals made from the earth elements of fire, water, soil, and air. Fireflies, fish, bears, birds, and many more beings who could live in harmony with the earth. Some of these creatures had antennae, some had scales, some had claws, and some had wings. Some were six legged, some four-legged, others two-legged, and still others no-legged. One of these was designed to care for all the other creatures. This one was called human.

But several of the dragons wanted to maintain power over their earthly creations. Rather than let humans decide how to live and allow free will to flourish, they turned to destruction and control instead. They became known as the *Drakoban*. Although few in number, they grew in power over time. Since the beginning, they have battled the Dragons of Light for authority over human souls—the Drakoban seeking to control through fear and the Dragons of Light seeking to free with love.

Over the past thirteen thousand years, the Drakoban have slowly been gaining power through the addictive use of chaos, conflict, and competition. Their energetic *Cloak of Fear*, which blankets the earth, is tightening its grip daily and is nearly complete in its dark coverage.

Now, only a human with great inner strength can tip the scales of darkness toward the light by mastering the dragon magic—the magic frequency woven through the fabric of all creation.

This human must learn all seven steps of the *Dragon Tail Breath*. And be able to breathe the seven colors of light through the seven energy centers of their body, igniting the dragon magic within.

Only a human who chooses to do this by her or his own free will, and then uses that magic to create for good, can prevent the Cloak of Fear from sealing over the earth and trapping human souls in darkness forever.

All of this must happen very soon because the ancient myth says,

> "Before seven moons pass
> in the twelfth year
> of the one human,
> all shall be complete."

Although many people have tried, many have failed. The last remaining hope of the Dragons of Light rests with one girl. She alone has the power to wield the dragon magic to shatter the Cloak of Fear.

Will she use it for herself? For the good of all? Or to destroy? Little does this girl know just how much of life hangs in the balance.

CHAPTER 1
TWELFTH BIRTHDAY

Balidova woke up with a start.

"Ugh," she groaned, "it's my turn to muck the stalls."

It was Saturday, and that meant two things. Well, three. One, it was her turn to clean the manure from the horse barn. Two, Saturday morning karate workout in the basement dojo with her dad and sisters. *Seriously? Training on a weekend? Why can't I be normal like any other kid and watch TV straight away?* Three, if she was lucky and there was still time... Saturday morning cartoons.

Then she remembered something. Something that eclipsed all the stuff she was complaining about. Today, December 31, the last day of the year, was special for another very important reason.

She sat up excitedly in bed. All groaning disappeared in an instant. "As of 9:06 a.m., I'll be my favorite number! It's my birthday!"

Balidova liked to talk to herself, whether out loud or silently, and this morning was no exception. Her inner dialogue—the voice in her head—was going strong already. As usual, it was quite a chatterbox.

There are two twelve-hour periods in a day, twelve months in a year, and twelve sets of ribs in my body! Twelve animals in the Chinese Zodiac. The Year of the Dragon is the best, of course—that's the year I was born.

"Hmm, twelve whole years on planet earth. I wonder what's in store for me today," she mused, sliding out of bed into her comfy slippers and glancing at the golden reading glasses on her desk. She loved her golden frames. Wearing them, she felt serene, smart, and strong, as if they gave her a different perspective on life. "First, how about some yummy breakfast?"

She stepped out of her fleece pajamas and put on a pair of torn blue jeans. Not 'fake' torn but actually torn from getting caught on the barbed-wire fence surrounding the pig pen. She pulled a purple long-sleeve shirt with a dragon on it over her head to complete her outfit. Beside it lay a purple scarf her mother had given her long ago.

"From a trip to Indonesia that we went on when you were a baby," her mom had told her. The scarf was one of Balidova's favorite things—she loved to wrap herself in it whenever she felt lonely.

On the way to the bathroom, she glanced at herself in the mirror. "Hah, my fav color on my fav day of the year. Purple on my birthday—burple!" she laughed, blending the words into one. She liked doing that. Blending things, transforming things, playing with things—to make something new. And she was good at it.

She had her rocks. She was always collecting rocks. All shapes and sizes. All colors and textures. Shiny, smooth, rough, cracked, dull, flat, round, jagged, pointy, sharp, even, and uneven. She especially liked the ones that no one else seemed to want. She liked things that were out of the ordinary. Not cast-a-ways, but extra-ordinary, she liked to think of them. Extraordinary. The rocks lay haphazardly in a pile on her desk, spilling out of a series of old glass jam jars.

Next to them was her slingshot, which she had made herself out of a perfect, Y-shaped spruce branch, notched at the ends and tied with a thick strip of rubber tubing and a small piece of leather in the middle. Together, the rocks and the slingshot made a dangerous combo—her weapon of choice. Balidova was a dynamite shot. She could hit a bullseye from fifty feet away.

Brushing her hair in the bathroom, she looked intently in the mirror, staring into her own eyes. Getting lost in their familiar milky brown depth, she looked at one eye, then the other. She noticed how her perception changed as if she were moving her whole body and standing in a different spot.

Balidova was a pretty girl, although she didn't know it. And didn't care, to be honest. She pulled her hair back into a ponytail, revealing an oval face, slender nose, and small ears. Her brown eyes merged with brown eyebrows and brown shoulder-length hair.

Except for the green tinge in my left eye, I'm a sea of brown.

As she looked intently in the mirror, her attention suddenly shifted to the delicious smell coming from the kitchen.

SHE RAN DOWNSTAIRS, following the scent of pancakes with whipped cream and strawberries that had wafted up to the second floor of the house where her bedroom was. She smelled it all the way down, salivating with anticipation by the time she reached the kitchen three seconds later.

Her mom was standing by the stove, flipping light brown, fluffy packets of dough onto a plate. Her once lean body had become stout over the years after bearing and raising four children from the age of twenty. Shoulder-length brown hair hung over her square face, revealing Scottish features, including a small indent under her nose, on the thin cartilage strip separating the two nostrils.

"Slow down. It's not a race," her mom said after watching Balidova gulp down a few large bites.

"But it's so good! I can't get enough of it. We don't get this every day, so I have to make the most of it. Especially today." Balidova waited for her mom to get the hint, but she didn't respond. She just continued dropping batter into the frying pan.

Huh, she must have forgotten. Oh well, could be worse. At least I got something yummy for breakfast.

"Good morning," her little sister, June, said as she sat down across the table from Balidova. Her baby pink shirt went perfectly with her position in the family. "Wassup?"

"Pancakes are good. That's wassup," Balidova replied. "Oh, and what time is karate workout this morning?"

"Workout's off coz Dad's not feeling well," her sister announced as she drizzled strawberry sauce onto her plate.

No workout? Another surprise birthday gift. But I wonder if anyone in this family will remember.

Just then, her two older sisters joined them at the table. April was older than Balidova by almost three years. May was barely a year older. All the Forester girls looked similar, with dark brown hair in various lengths, brown eyes with a crease above the lids, and Eurasian features. They were all of average height, although Balidova was the tallest, despite being the third child. And they had good muscle tone underneath their smooth olive-colored skin.

Neither of them said anything when they sat down for breakfast. The two older girls glanced at the two younger ones as if they barely existed. As Balidova and her sisters chowed down, only the sound of forks clinking on plates and hungry mouths chewing could be heard. The four girls ate in silence.

Looking around the table at her sisters, Balidova couldn't help wondering... *Why's my name so different from everyone else's? Ba-li-do-va is four syllables. And it's a weird name. All my sister's name's are one or two syllables. They're named after months of the year. And in order! April's the oldest. May's in the middle, like me. June's the youngest.*

Suddenly, Balidova's mind snapped back to the fact that it was her birthday.

I guess nobody remembered.

She got up and put her plate in the dishwasher, ready to head out to the barn.

Well, that's just awesome. My one special day of the year, and no one clues in. I've always felt like I don't belong in this family, but this is too much. I'm done with this.

BY THE TIME she made it out to the barn, Balidova was more than a little upset. Her indignation had risen to a fever pitch as she put on her thick wool socks, hat, gloves, gumboots, and a heavy jacket to protect against the bone-chilling winter weather. The last day of the year was traditionally also one of the coldest, with temperatures dropping well below freezing. She exited the house and stomped across the yard, through a well-worn path in the deep snow to the reddish-brown barn that stood on the far edge of the property, bordered by an unending forest of evergreen trees. Behind that barn lay hundreds of miles of wilderness, stretching up the British Columbia coast to the Yukon and Alaska. The cold, white, snow-covered landscape was a stark contrast to the raging fire that burned within her.

Before opening the large double doors, she stood fuming. *Everyone's forgotten my birthday. How could they?* She felt like crying, she was so mad. Mad and sad at the same time—*smad*. She stood there all alone, shaking.

A single tear rolled down her cheek.

And then another.

The barn cat, Boots, sauntered up and rubbed against her leg, purring loudly as its black, white, and grey calico fur stood out against the snow. She bent down and touched her hand along its back.

All of a sudden, she heard whinnying from the other side of the doors. The horses knew she was there, and they were calling for her. *Her* horse was calling for her. Balidova wiped her tears and leaned into the heavy wooden doors, sliding them apart. She took in a deep breath as she entered the dusty hay and manure-smelling space of the barn. With that one breath, she was transported to a whole different world.

She loved the musty smell of last season's hay, stacked high to the cobweb-filled, swallow-pooped roof beams holding up the deep red barn. Somehow, she felt closer to the ground they lived on walking into this building—home to horses, cows, pigs, chickens, goats, dogs, cats, owls, mice, and the occasional rat. As if stepping into the place that housed the earth's creatures brought her closer to the earth itself.

Balidova walked down the barn hallway, saying good morning to the horses as she passed by. The old mare, Gypsy, stuck her big brown head over the stall door. Balidova stopped to pat her, rubbing the white mark between her soft eyes.

Gypsy was a gentle giant. As a young girl, her mom had raised Gypsy with her father—Balidova's grandfather. Together, over the years, they poured so much love into that little filly and, at the same time, taught one another what a loving relationship could be like. Now, Gypsy was an old mare with the great big hooves of a Clydesdale and delicate eyes of an Arabian. An unusual mix of breeds.

Kinda like me, Balidova mused.

Balidova continued down the aisle way of the barn, talking to each horse in turn. Harmony, June's horse, was on the left. Hurricane was next to her, belonging to her second sister, May. April didn't have a horse—she just wasn't a horse person. Last but not least was Balidova's horse, Melody, at the far end.

Melody poked her head out of the stall curiously to see who was coming. When she saw Balidova, her ears perked forward, and she whinnied softly, her big brown eyes sparkling with delight.

Seeing the four-legged beauty, Balidova was immediately grateful to her mom. Her mom was why they had moved from their small house in town to a larger property in Cablecar, with lots big enough to accommodate large animals. Because of her mom's dogged persistence, the family brought Gypsy up north in the back of a pickup truck, on an eighteen-hour journey from Vancouver, through central British Columbia. Her mom insisted they have horses and would have it no other way. She loved that mare and wanted to share her love of horses with her children.

Balidova's dad argued that horses were too expensive, too impractical, and too time-consuming. But her mom knew the gentle animals could provide a kind of unconditional love that her daughters couldn't get elsewhere. Eventually, she found the right argument to convince him.

"If you get to share what you love with our daughters—martial arts—why can't I?"

Finally, he had given in. After Gypsy's arrival, more horses arrived too—from other farms. A few years later, Gypsy had a baby—Melody. Before long, each of the girls had their own horse to love and be loved by.

"Time for breakfast, eh?" Balidova rubbed her hand over Melody's face, allowing her fingers to outline the perfect white diamond between Melody's eyes—just like her mama—then follow the white stripe down to the little mare's muzzle. She loved caressing the soft skin around Melody's nose and especially loved cupping the egg-shaped skin under her mouth.

Just as Balidova was losing herself in the softness, Melody pumped her head up and down impatiently.

"Okay, okay, I get it. You want breakfast," Balidova responded, jumping into action with the morning feeding routine. She was well-versed in what to do as the four sisters took turns feeding horses and mucking stalls in the morning. Saturday was Balidova's day, which was good and bad. Good, because she knew she wouldn't be disturbed in her peaceful haven of the barn. Bad, because she couldn't sleep in on the weekends.

Opening up the feed room, she threw a hay bale into the wheelbarrow and proceeded down the barn aisle throwing two flakes of hay into each stall. She sang, "Two for you, and two for you... hay for you to eat and poo!"

Although Balidova was only twelve, a fifty-pound bale of hay was no problem for her to throw around. She had already been training karate for a decade—as soon as she could walk and run, she learned how to kick and punch. She had well-formed muscles on her arms and legs, chest, and back. Karate requires both upper and lower body techniques in equal measure, and after thousands of sit-ups, the core of her body was quite literally as strong as a horse.

After feeding all the animals, Balidova got busy with the next part of the morning barn routine—mucking stalls. She grabbed a pitchfork and wheelbarrow, stationed them in front of Gypsy's open stall door so the horse couldn't get out, and proceeded to scoop round, dry pellets into the wheelbarrow, lifting then shaking the pitchfork so the good sawdust could escape. When all the large clumps of manure were collected, she went after the wet bits, where the sawdust was a darker color. She stabbed deep down to the floor to get the wettest, poopiest parts of the stall.

Each time the wheelbarrow was full, she hauled it out to the manure pile and dumped it unceremoniously.

She took out her anger and frustration toward her family on the muck—attacking it with the pitchfork and flinging big chunks of manure into the wheelbarrow as if shoveling poopy thoughts and feelings out of herself. Working up a sweat with her vigorous labor, she felt better as each drop fell from her forehead.

Exercise had a way of doing that for Balidova. Moving her body moved bad feelings around too, so they could work their way through.

After all, emotion is just E-motion.

Energy in motion.

She remembered her karate sensei telling her.

I'd better put my body in motion to move these feelings around and outta me.

Around the fifth wheelbarrow, as she finished the job of mucking stalls, a feeling of relief came over Balidova. She put down her pitchfork, said goodbye to the horses, and returned to the house. It was lunchtime, and she was getting hungry. Although there was a lot of horse food in the barn, there was nothing *she* could eat.

She sighed at the thought of returning to the people closest to her—the same people who'd forgotten her birthday—her own family.

"Oh well, I still love them, I guess."

Somehow the sting didn't feel as bad as it did earlier. She had simply let go of most of it into the manure pile.

BACK IN THE HOUSE, Balidova rounded the corner of the hallway into the kitchen and spotted a brown and white round object, about six inches high and a foot in diameter, sitting on the countertop.

"Is that what I think it is?" she said aloud, thinking she was alone.

"Yes, it is." her mom replied. "You thought we forgot, didn't you?"

"Well, uh, yeah. I did. No one said anything."

Her mom looked up and smiled, revealing stress lines around her eyes. "We wouldn't do that, Balidova. I may be absent-minded, but I'm not that thoughtless."

"I thought you didn't care," Balidova's lip trembled, still tender from the earlier hurt.

"No way, we just wanted to surprise you."

Balidova grunted, unconvinced, biting her lip to fight back the tears.

A delicious, large, wonderful-looking black forest cake stood staring at her from the counter, complete with whipped cream, chocolate sprinkles, and red maraschino cherries, making a ring of twelve around the top.

"We have another surprise for you, too," her mom continued as she handed Balidova a large package wrapped in a brown paper bag with a gold bow on top.

"What is it?"

"Go ahead, open it."

Balidova ripped open the paper to reveal a bright red, puffy, down jacket. She held it up against her body, beaming from ear to ear. "It's brand new!"

"It'll come in handy out there with all the cold weather," her mom chuckled. "I thought you'd like your own, not one of your sisters' hand-me-downs."

Balidova tried the jacket on. It fit perfectly. Looking at the coat and the cake, thinking about what they represented to her—the love and acknowledgment of her family—a smile of deep satisfaction slowly spread across her face.

Funny how you can want something so bad.

And it doesn't come.

But when you finally let it go, it rushes in.

She looked up. "Thanks, Mom. I guess this isn't such a bad birthday after all."

Neither of them had any idea just how important this birthday, or the red jacket, would become.

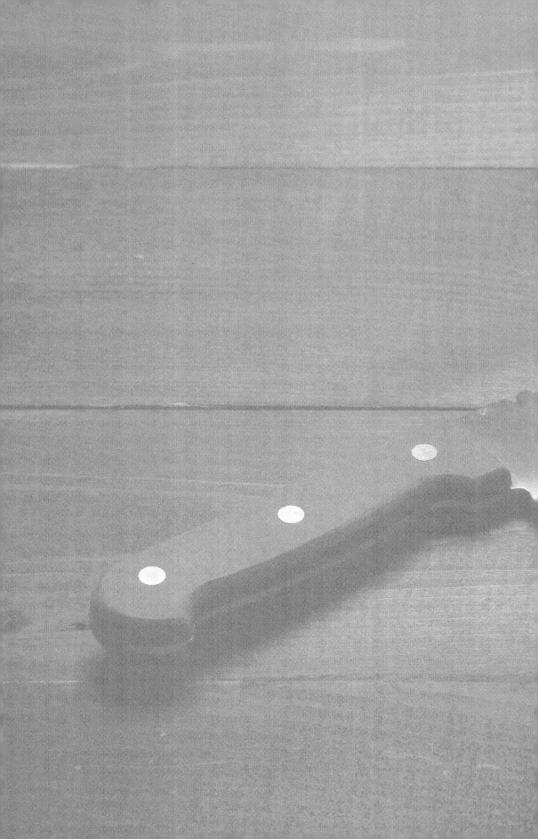

CHAPTER 2
THE BUTCHER KNIFE

Balidova couldn't decide what to wear. Her whole family, all six of them, were going to a New Year's Day celebration at the Community Center. The place where they lived—Kitimat—was a small town on the Pacific coast, at the head of a long seagoing channel, way up in Northern British Columbia, Canada. The name meant "People of the Snow" in the language of the Indigenous peoples who first settled there and still had their own Kitamaat Village nearby. Although the spelling had changed, the name stuck, and a white snowflake on a blue background became the Kitimat municipal flag.

A single winter could bring up to fifty feet of snow. Clouds heading east from the Pacific Ocean dumped their load upon hitting the coastal mountain range. Because the town was so far north, that meant a lot of snow in winter and a lot of rain in summer. This unique climate, wet year-round, created an old-growth rainforest home to one of the tallest trees in the world—the Giant Sitka Spruce.

At the community celebration, Balidova's dad would be talking to many people because he was the town doctor, so she couldn't just wear her grubby jeans and t-shirt. She had to look "presentable," according to her mom.

She stood in front of her messy closet in her underwear. Muscles rippled along her strong, lean body as she struggled with her options. *I like my purple shirt. AND I also like this orange one. My two favorite colors. Which one will it be?* She couldn't decide and went back and forth until she finally gave up. She could feel in her gut that she wanted the purple one, but her head said, *You wore that yesterday,* so she was stuck. She didn't trust herself over such a small decision. She hated wearing dresses and never wore pink, but deciding between her two favorite colors? She was torn between her gut feeling and her brain logic.

My gut and my head feel like they're in a tug-o-war.

Balidova could feel something pulling her toward the purple shirt but let her mind override it. She grabbed the orange one.

As she got dressed, she noticed something that surprised her—how quiet the house was. Unusually quiet. Peaceful even. She got still and listened closely—she could hear the clock ticking in the living room, the birds chirping outside her window.

Balidova smiled.

It was a rare peace she desperately craved that didn't often happen amidst the daily emotional chaos of four strong, active girls and a very opinionated and stubborn set of parents.

Just then, she heard loud voices coming from downstairs. She peeked over the railing outside her room and noticed it was her mom and dad, shouting at each other in the kitchen.

Well, so much for peace. That quiet didn't last long.

She quickly threw on her shirt and jeans, then crept down the stairway to overhear their conversation. Her parents yelling at each other was nothing new to her, but she was curious about what they were fighting over this time.

"I don't like the sound of it," her dad said. His brown eyes squinted in annoyance on his square face.

"But it's not that loud," her mom replied.

"It's too loud for me, and we don't need it. You can do them by hand!" her dad continued, his short, black hair shaking as his temper rose.

"Easy for you to say, you don't do them!" her mom replied, also getting angrier by the minute.

"What the heck are they talking about?" Balidova wondered.

"Get the kids to help out! Do them by hand, woman!" her dad shouted, pounding his fist on the table.

Balidova's father was a short, stocky man with forearms like logs from practicing martial arts. His legs were just as big, accustomed to hard labor, even as a medical professional. He loved to work with his hands and build things out of wood—barns, houses, sheds, and doghouses. He was made like an oak tree. Solid and strong.

Suddenly, Balidova realized exactly what they were talking about—the dishes. Her mom wanted to use the dishwasher to clean them. Her dad wanted them washed by hand in the sink.

"Seriously, guys, do you have to fight over everything?" Balidova muttered to herself. "Can't you agree on something as simple as how to wash the dumb dishes? This is ridiculous."

Her illusion of peace completely shattered, Balidova sat on the stairs, thinking about all the other things she had heard her parents fighting about: Whether the girls needed to practice piano (which her mom wanted) or do karate (which her dad wanted). Money—she always heard them arguing about money. Her mom was always asking for money from her dad because he worked at the hospital while she stayed home to take care of the kids. It seemed like a great injustice to Balidova that her mom had to ask for money when she was doing just as much work as him.

Her mom always seemed to oscillate between being angry and sad. Her parents fought all the time about everything. Most of the time, Balidova saw her mom lose those fights. She saw her mom lose the money fight, lose the battle about practice time—that's why the four girls had karate workouts every other day, sometimes before school and definitely on the weekends—and lose the fight about willpower. After all, her dad was a martial arts expert—judo, karate, aikido, weapons—and her mom didn't know one bit of martial arts. She didn't even know how to do a basic kick, punch, or block. She couldn't defend herself at all.

All these thoughts ran through Balidova's mind as she sat at the top of the stairs, listening to her parents argue. Her sisters had already fled into their rooms and shut their doors. Hide—that's what they all did when fights broke out.

But this time, Balidova couldn't stand it anymore. She was twelve now. And it was New Year's Day. Was this the way to start a whole new year? She decided to go downstairs and break it up. She walked down the stairs slowly, step-by-step, gathering courage as she rounded the pillar in the middle of the stairwell and descended the last half of the stairs.

Just as she was at the kitchen doorway, she saw her dad grab a butcher knife from the counter and hold it high in the air. By now, he was beside himself with rage. He looked so upset, Balidova didn't know what he would do with the knife. Her mom was standing just a few feet away.

For a second, Balidova's whole world turned upside down as she witnessed a new level of aggression she didn't know her dad was capable of.

"Give me the cord, or else put it away," he said with a steely tone. Her dad's jaw muscle tightened, creating a small crease on the lower side of his face, a sign that his patience had worn out.

"No! I want to use it. It's my kitchen," her mom said defiantly.

"I said give it to me." He spoke each word slowly as he stepped toward her with the knife.

"NO," her mom said with stone-cold calm in her voice. Balidova wondered where her mom's resolve came from, despite the danger she faced.

That was it. That simple, two-letter word sent him over an emotional cliff. Lunging forward, he grabbed the rubber tube from her hand, threw its black length down on the wooden chopping block, and WHAM! Brought the silver blade of the butcher knife down on it with incredible force. Within a split second, the cord was severed in half.

The portable dishwasher stood alone in the center of the kitchen. A black cord pulled out and attached to the kitchen faucet from the side of the machine, a few feet away. The dishwasher was not built into the countertop. It was separate.

Now it was even more separate.

"There, NO MORE DISHWASHER!" he shouted. "You can do dishes the old-fashioned way, with some elbow grease." He dropped the knife on the chopping block and stomped out of the room.

Her mom looked aghast. She couldn't believe he'd done it.

Balidova too, was shocked. Scared. And furious.

How could Dad do this? How could Mom let him do this? How could she be so powerless, even in her domain—the kitchen! The kitchen is HER space! He came in here and told HER how to run it. Why didn't she stop him? Now we'll be doing dishes by hand forever! We'll NEVER get a new dishwasher. Mom doesn't have the money for it, and Dad will never buy one again.

Balidova gritted her teeth, looking her mom in the eyes. Her mom looked beaten down but not broken. There was a steely gaze in her green eyes as she looked at nothing in particular. Balidova's mom was the only one in the family whose eyes were not brown.

Balidova had not seen this look in her mother before. Her mom turned away from Balidova and put her hands on the edge of the sink. Her whole body trembled, but she did not cry. Balidova had seen her mom cry plenty of times before and wondered, *Why not now?*

UNBEKNOWNST TO BALIDOVA, her mother was undergoing a transformation of her own. She had reached the end of her rope. In the next few breaths, fear and panic settled down in her, transforming into a hardened resolve, like setting concrete. Shoulders hunched, fingers gripping the aluminum basin, she withdrew her fierce spirit and contracted it into a small box deep within.

Don't give up. Find a way. You have to. For the girls.

She retreated into survival mode, yet she was bound and determined to have a continuing relationship with her husband because of her daughters. She wasn't going to be a quitter. If she knew one thing and one thing only, it was that she would see her job of raising her girls through to the finish. She would never be able to face her own father if she did not fulfill that obligation.

At her lowest points, when things were very, very difficult, what kept her going was her desire not to disappoint her own father. He had shown her what loving another creature looked like by raising their beloved Gypsy together. That's what kept her from abandoning her girls. She was so emotionally exhausted and beaten down that she couldn't even do it for herself. She had to do it for someone else.

NOT KNOWING ALL that was happening inside her mother, Balidova thought she was simply recovering from yet another altercation with her dad. Balidova wanted to run over to her, console her, hug her, and tell her it was okay. But she'd done that so many times before, and look where it had gotten them? She stopped and braced herself instead. *Now we'll never be able to use the dishwasher. She couldn't protect me from having to clean dishes by hand forever! What else can't she protect me from? If he's stronger than her, what side of that equation do I want to be on?*

Balidova's mind went in circles, back and forth, oscillating between feeling sorry for her mom and being furious with her. In a flash, she caught a glint of the silver blade of the butcher knife as a speck of light entered through the kitchen window and reflected off its shiny surface. She saw the chopped cord, broken and useless, lying hopelessly beside it. Right then and there, she made a decision, secretly and silently, in her head and heart.

That's never gonna happen to me.

I'm never gonna get beaten down like that.

I'm never gonna be like my mother—weak and powerless.

BALIDOVA LOOKED at her mom's trembling body, partly in sorrow, partly in disgust. Little did the girl know that the trembling was rooted in a deliberate resolve by her mother never to let this occur again. Whatever happened, the woman had a profound flow of life within her that nothing could touch—something beautiful the woman had learned from her time spent with horses. That's what Balidova's father lost when he became violent. When the dishwasher cord was severed, something between Balidova's mom and dad was also severed. The mother put up a wall and cut that flow off from him.

But in doing so, she also cut it off from herself. There was a part of her that she shut down and put on a shelf to protect from him. In this way, her Scottish stubbornness served her well. The woman would not allow her spirit to be crushed.

Balidova squeezed both fists tightly, turned around, and marched back toward her room. Before climbing the stairs, she looked down the hallway toward her dad's office. She didn't understand everything going on, but she knew one thing—her dad was in charge of this household.

Dad's the powerful one. And I'm gonna be too.

Eyes staring straight ahead, jaw clenched, Balidova climbed slowly, deliberately up to her room. "I'm done talking to you, Mom," she whispered to herself as she placed one foot after the other on the green-carpeted stairs. "Birthday cake or not, I have nothing to say to you anymore."

In that instant, Balidova decided that aligning herself with her father was how she would get what she wanted in life.

Yet, deep within, unbeknownst to either one of them, there was something she and her mother shared—they both had a place inside that nothing and no one could touch. The mother knew this about herself but couldn't put it into words.

The girl had yet to discover it.

CHAPTER 3
FIGHT FOR APPROVAL

The next morning, Balidova woke up to the smell of freshly baked chocolate chip cookies. It was early on a Monday morning, and she knew what that meant—karate workout before school. It was something she could count on every Monday, Wednesday, and Friday.

"Oh no," she groaned. But there was no getting out of it. Her dad always insisted they train before heading off to class, especially since they had missed their weekend workout.

"The pen and the sword must be in accord" was one of her dad's favorite sayings. It meant that academics and athletics went hand in hand and were of equal importance. Also, that your words and your actions had to match.

Who works out before school?!? I just wanna sleep in and get to class on time like a normal kid. She let out a big yawn, interrupting her very loud inner dialogue. *But nooooo... early morning workouts are mandatory in our house. All four girls training with Dad. It's a thing in our family. An expected thing that you don't argue with—or else.*

Letting out a big sigh as she got out of bed, Balidova took off her fleece pj's and put on her white karate uniform. She tied her green belt around her waist and headed to the bathroom. Examining herself in the mirror as she brushed her teeth—pimples, buck teeth and all—she didn't like what she saw today but thought, *Oh well... it is what it is.*

She tiptoed downstairs into the kitchen to see if she could scoff a cookie before the workout.

"I know you're there, Balidova," her mom said absently, without turning around.

The strange thing was that the woman sounded like *she* wasn't fully there. Balidova stopped in her tracks, looked at her mom, but didn't say anything. She remembered her promise from yesterday. *I'm not speaking to you.*

Her mom didn't know Balidova had made this promise to herself, but Balidova did. And she was determined to stick to it. *If I can't trust anyone else in my family, I've gotta at least be able to trust myself, right?*

"You can have one after your workout. Go downstairs. Now. Your dad's waiting for you."

For a brief moment—at the thought of sweet, chocolaty goodness melting down her throat—Balidova perked up on the inside, careful not to show her mom the positive reaction. *Really? Thanks, Mom.*

Then she immediately returned to her critical thoughts. *Just like that, Mom acts as if yesterday never even happened. What?! Parents are weird. They're in cahoots together about doing karate even though they seem to hate each other. Mom baking cookies and bribing us while Dad cracks the whip. Even though they were fighting like crazy yesterday! Did she already forget what happened with the dishwasher? Why's she helping him?*

She looked longingly at the cookies, taking in a whiff of their sweet smell. *Oh well, whatever.*

What Balidova didn't know was that her Mom *liked* the way her daughters looked right through her when she interrupted their practice on occasion, such was their focus and concentration. She liked that her girls were learning how to channel their energy in such a fierce and determined way—even if it scared her a little. For that, she gave her husband credit. Even though he could be way out of control sometimes, he was teaching their daughters something powerful and good.

BALIDOVA HEADED down the stairs to their basement dojo. The grey concrete floor was covered with light green tatami mats ringed with two by six wooden boards to keep the mats firmly in place. A huge mirror covered the whole white wall at the far end of the room. You couldn't stand anywhere on those tatami mats without seeing yourself in the mirror. That was the point. The girls were supposed to perfect their technique by knowing what the movements felt like and what they looked like.

"Practice doesn't make perfect," her dad used to say. "*Perfect practice makes perfect.*"

Well, his meticulous attention to detail worked. The Forester girls were all club champions in their town. No one else even came close.

A faded, brown leather punching bag hung from a wooden beam at the opposite end of the room from the mirror—its long bulk stretching almost the five-foot length of Balidova herself. The dojo was right beside the room with the wood stove, so there was no worry about it getting cold down there. It was one of the hottest rooms in the house. This made for a lot of sweating during karate workouts—probably a good thing to eliminate toxins from the body, but not always welcome.

Peeeeyew! Smelly! Balidova wrinkled her nose as she passed by a large white towel that was used for wiping sweat in an attempt to reduce the noxious smell of perspiring kids. It lay draped over a puffy, flower-print, orange and gold polyester rocking chair positioned just outside the edge of the mats. When they were tired, the girls could take a break to wipe the sweat off their brows but didn't dare sit in their dad's favorite rocking chair for fear of being seriously reprimanded and labeled with just about the worst word in the Forester household—lazy.

Various weapons hung from the walls along the side of the dojo. Light brown bamboo sticks (shinai) stood out against the white wall. Her dad would whack them with the shinai when they didn't stand or punch properly. It sounded horrible, but it didn't hurt that much. It was mainly meant to scare them with the loud noise. Small wooden sticks (tonfa), long wooden sticks (bo), and two short sticks linked by a chain (nunchaku) were lined up vertically in a neat row.

Balidova glanced at the middle of the room and saw her three sisters kneeling in age order. She stepped onto the dojo floor and took her place, where there was already a space left for her. Third in line out of four. Oldest on the right, youngest on the left. All facing the mirror and their dad. Their dad facing them.

"Nice of you to join us, Balidova," her dad chuckled.

"Hmph," she replied silently. *Cookies or not, I'm still not happy about having to work out before school, especially on a Monday.* She didn't dare speak these words out loud for fear of displeasing her father.

They all sat in *seiza* position—their legs folded underneath them, sitting on their heels, barefoot even in winter when the floor was cold. Backs straight, chin tucked in, shoulders square, and hands resting neatly on their laps. They had gotten used to sitting in this position. At first, they could only hold it for a few seconds before their ankles, shins, and knees hurt. Now, it didn't bother them at all. Their hip, leg, and ankle flexibility had increased dramatically. Their body strength had risen steadily. Their discipline had doubled and doubled again. Having trained for years since they were toddlers, they could now sit like this forever.

She looked to her right at her two older sisters. *Mom told me that I was supposed to have been a boy, that Dad, being Chinese, desperately wanted a boy but got all girls instead. And after four kids, Mom, being Scottish, said, "That's it, no more. The gate is closed." So, Dad had to make do with what he had, raising us all like sons—just like he adapted by anglicizing his last name when he first came to North America as a teenager. How else do you have a name like "Forester" when your dad's Chinese?*

The four girls grew up doing all the things boys would typically do with their father on a farm—run the tractor, use the chainsaw, chop wood, build barns, fix the car, and study martial arts. Despite the vigorous, challenging nature of all these tasks, beneath the activity was an underlying tone that girls were somehow "less than" and needed to work twice as hard to be better than boys. Despite raising his family in Canada, her dad's desire for male progeny ran deep. Thousands of years of Chinese history deep. Balidova always felt she had to prove her worth—it wasn't a given.

As a boy, her father had seen the monks in the temples—of the small town in Malaysia where he grew up—practicing traditional, weaponless forms of self-defense involving great physical skill and coordination. He had wanted so badly to join them but needed to work tapping rubber trees so his family could eat. Now that he had kids of his own, he was determined to realize his childhood dream by teaching his children martial arts. Since he didn't have any sons, he wanted his daughters to be able to take care of themselves in any situation, just as sons would do. Each Asian country has its version of martial arts—kung fu, judo, kalarippayattu, kickboxing, tae kwon do, tai chi, aikido, and jujitsu, to name a few. Balidova's father settled on teaching his daughters karate, a martial art originating from Japan that he had studied while in medical school.

"Mok-so," her dad barked.

Balidova sighed and closed her eyes on command. The class had begun. It always started with a short meditation to collect your energy, thoughts, and focus. It helped you get ready for the training session ahead by bringing you right here, right now.

She inhaled through her nose as her eyelids shut. Automatically, her focus shifted inward, as if the lenses of her eyes had promptly turned around and were now scanning the inside of her body. A quiet descended upon her entire being, and she relaxed slightly. She felt a brief respite from the outside world and what everyone else wanted of her. Just as she could feel her body relax and was beginning to enjoy this tuning into herself...

"Mok-so yame!" her dad commanded.

She opened her eyes abruptly. That was the problem with karate workouts. Well, one of the problems—she didn't get to decide how long she meditated.

"Shomani rei!" he continued.

She leaned forward, placing one hand on the mat, then the other. Her forefingers and thumbs formed a triangle on the floor, into which she leaned down and put her forehead. Bowing toward the front of the dojo was a sign of respect for the teacher. During the workout, he would no longer be Dad but referred to as *Sensei*.

"Otogani rei!"

She turned sideways, facing her youngest sister, repeating the same steps. Each pair of siblings bowed to each other, showing respect for the other person and the training they were about to take part in.

"Who would like to do the warmup today?" her dad asked gruffly, eager to dispense with formalities and get moving.

"I would," her little sister, June, chimed in. She was four years younger than Balidova but had the nerve of all her sisters combined. Being the youngest, she always tried to prove she could do as much or more than her older siblings.

She came to the front of the class, faced her sisters, and smiled. She was happy to be the boss for a few moments. Without saying a word, she led them through a well-rehearsed series of movements, opening and loosening up all the major muscles and joints in the body. A few moments later, all parts of their bodies were limber, awake, and ready to go.

"Thanks, you can line up again now," her dad said to June, motioning her back to her spot.

"We need to get ready for the tournament next month," her dad continued. "Let's practice your katas."

Balidova groaned internally.

There are two main events in karate—*kata* and *kumite*. Kata is a series of pre-arranged moves that you do on your own against an imaginary opponent. You are in a ring, by yourself, with judges who sit on the four corners of the ring. When you're done, the head referee blows a whistle, and they all hold up scorecards. They give you a score based on your style, balance, speed, power, strength, flexibility, sharpness of movement, agility, and correct application of the movements.

Balidova's oldest sister, April, loved kata and was the best at it. Balidova, on the other hand, thought it was boring. But she did it anyway since it was part of the basic foundation of karate. It gave her all the basic movements to do what she really liked —kumite.

Kumite is free sparring, in a ring, with an opponent. You don't know what the other person is going to do. There is nothing pre-arranged about it. Kumite is completely spontaneous.

That's what Balidova loved about it! Everything you practiced came out in the ring. And if you didn't practice, it showed. But even with a ton of training, you had to let it all go and just pay attention—pay very close attention—to your opponent. You had to be 100% present and focused because if you got too fixed in your mind about what you were planning to do, you'd get destroyed. You wouldn't be flexible enough to anticipate moves coming from your opponent. On the other hand, if you had no plan at all, you wouldn't be able to defend against the other person's strengths or capitalize on their weaknesses.

Kumite is sort of like improvisation in music. You have to be flexible yet fixed at the same time, making up movements as you go along—something incredibly difficult to do. Like any creative discipline, it takes an awful lot of practice to make kumite look easy.

Balidova was drawn to the unpredictability of kumite training, even though it scared the heck out of her. She was always riding that thin line between fear and excitement. She loved and feared looking her opponent in the eyes—staring them down—standing on their marks, knowing that when the referee said "go," they were going to exchange blows.

Yes, it was exhilarating, AND it was scary. She never knew which side of that line she would be on.

But that's part of the fun, to feel afraid and then conquer it, she grinned mischievously.

To be honest, she didn't have much choice. Her dad would have been very disappointed if she had shied away from difficult things. It was a badge of honor in their family—to face your fears and do stuff anyway.

The alternative was grave displeasure from their father. And she definitely didn't want that. Like it or not, the intense pressure from their dad and fierce competition amongst the sisters made them all better.

How else were they supposed to develop the tiger-locked-on-its-prey focus that all the girls possessed?

But they weren't doing kumite today. That would be left for the next practice. Sparring with her sisters wasn't always a good idea. Tensions could rise and carry outside the dojo, into the house, and their lives on the farm and at school. The three older sisters went to the same high school—the only one in town—so it wasn't good if lingering tensions were spreading among them like slime.

Kata, on the other hand, didn't incite the same level of face-to-face conflict amongst the sisters. At the tournament, there was an event called "team kata," where three people standing in a triangle formation did a kata in unison. Part of what they were scored on was the synchronicity between the three, in addition to the other individual qualities of speed, strength, timing, agility, and explosive power. Because there were four girls, the sisters practiced with one extra person, forming a diamond shape so they could all do it together, even though the fourth person—June—was not included when they performed in tournaments.

BALIDOVA COULD FEEL a heaviness in the air as if each girl's exhale spread little particles of resentment in the air. With a decade of martial arts under their belts, Balidova and her sisters had executed thousands of punches and kicks. They repeated the same kata and kumite techniques hundreds of times. They all wanted to quit, but no one had the guts to tell their dad. Despite their displeasure, there was a certain solidarity amongst the four girls. They would bear the burden of this workout together.

As Balidova looked around the room at their diamond configuration—oldest out in front, the two middle kids on the sides, and the youngest at the back—she couldn't help thinking, *At least I'm not last in the order.* She glanced back at her youngest sister. *But I'm pretty close. There are advantages to being third, I guess. My older two sisters already broke most of the rules—like staying up late or having friends over. So I don't have to break so many.*

For a brief second, she felt a pang of gratitude toward her two older sisters for protecting her from the brunt of her dad's wrath and control. Her oldest sister had already conformed to her dad's wishes. Her second eldest sister had rebelled. Between those two opposites, everything had already been done. What else was there to do?

As they started doing their team kata—a form called *Basai-dai*—all four performed in unison—turning, punching, blocking, kicking in perfect synchronicity. Halfway through, Balidova was distracted by a piece of her hair flying into her eye and got out of sync with her three sisters. She stumbled and fell.

"Can't you do it properly?" April said, glowering at her.

"Seriously, what's wrong with you," May chimed in with a disgusted look.

"It's okay, Dova. You'll get it next time," June added sympathetically.

Being a middle child, Balidova simultaneously felt the scorn of her two older sisters, who thought she could never do anything right, and the idolization of her youngest sister, who thought she could never do anything wrong. Plus, she didn't even want to be there. Amidst all this internal confusion, she exploded.

Balidova flopped her arms down and finally let her true feelings gush like water from a broken faucet.

"I don't even wanna do this anymore. I don't even wanna do karate. I just wanna quit!" she yelled.

Her sisters couldn't believe she'd said those words out loud. Did she dare oppose their dad?

He glared at her for a long moment. He seemed to be deciding how to respond, then slowly softened his gaze.

"But Balidova, just think of all the fun you'll be missing. All those medals and trophies you get to bring home. You won't have any of that."

"I don't care. I don't need any more medals. I've already got enough. Besides, they just sit there in a pile in my room. They don't *do* anything."

Sensing that the gentle approach wasn't working, her dad tried another tactic. "Well, you'll be left out." His tone was harsher now. "You'll be left out of all these family workouts. All these family trips. You'll be the only one of your sisters who doesn't do martial arts. What will you be good at?" He looked at each one, making it very clear that they were not-allowed-to-quit.

Balidova heard the steely tone of his voice. She heard the iron fist beneath the velvet glove. And his question, "What will you be good at?" stung her deeply. *I'm already not talking to Mom. I don't get along with my sisters that great. Do I want to peeve Dad off too? Am I prepared to be a complete outcast in this family?*

She glanced around the dojo, looking at the punching bag, which was probably her favorite piece of equipment because it withstood her poundings when she was mad.

Well, I guess it's not that bad, she told herself. *It's just a few workouts a week. I can handle it. And after all this kata stuff, I will get to do some kumite. I'll just go to this tournament and see.*

She talked herself into it in her mind but didn't say anything. She clenched her jaw, glared at her dad, stepped back in line, and continued doing team kata with her sisters. She poured her frustration into an intense focus on the sequence of moves and got the timing perfect. When she sat down, satisfied with her performance, she started thinking. *If I'm gonna do this, I'm gonna be the best. I'll show you what I'm good at. I'll do it— perfectly.*

Balidova instinctively knew that she and her sisters were all competing, not just for karate medals, but for something much more important—something that eclipsed the biggest trophy of all yet was tied directly to it. Whether they liked it or not, the four Forester girls were all locked in a battle, competing for their dad's approval and love. Balidova sat there, looking around the dojo, waiting for her turn to perform her individual kata, nodding her head on the inside. *I'm gonna be better than my sisters at this. You'll see, Dad. You'll see...*

Extreme competitiveness in everything taught her always to aim to be the victor. If one person wins, the other loses. And it felt terrible to lose. So why wouldn't you want to be the best? The champion? Winning was everything. She scoffed at those who could not compete. She looked down upon those who did not have the skill, endurance, strength, adaptability, or discipline to win.

Hmph. Weaklings. Not me! I'm strong. I will NOT be the one squashed to pieces and left behind. I will be the one who stands up at the end—the winner.

IN THAT MOMENT, deciding to go to the karate competition even though she didn't want to and put her desires secondary to those of her father, Balidova implicitly decided how she would survive. Shunning her mom and aligning with her dad, she would win by the rules of the power game. She would gain her father's approval and collect a lot of trophies along the way.

After the workout ended and everyone went upstairs to eat chocolate chip cookies, Balidova lingered downstairs. Even her dad had left, but she remained. She stayed and practiced her punches and kicks—just a little more—by herself, in front of the mirror. She perfected her form, strengthened her legs and arms, doing a little extra, a little more than her sisters. After finishing her last set of pushups, she walked up to the large mirror at the front of the dojo, still breathing heavily from the effort. Only inches away from the glass, her warm breath steaming up the mirror, she stared intensely into her own eyes and made another promise to herself.

If I'm gonna do karate, I'm gonna win, whatever it takes.

CHAPTER 4
TRAPPED IN HER HEAD

When Balidova finished her extra practice, she came upstairs and grabbed a couple of chocolate chip cookies, still warm from the oven, then quickly changed out of her white karate uniform. It was still only 8 a.m., but she had to catch the bus by 8:15 for the twenty-minute ride to school.

The Forester family lived in a subdivision about five miles out of town called Cablecar. She couldn't miss the bus, or she'd be in BIG trouble. Her dad would be heading to his clinic at the hospital, but not till later that morning. If she caught a ride with him, she'd be late. Her mom would be going out to the barn to do the morning feeding any minute now, as soon as all the girls headed off to school. And although she could technically drive Balidova, she would not be happy about it. Asking her mom for a ride would undoubtedly cost her later on—with extra chores, an angry outburst, or something. Besides, she wasn't talking to her mom.

Balidova threw on the same orange t-shirt from the day before because it was on top of the pile and pulled on her favorite pair of torn jeans. As she ran past the kitchen, she grabbed her lunchbox from her mom, standing by the kitchen doorway, and stuffed it into her backpack.

"Aren't you going to say thank you?" her mom asked.

Balidova didn't speak. They looked at each other briefly—two proud and unrelenting spirits.

Her mom could sense that something had changed within Balidova, just as something had changed within her. She noticed that the girl had not spoken to her since the butcher knife incident. Both had strong cheekbones and symmetrical lips with a well-defined cupid's bow. Both could be incredibly stubborn. Neither smiled or said goodbye.

Then Balidova looked away. She threw on her jacket, hat, and gloves and ran out the front door down the long semi-circular driveway. She made it to the bus stop where her sisters were waiting just as the school bus came rumbling up the street. As she boarded, she looked back to see if her mom was standing by the front door watching her go as usual, but she wasn't there.

"Late again, eh Balidova?" the bus driver, Mrs. Hornby, said. The big lady reached over and grabbed the door handle, pulling it closed with her tremendous weight.

"Not late—just in the nick of time," Balidova smiled mischievously as she climbed up the steps of the big, black and yellow bus. It had the words *Kitimat Valley Public Schools* written on the side. She walked down the aisle and found an empty seat about halfway down. She liked sitting by herself on the bus. It gave her time to daydream and think about nothing at all before she got to school and had to think about a whole bunch of stuff whether she wanted to or not—like the definition of hyperbole, or who the first Prime Minister of Canada was, or the difference between white, brown and black bears.

The bus rumbled along, through the streets of Cablecar and then onto the main highway, where she spotted her favorite group of trees. All around, the land had been clear cut by loggers, yet one large grove remained. As she stared at the cedar, spruce, and pine trees through the bus window, they turned into a blur of forest green. Her mind drifted off as she imagined their woodsy aroma filling her nostrils.

The forest is one of my favorite places—full of mystery—but scary too.

"Don't get left out in the woods at night," Dad always says. "The night animals might come for you—bears, wolves, owls, and lynx hunting under cover of darkness—it's no place for a kid."

I wonder what I'd do if I ran into a bear.

ALL OF A SUDDEN, the bus lurched to a stop. They had arrived at Mount Elizabeth Secondary School, otherwise known as M.E.S.S., the only high school in town. Before them lay a sprawling, light and dark grey expanse of rectangular one-story structures, connecting like words on a Scrabble board. Inside, long, locker-lined hallways converged on a big lump in the middle that rose above everything else—the gymnasium. A vast field surrounded by a running track lay just outside the gym, with wide open grassy areas surrounding the rest of the school. A large parking lot, made of gravel and black asphalt, acted as a border between the school and the wooded trails of the forest beyond.

Balidova entered the building through steel and glass doors and walked down the hallway to her locker. After putting her backpack and jacket in, she took her English notebook out, then closed its ruddy blue full-length metal door. She turned around to join the masses of kids—over a thousand—heading to class. She was one of the youngest in her Grade 8 class, having skipped a grade in elementary school. Although she liked the hustle and bustle of high school, it took her a minute to get used to it in the mornings. She'd had four months of acclimatization already last fall. Today was the first day back to school in January—a brand new calendar year.

"Hey Balidova, whatchu up to?"

A familiar voice sounded behind her. It was Angel. Somewhat chubby, kinda quirky, always reliable, Angel. She was a short, stubby kid with strawberry blonde hair cut in a bob, a round face, and a big smile. She looked like a cherub—plump and happy.

A theatre geek, Angel was artistic, not athletic—the opposite of Balidova in many ways. Yet they had been best friends since third grade when they met while arguing over whose turn it was to ride the playground swing.

Arguing had quickly turned to laughter when they realized there was a whole new set of swings they'd forgotten about that were empty. That marked the beginning of their friendship—anger turned to embarrassment and then fun—a good marker of things to come. Although they seemed very different at first glance, both girls had big hearts and even bigger imaginations.

Now, in eighth grade, they were still friends, even though Balidova had moved out of town while Angel remained in town.

"Did you do your karate workout this morning?" Angel chuckled, adjusting her dangly earrings—something Balidova wouldn't be caught dead in, especially since she didn't even have her ears pierced.

"Yeah, it's Monday. Whaddya expect?" Balidova snickered.

Angel's parents were the opposite of Balidova's. They were super laid-back, casual, and didn't have much of a schedule.

"Ah, if only I could have your life," Balidova mused. "Wake up late, eat breakfast, and go to school like a normal kid."

"Yeah, but then you wouldn't have all your fancy trophies and medals. You wouldn't be the big karate champ around here." Angel laughed, her strawberry blonde hair swishing around her soft, squishy neck.

"Big champ, my butt." Balidova scoffed. "That means nothing

in my family. You gotta win it ALL just to keep up! And it doesn't mean much here, either. We're the youngest in the school—the peons—in case you haven't noticed."

A tall boy wearing a space grey t-shirt and beige cargo pants walked by with his gang of friends. He brushed past Balidova, then pushed Angel in a way that seemed to be on purpose. Angel fell toward the floor and banged her head into the blue metal lockers. All her books tumbled to the ground.

"Ow, watch where you're going!" she shouted.

The boy swiveled his head to have a look, scoffed, then kept walking with his friends as they pointed their fingers at Angel on the floor and laughed. He didn't slow down one bit. And he certainly didn't apologize.

He was a tallish skinny kid with long, dirty blonde hair—attractive in a wild way. He had blue eyes that spoke not of the expansiveness of sky or sea, but the cold starkness of polar ice. As if all the warmth had been drained out.

Balidova just stood there. Partly in shock. Partly in fear that they would come after her next.

"Aren't you gonna do something?" Angel said, annoyed with her friend. "Help me up." She reached out her hand. Balidova shook her head as if to snap herself out of her stupor and reached her arm down.

"You okay?" Balidova asked, pulling Angel up.

"Not really," Angel said, rubbing her head, looking dazed. "Why didn't you say anything? Or do anything?" Angel asked, dumbfounded. "You know karate—you could have decked those guys—Gus Polter and his gang. Good thing that locker door was shut. Otherwise, it would've cut my face open."

Balidova looked at her best friend. She still felt afraid. It was strange. She knew she could have defended Angel, but something held her back. Or maybe she couldn't? There was a whole gang of them, after all, and she was just one girl—karate or not.

She looked down at her hands sheepishly. "Uh, uh, I gotta get to class," she muttered. Then quickly turned and walked off.

"Thanks," Angel called after her. "Nice friend you are." There was an unmistakable tone of disgusted sarcasm in her voice.

BALIDOVA JUST WALKED AWAY FASTER, pretending she couldn't hear, and didn't look back. But during English class, she couldn't get over the feeling that she had done something wrong.

Balidova remembered when she and Gus used to catch butterflies together years ago when they lived near each other in kindergarten. They had the same adventurous, energetic spirit. But then everything changed. His parents divorced, and he went to live with his dad, an alcoholic.

That's when he became a jerk. It must have been tough—having a dad who drank that much. I don't blame him for taking out his bad feelings on others. I've been known to do the same. Balidova's head felt like a battleground—opposing ideas wrestling each other in a tug-o-war.

"Balidova Forester! Pay attention!" her English teacher—a strict disciplinarian and one of the meanest teachers in the school—barked. "What is onomatopoeia?" He deliberately put the girl on the spot precisely because she was not paying attention.

Balidova squirmed in her seat. "Uh...uh... automatic peeing??" she said hesitantly.

The entire class burst into laughter. "Oh my gosh," she muttered. "I just embarrassed myself in front of the whole class! This day is going from bad to worse." She buried her head in her hands.

"No, that's incorrect," her teacher replied, shaking his head and muttering, "idiot." Frustrated with her, he explained the correct definition. "It's when you use a word to imitate the sound that it describes."

Kinda like poof? Balidova thought. *Coz that's what I wanna do right now, disappear.*

Luckily, her teacher didn't call on her for the rest of the class. When the bell finally rang, and swarms of high school students crowded the hallways, Balidova did her best to stay incognito. She avoided Angel the whole day, even at lunch. Not able to bear seeing her friend or looking her in the eye, she ducked into the library instead of heading to the cafeteria. She felt ashamed for her lack of action. When the last bell of the day rang, she ran to the bus and got home as quickly as she could.

WALKING through the wooden front double doors, she avoided her mom by not getting a snack in the kitchen and went straight to her room. Later, after settling into the safety of her own space, she snuck downstairs, quickly made herself a peanut butter and banana toast while her mom was out of the kitchen, then headed back to her room. Aside from not wanting to speak to her mom, Balidova never knew what mood her mom would be in and didn't want to deal with her increasingly volatile emotional outbursts.

The other day, Balidova had witnessed June asking her mom a simple question, only to have her mom explode in anger at the girl. Since the dishwasher cord chopping incident, her mom's moods had grown more extreme. As if she had retreated to a place inside where she was protecting herself not only from her husband, but even from the demands of her children.

Her mom had a habit of keeping things buried inside her, letting them build up. At the same time, she created stories in her head, then exploded like an erupting volcano when triggered by whichever unfortunate kid happened to be in her vicinity. Her sisters almost felt like they "took turns" being the object of their mom's wrathful outbursts. It was as if a part of her were unhinged.

A soft-spoken city girl, she had left the world she knew, married a strong-willed man, and traveled up north where she had little to no support caring for four children. The first three daughters were all about a year apart. At one point, she had three kids under three years of age—enough to drive anyone insane! Add in the long winters, spent mostly indoors, where getting dressed to play outside was an ordeal in and of itself. By the time the last kid had her gear on, the first one had to go to the bathroom! Which meant, in a full-body one-piece snowsuit, starting right at the beginning again. Even gloves, attached by a string so they didn't get lost, had to be reinserted through jacket armholes once the jacket was removed—frustrating, to say the least.

Balidova snuck upstairs with her toast. The kids weren't supposed to eat outside the kitchen, but she wanted to be in the privacy of her room. Just when she was about to bite into her sticky, crunchy, peanut butter banana bread, her second sister, May, called out from downstairs, "Balidova, where's that pen of mine you borrowed? I want it back!"

Oh, great. Another person who's annoyed with me, she groaned.

Balidova looked around her bedroom—clothes strewn everywhere, scraps of paper scattered across her desk, books lying open on the floor. She got up and searched everywhere.

I can't find it, she thought. *Uh-oh. Yet another thing I did wrong.*

She kept searching—dumping out her jars of rocks, sifting through a pile of shells she had collected from a beach vacation on Vancouver Island long ago, even trawling through her stack of karate medals and trophies.

"Oh girl, your sister's gonna be mad at you," she muttered under her breath. Balidova was the only one in the room. *Her* room. But that didn't prevent her from talking to herself. And not just silently in her head, but out *loud*.

She stopped for a moment, grabbed the toast, and took a big bite. The stickiness of the peanut butter on the roof of her mouth forced her to pause amidst her frantic search and get a grip.

"Okay, girl, slow down. Just slow down. Where did you have it last?" When she got stressed, Balidova referred to herself not with "I" but with "you," switching from first to third person to keep herself and the anxiety inside her arm's length away.

She took another bite of the toast, and the soft sweetness of the banana jogged her memory. "You put it in your backpack during the last period at school. Then, you got on the bus and came home. When you arrived at the house, you dropped your backpack in your room, then came to the kitchen to eat a peanut butter banana toast snack. Then you went back to your room to do your homework, and it wasn't there. Where could it have gone?"

Balidova retraced her steps in her mind with sleuth-like precision, carefully leaving no stone unturned. Others had called her obsessive-compulsive—OCD for short—a disorder where you obsess over small details. She smiled, thinking that those qualities came in handy sometimes.

How was she ever going to find her sister's favorite pen? Her sister got it as a birthday present last month and fell in love with it. It was one of those pens with multiple colors in it. *Did she leave it at school?* No. Most definitely not. *Did it drop out on the bus?* Unlikely. She didn't hear anything fall. *Did it come out in her room?* Maybe. Probably. Most likely. It was the only explanation she could think of. Thus, she found herself sifting through the mess.

Just then, May walked in. She was less than a year older than Balidova (363 days to be exact), but acted like she was several years older.

"Hey, can I have my pen back?"

"Uh, yeah, sure. Just as soon as I find it."

"What! You lost it? You promised me you wouldn't when you begged me to use it last week! You better not have lost it," May growled.

"Just, uh, give me a sec. I'm sure it's here somewhere." Balidova said hopefully. "I know I had it when I left school, so that's a good thing, right?!"

"Hmph. Not good enough. You're dead meat if you can't find it. I'm gonna lose something precious of yours, like that dumb piece of jade," her sister threatened as she pointed to the emerald green stone sitting on Balidova's desk—the pride and joy of her rock collection—a special gift from her grandmother on her dad's side that she had slipped on a black string and often wore around her neck.

Balidova paused for a moment, eyeing her sister carefully. "Naw, you wouldn't do that, would you?"

"Try me," May said in a low voice, slowly and deliberately.

"I didn't lose it on purpose!" Balidova retorted.

"So what? It's still gone," May grumbled.

Yikes! Balidova ran downstairs to see if the pen had dropped out of her bag somewhere along the way. She bumped into her dad, who was emerging from his office at the end of the hallway, opposite the kitchen, near the side door of the house.

"Balidova, when's the last time you vacuumed the house? It's looking pretty dirty, and it's your turn this week, isn't it?"

There was a chart of each child's chores posted on the fridge. Balidova was a little surprised her dad knew what was on it. Her mom usually kept track of it while her dad enforced what mom declared—one of the small victories in the constant battle of their relationship that her mom claimed.

"Yeah, I know," she replied. "I'll get to it."

"You'll get to it?" he raised his eyebrows. "What does that mean?"

"I said I'll get to it!" she glared at him.

"Don't you raise your voice with me, young lady," her dad said firmly. "You don't want to go there, believe me."

"Just get off my case," she muttered under her breath.

"What's that?" her dad asked.

"Nothing," she turned and walked away.

Balidova entered the kitchen, looking for a safe haven away from all the craziness—and something else yummy to eat. The cookie was a good start, but it wasn't nearly enough to satisfy her hunger.

"Hey Balidova, how was school?" her mom asked cheerily.

Wow. She's obviously in a better mood than she was this morning. Balidova didn't answer, just nodded her head.

"That good, huh? Anything interesting happen?"

Balidova shook her head.

"Hmm, okay. Cat got your tongue?" Her mom kept chopping vegetables in silence. Then asked, "Could you help me with these?"

"Oh geez, do I have to? Can't I have a little peace and quiet, please?" she blurted out, forgetting her vow of silence toward her mother.

"What's that? Was that a yes?" Her mom furrowed her brow.

Balidova just glared at her.

"Don't look so enthused," her mom chided.

Balidova grabbed a knife and started in on the carrots.

"Not like that," her mom said immediately.

What? Since when is there a proper way to chop carrots? She thought sarcastically as she glanced sideways at her mom, rolling her eyes.

Her Mom didn't like Balidova's expression. As if reading her mind, she said, "It's not that difficult. Just cut them on an angle like this, so there's more surface area for them to stir fry in the pan and soak up the flavor."

Honestly, does it really matter, Mom? Balidova rolled her eyes again. She might have vowed not to talk to her mom, but that didn't mean she would stop thinking...

"Look, if you're gonna give me so much grief, you'd better go. That's not any help at all."

I'm trying my best. Aren't I allowed to do it my way? Balidova glared at her again.

"Go. Just get out."

Okay fine! I will then! Balidova stormed out of the kitchen in a silent huff.

SHE RAN up to her room and slammed the door. Standing in the middle of her private space, she scanned the mess: her bed unmade, books strewn all over the floor—pens, papers, stones, and markers scattered across her desk—old wrappers and even a banana peel lying in the corner. Her waste bin was piled high, unemptied for who knows how long. Stacks of karate medals, paraphernalia, do-dads, and knick-knacks lay scattered on her shelf.

This place is a pigsty. I can't stand it anymore.

Her mind was swirling, her heart boiling over.

"Aaaaaaaaaaaarrrrrrgggggggggghhhhhhhhhhh!"

She did a semi-silent scream—opened her mouth with only a tiny sound coming out, even though it was a loud scream on the inside. Seething with rage, she stomped violently, pounding on the floor and then on the wall. Before she knew it, she had put her fist through the wall, right by her door. The power she could generate in her martial arts-trained body was no match for the thin surface. She pulled her hand out, covered in white dust from the broken gyproc.

"Oh no," she moaned. "Now I'm in trouble." She wanted to

shout until this feeling stopped. And yet she knew from experience that if she did that, it might make it worse—she might break something else.

So, she sat down.

Deep breath. She inhaled, and let the air rush out. She remembered the technique she used to calm herself down at the beginning of a karate fight.

Inhale.

Exhale.

Swirls of anger and confusion roiled through her veins, pulsing from every cell in her body.

She breathed heavily again.

She had grabbed the reins of the wild horse of her mind again —slowly pulling on the bit and bringing it under control.

Well, at least my karate training's useful for something, she thought.

"Who cares about all these dumb medals. I don't."

Inhale.

Exhale.

Win all these medals and still feel like crap. What's the point of that?

She sat on the floor, steam coming out of her ears.

Balidova just couldn't understand why all these people were upset with her. She wanted this horrible feeling to go away, but it kept swirling inside her like a perpetually draining bathtub. She tried to find a way out. She went around in her head, thinking of who was right and who was wrong.

After a while, the anger subsided—it just couldn't keep up that level of fury. Gradually, the same energy that had driven her fist through the wall turned into tears. She leaned forward and pressed her head against the floor, head cupped in her hands, and started to sob.

"There we go again," she thought. "Sad and mad at the same time—SMAD. I hate this."

There's no way out. How do I get out of this maze of thoughts about who's right and who's wrong? It just doesn't work!

And now even my best friend, who I can always count on, hates my guts too. What is wrong with me?

She got up again, pacing back and forth in her room.

"Was I right? Was I wrong? About Angel? Couldn't she have done something for herself? Why'd she expect me to do something? If I'd said something to Gus, his gang would have come after me, and we'd both be toast." She flung her arms around wildly, going off on a tangent again.

With such aggressive internal energy wearing her out, she suddenly stopped pacing and crumpled to the floor. She sat there with her knees curled up to her chest, her arms wrapped around them, rocking back and forth.

ON THE INSIDE, she sank lower and lower, to a darker place, until she felt utterly lost and alone, angry and afraid. The hairs on the back of her neck stood up, and her whole body tightened as she felt smaller, like something was pressing on her, restricting her. Something not good. As if a Cloak of Fear were descending upon her, wrapping itself around her shoulders. *What is the point? What's the point of even being here if this is what it's gonna feel like? It's all pointless, anyhow.*

Completely lost in despair, she fell into a black hole in her mind. The cloak's grip was complete now—she was in full-on self-loathing mode. Resting her head against her knees, she continued sobbing, her whole body shaking. *My heart hurts—it's so tight—I feel like my whole body's being pulled apart.*

She couldn't think—couldn't make sense of anything—

couldn't even decide what to do. She felt trapped in her head like a bug stuck in a spider's web. Even more than the conflict with everyone else, the conflict within herself was killing her.

I hate fighting with everyone.
I hate feeling like this.
I hate this family.
I hate my life.
I hate me.

CHAPTER 5
UNEXPECTED ENCOUNTERS

Balidova couldn't take it anymore. She dried her tears and got up off the floor of her room. *I can't just sit here crying forever.* She snuck downstairs, put on her brand-new red winter jacket, snow boots, hat, and woolly mittens, and silently exited the house through the side door. It was only 5:00 p.m., but already dark out.

Sunset arrived early during the winter months this far north, but she didn't care. She needed to do something to get rid of the awful feeling inside her. Behind their house lay miles of pure wilderness that stretched as far as the eye could see. Five hundred miles of wilderness that stretched up the provincial coast to the Yukon border, to be exact. She intended to lose herself in it.

A large brown and white Japanese bear dog, an *Akita*, bounded up to her, wagging its tail—the family guard dog. For a moment, she thought of taking him with her, but then decided against it.

"No, Nutmeg, I can't take you with me this time. I need to get outta here and be alone." She patted him on the head as she tied him up. Feeling his thick fur against her skin, another thought came to her. *I'll show them, make them pay. They can all be scared that I'm gone and know that I don't have a dog to protect me.* She had no plan. She just needed to get out of the house, out of the family, out of her mind, and out of this feeling.

Outside was bitterly cold, with winter wind gusting from the north. The wind chill factor quickly dropped temperatures by over 20 degrees so that -10 degrees Celsius felt like -30. But Balidova knew how to protect herself from the freezing weather. She zipped her down jacket up to her nose and pulled her grey and white toque down to her eyes, leaving only a thin strip of skin exposed to the elements so she could see. She wiggled her fingers in her mittens to generate heat, remembering that bare fingers pressing on each other inside mittens generated more heat than gloves did.

Long, thin icicles tapering to a point like spears hung from tree branches. Balidova grabbed one clumsily through her mittens, broke it off with a snap, then sucked on it as she trudged through the snow toward the barn. She slowed down by the large red structure, one of her favorite places in the world, but didn't stop. Instead, she continued past it, down the tree-filled ravine, and into the lagoon behind their house.

All at once, the dense snow carpeted forest opened up to a wide, frozen pond. By the middle of winter, the lagoon had become a solid block of ice covered with several feet of snow. She looked to her left and her right. All she could see was snow. She looked up and saw the moon casting elegant silver rays onto the vast, white expanse. It seemed to be illuminating a path in front of her. She followed the light with her eyes and looked down at a sea of ice crystals at her feet.

Tracks. In the snow. What kind are they? A dog? Nutmeg?

She noticed the footprints were not of just one animal but several. *Hmm, that's weird. What're a whole bunch of dogs doing down here? Wait a sec. Those aren't Nutmeg's paw prints. There are too many of them. And they're deep.*

She knew wolves traveled in packs and tended to step in the tracks of the wolf in front of them when possible, deepening the prints. Wolves did this to save energy when covering long distances and conceal the pack's number. On the other hand, domesticated dogs meandered aimlessly, following whatever scent caught their attention, resulting in shallow tracks.

She knelt next to one of the footprints and examined it closer. The prints showed four toes and a paw in an oval shape, about four inches across and four inches down, but the four toe prints were the same size. Balidova knew from going deer hunting with her dad how to differentiate between wolf and dog tracks. Dogs had uneven toe prints—the two toes in the middle were larger than the ones on the side. These were not dog tracks.

As she walked on, she saw thin, round holes that went down two to three feet below the snow bed. These were the tracks of a heavier animal with long legs—one that was not light enough to tread on the surface.

Huh, I wonder what this is?

Curiosity, combined with anger, made her cast fear aside. She followed the tracks further. Even though it was cold, she worked so hard trudging through the deep snow that she was sweating under her down parka. Luckily for her, she lived in sports shirts, so she wore material that wicked sweat away from her skin. Otherwise, she'd have become very cold, very fast, even with a thick jacket. It was one of the paradoxes of living in the North. You could be dry on the outside but get completely soaked from the inside out.

ANOTHER QUARTER-MILE AWAY, she stopped abruptly. *Now I know what made those deep holes in the snow.* As she looked across the frozen lagoon, she saw the half-eaten carcass of a dead animal ahead of her. Its blood was still red and runny against the white snow, which meant it had been a recent kill. Startled, she knew there was only one animal that could have brought down as large a creature as a moose—and it hunted in a pack.

She looked around for signs of the grey beasts. *I wish I'd brought the dog. How could I be so dumb?* She clasped her hands together, searching for some idea to support herself. Then she found it, a thought that felt better. *Well, at least the wolves are full. They're probably sleeping somewhere.*

For a brief moment, she felt a sense of relief, but then the reality of her situation sunk in. In that instant, her idea of running away so that her family would be scared and she would make them pay for fighting with her vanished.

She was deep down in the lagoon on a frozen pond, covered with snow. Home was across an enormous, open expanse, up a hill, and through the forest into their backyard—more than half a mile away. She took one more look at the moose, its eyes staring lifelessly at her.

A bolt of terror shot through her heart as the image of a vicious wolf pack bringing down this large creature to its death flashed through her mind.

She turned around and started back home right away. But at the edge of the lagoon, she spotted something moving in the forest. Yellow eyes stared at her from a distance. She'd seen them before, in the night, as she looked out her second-floor bedroom window toward the forest.

Wolves had been known to hunt cattle and prey on her family's livestock. She looked to her left side, knowing wolves hunted in packs and spotted another pair of eyes. Looking to her right, she spotted even more eyes.

Oh my gosh, they've surrounded me. They know I'm here, and they're not sleeping at all! They've been stalking me!

Fear gripped her throat as her entire body tensed up, frozen in place. But then she remembered what her mom had told her about animals—*they can sense fear.* She tried to calm herself down without much success.

Less than fifty yards away, a big grey wolf stepped out of the forest in front of her. It must have been the alpha—leader of the pack—because it looked at her with its beady eyes and came toward her, first at a walk and then a trot. The other wolves followed suit and emerged from the forest on both sides of her. The hunt had begun.

She closed her eyes for a second and prayed. It was the only thing she could do. It was pointless to run—the pack would catch her. She was sinking into the snow with each step, but the wolves ran on top of it. Four-legged creatures had lighter and more even weight distribution than two-legged ones.

The wolves were close now, making their final approach toward their prey. But wolves have a complex social hierarchy, and the pack would not attack until the lead wolf gave the signal through sound or body language.

When they were about fifteen feet away, the largest wolf stopped abruptly. It growled at her, baring white fangs through curled lips. The beast was so close that she could see saliva dripping from the sides of its mouth. She knew this was the final signal before the kill. In one last, desperate attempt at survival, she thrust every bit of energy she had into aggression—something she instinctively did when backed into a corner.

A bloodcurdling scream erupted from Balidova's mouth as she made one last-ditch attempt to scare the beasts away and save herself.

Miraculously, the lead wolf lowered its long snout and crouched down.

But then it lunged forward at her. Summoning all the skill she had gained through her karate training, she instinctively ducked out of the way just as its claws sliced through the left arm of her jacket and grazed through her shirt down to her skin. She had almost made it, but not quite.

She felt the sharp sting of a fresh cut on her arm, and as she touched the place where she was cut with her other hand, she felt something wet. She looked at her arm and saw that it was bleeding like the moose. Having missed its mark, the big grey wolf skidded to a stop behind her and turned to face her again as the pack closed in, forming a tight circle. There was no escape now.

At that moment, something unexpected happened. Balidova had all but given up when she suddenly became aware of the wind. The wolves had approached from the south, downwind of her, which is how they had picked up her scent. Like dogs, wolves have an excellent sense of smell, more than one hundred times stronger than humans.

The gusts of air seemed louder than before as if they were whispering a strange language to her. Time seemed to slow down as the grey wolf perked up its ears and raised its head to the sky, listening to the wind. For a moment, she thought it would howl, but the other wolves also stopped in their tracks and lifted their snouts skyward, searching for something.

The gale picked up again, even more intensely than before, whistling in her ears. A huge gust of snow flurried around her as if enveloping her in a protective sheath. And the wolves, in one simultaneous yet silent communication, turned tail and ran, scattering in all directions, disappearing into the forest just as quickly as they had come.

Balidova stood in the middle of the lagoon, looking around in shock. *What just happened? The wolves are gone!* She couldn't believe her luck. She saw a mist by the tree line. It was moving toward her, coming closer. The hair on the back of her neck stood up, and goosebumps erupted down her arm.

Something was here—a presence much larger than the wolves. Instantly, her relief at the wolf pack's disappearance turned into fear.

But when the snowy mist curled itself around her body, her feeling changed again. Whatever it was, carried by the wind, touched her skin with a gentle stroke, then surged around her until it filled the airspace surrounding her body.

AN IRRATIONAL CALMNESS came over her. As she breathed, she felt like she was riding an elevator from her frazzled head down into her heart, and then even deeper into the belly of her body and all the way down her legs. She shivered as a bolt of energy passed down her spine and left a buzzing sensation on the soles of her feet. She felt settled and steady, deep into her bones. She felt centered in herself in a way she had not felt, ever.

SHE CLOSED her eyes and lifted her nose to smell what was in the air. The scent of pine and fir trees filled her nostrils, but there were no other olfactory clues. Opening her eyes again, hoping to see what had brought this wind of peace, all she saw was snow blowing in small gusts around her. It seemed to be whispering in her ear:

Whoosh—whoosh—whoosh...
What's it saying?
She listened closely and thought she heard the words,

"You—are—the—one...
Meet—full—moon...."

She breathed in deeply.

She breathed out deeply.

And felt her focus shift from her mind down into her heart again.

She felt her heart space open up as all the fear left her body. And a warm, tingly feeling entered—a sensation of pure peace. *It feels like the wind is alive and hugging me. What is that? A wind spirit?*

A speck of blood blew onto her face and she remembered the cut on her left arm. Suddenly, it hurt now—the rush of adrenaline through her body while facing the wolves had numbed the pain of the injury, but now the immediate threat had passed, and the pain returned.

A smile crept across her face. She didn't know why, but she felt safe. *Maybe the wind spirit is real, after all.* Even though the wolves had cut her, they had not killed her. She couldn't help feeling like she owed her life to whatever had scared them away.

A moment later, she noticed the wind had died down, and a snowy owl appeared out of nowhere, flying majestically overhead, its full wingspan on display. Dipping low toward the ground, its white underbelly blended in with the snow, save for black speckled wings. She noticed that its eyes were a piercing yellow, even more so than the wolves. As the owl flew off, a little blue bird with white wing tips flitted around her as though wanting her to notice it too.

That's weird. These little birds normally aren't here in the winter. They migrate south to get away from the cold. And owls usually eat them.

Suddenly, Balidova realized that the world was not as it seemed. *How could I go from being terrified to feeling so calm, just like that? How could things go from being so bad to so good in a split second? How could birds appear out of nowhere? Birds that aren't supposed to be here?*

A new world had just opened up to her. A world full of possibilities she hadn't imagined. In that moment, Balidova knew her world was not ending as she thought it had been. Quite the contrary, it had just begun.

She looked down at her feet, stuck in the snow. She pulled one boot out, then looked around for signs of other creatures. She grabbed a handful of snow and placed it on the gash on her arm to stem the flow of blood. She had been cut often enough doing farm chores to know that cold made blood cells coagulate, which slowed the bleeding. It would give her enough time to get back and bandaged up before anyone at home noticed she was gone. Although she could feel the injury was superficial, a few drops of blood fell onto the snow, reminding her how close she had been to facing the same fate as the moose.

With the strange feeling that something inexplicably magical had just happened, she tore home as fast as her white and black snow boots would carry her.

CHAPTER 6
CHOPPING WOOD

The next day, Balidova woke up groggy—her whole body ached. The stress and tension of the emotional roller coaster the night before had seeped into her muscles. A fog hung over her mind like a cloudy day.

As she stretched out and rubbed her eyes, the memory of the wolves returned. A pang of fear shot up her spine as she imagined white fangs staring at her. But then she also remembered the whispering wind—the invisible presence that felt like a peaceful wind spirit. It had spoken to the wolves, made them scatter, and saved her life.

Her arm stung. She had bandaged it up when she got home last night after sneaking back in the house, cleaning the cut with an antiseptic solution, and realizing it wasn't that deep. Her reflexive dodge of the lead wolf's attack had worked, turning what would have been a near-fatal slash into a skin scrape.

There were loads of product samples in their bathroom—everything she needed to dress her wound—that her dad brought home from his medical office. She knew smallish injuries didn't warrant anything more than bandages and tender loving care.

Trips to the hospital were rare in their family. They were reserved for near-death injuries or deep cuts that required stitches. Afraid of the potential repercussions, she had not told anyone in her house about what had happened down in the lagoon last night or even that she had gone down there, which she wasn't supposed to do.

She sat up in bed and remembered she had work to do. Even though it was a Tuesday, there was no school today. It was a teacher workday, and a workday for her too—farm chores. It was her turn to load up the basement with freshly chopped wood. Figuring she might as well get it over with early and then enjoy the rest of the day, she took a deep breath and decided to get to it right away. She changed out of her pajamas, brushed her teeth, washed her face, and headed downstairs.

In the kitchen, she helped herself to something yummy her mom had made and left in a pot on the stovetop—hot porridge sweetened with raisins, maple syrup, and a little cinnamon. A few minutes later, her belly full and warm, she put on her steel-toed work boots, red jacket, grey hat and gloves, and headed outside. Although her left arm was sore, it was not broken. And unless there was something seriously wrong with you, there was no getting out of chores. So, she didn't even bother asking her dad for a reprieve. He wasn't going to give it.

A HUGE PILE of logs lay on the snow beside the basement window in the backyard. Her dad had felled a tree, cut it into large pieces with a chainsaw, and deposited those pieces near the house with the tractor bucket.

The non-mechanical grunt work began—splitting each log into smaller pieces that could be stacked inside the house to dry out and fit into the wood-burning stove in their basement to heat the whole home all winter long.

As she grabbed the ax with her right hand and lifted it high, adrenaline surged in her veins. She brought the ax down on the log with a big thud. Crack! The log split down the middle. Another swing of the ax, in just the right spot, and two halves of the log tumbled off either side of the chopping block.

She breathed in deep lungfuls of air with each inhale, not to calm down, but just because her working body needed that much oxygen. Chopping wood with an ax was tremendously hard work. It took a ton of energy to split each log—even if you were good at it. And Balidova was good at it.

At age twelve, she'd already had a couple of years of practice. No one in their family, no matter how young, was spared from farm chores. There was simply too much to do. Several acres of land, a large vegetable garden, the barn, horse paddocks, farm equipment, all kinds of animals, and a family of six added up to a whole lot of jobs. Chopping wood was one of her least favorite tasks, but she knew how to do it well. Little to no choice was given to them by their dad over which jobs to do. They just had to get them done.

Balidova knew to place her feet in a wide stance in case she missed the block—so the ax would swing harmlessly between her legs and not hit her foot. She knew to wear gloves so her palms would not blister as quickly as they rubbed against the wooden handle with each rise and fall of the ax. She learned to first place the ax on precisely the spot she wanted to strike and then raise it while focusing on that spot, allowing her the greatest chance of hitting her target the first time without wasted effort.

She felt good working like this. Her body was strong, supple, and stamina-filled from years of karate training in their basement dojo and at the Kitimat Karate Club. She liked feeling her strength. Wielding an ax and splitting logs with a single stroke made her feel powerful. Not just in her body but in her mind too. Over the years, her physical stamina had translated into mental stamina, making school work easy for her.

After going through a quarter of the log pile, she paused, lifted her right arm in a blocking motion, and wiped annoying beads of sweat from her brow. Then she continued working and moved on to a different part of the task—loading cut pieces of wood into the basement wood room. Even though she was nowhere near finished chopping, she wasn't a machine—she needed a change of pace.

A TREMENDOUS AMOUNT of wood was required to heat a home in Northern Canada for the whole winter, especially when winter stretched a good six months from October to March. The Forester family warmed their entire, three-story, 4000 square foot house with a single wood stove. Hot air travels up, so the wood stove was placed in the basement, enclosed in a makeshift room with pine boards for walls that her dad had constructed. He cut a hole in the wall of the nearby stairwell so that heat could travel up into the rest of the house. When that stove was loaded up with wood, burning steadily in a rip-roaring fire, it was hot!

Loading the chopped pieces of wood into the basement was a tricky job. Blocks of wood had to be passed through the open window and stacked up in the wood room. The driest wood went in front, ready to go straight into the fire. The wettest wood went in the back, so it had time to dry out before being burned.

Balidova's youngest sister, June, joined her, working together as a team. June was strong and wiry, with well-honed reflexes, like her sister. The girls got into a rhythm with Balidova throwing the pieces down into the basement from outside. June sorted and stacked them in the wood room from inside. During a break, June noticed something flapping on Balidova's red jacket.

"Why's your sleeve all ripped?"

"Uh, well, I," Balidova hesitated. Should she tell her sister about the wolves? And the wind spirit? Could she trust her with this information?

"What's the matter?" June persisted. "Are you hiding something? You're gonna be in big trouble for destroying your new jacket so quickly."

"Oh, alright," Balidova muttered. "I ran away last night and got attacked by a pack of wolves." She said it so matter-of-factly that it caught June off guard.

This was not the answer her little sister was expecting. June gasped, and her jaw dropped open. Then she looked at Balidova intently, cocked her head sideways, and started laughing.

"Ha, you almost got me, you trickster!"

"Whaddya mean, I'm not tricking you, I'm telling the truth! That really happened!" Balidova said defiantly.

"Then why aren't you dead? Huh?" June placed both hands on her hips and looked up toward her sister from the basement floor.

Taken aback, Balidova paused for a second before continuing. "Because something swooped down and saved me. It scared the wolves away."

"Really?" June looked skeptical. "What was it? What's scarier than a pack of wolves?"

"I don't know. I couldn't see it."

"Why, coz your eyes were closed?" June said, genuinely confused. "I don't get it."

"No, my eyes were open, but it wasn't visible. It was just a mist— something big, carried by the wind." Balidova paused, "a kind of wind spirit."

"Ha, you're joking, right?!" June insisted. "Come on, just tell me the truth, Dova. What're you so worried about?"

"I AM telling you the truth!" Balidova was annoyed at her little sister now. "Why don't you believe me!"

"Well, gosh, I dunno, it just isn't easy to believe—you almost dying in a wolf attack only to be saved by an invisible wind spirit. I mean, the wolf thing, yeah, I get that. That happens around here. But the invisible creature? That's a little far-fetched. Very creative, though. You definitely get points for that."

"Okay, forget it. I'm not telling you anything else." Balidova felt embarrassed and annoyed. She had just shared one of her most dramatic and magical moments—something very personal and meaningful—and her sister just crapped all over it.

"Aww, come on, just tell me. Or how about I guess? Did you rip your jacket on the barbed wire fence next to the goat shed? Huh? That's it, isn't it? And then you made up this big story so you wouldn't get in trouble for ruining your new jacket?"

Balidova turned away. She was mad now. She grabbed a piece of wood and flung it in the direction of her sister, hoping it would hit her. Unfortunately, it hit something else instead.

CRASH!!

The sound of glass smashing into a thousand pieces filled the air. One of the shards flew into Balidova's hand, and she yelped in pain. As she looked down, she saw a single piece of glass sticking out of the middle finger of her left hand, blood dripping into her palm. The basement window was destroyed. Bits of glass lay everywhere, and blood spilled onto the white snow in a trickle of red. She was reminded of the moose for a moment, but the pain in her hand brought her back.

"Help! I'm bleeding! I'm cut!" she shouted. "You idiot," she glared at June. "You did this."

"I did not!" June protested. "I didn't do anything!"

"Just go get Mom," Balidova growled.

"You could ask if I'm okay!" June shouted back through the

broken window. "You're lucky I'm not cut too!" She stormed off inside the house, heading upstairs toward the kitchen.

"Great, just what I need," Balidova scowled, "another reason for mom and dad to be mad at me."

A few moments later, her mom arrived.

"What is going on here, girls? That window's completely smashed! What are you two doing?"

She was *not* happy. Then she saw the pool of blood on Balidova's hand.

"Oh my goodness, you really did it this time, didn't you?" She examined Balidova's hand. "Looks like you're gonna need stitches," her mom said. "That's the last thing I need—driving you to the hospital on your day off school."

Then she realized what she was saying and changed her tone. "Does it hurt?"

Ugh. Well, duh, of course it hurts! Balidova was tempted to unleash all her pain on her mom, but she bit her lip to stop herself from speaking. *It's not gonna do any good. Besides, I'm not talking to her.*

A FIFTEEN-MINUTE DRIVE LATER, they were at the Kitimat General Hospital, right in the center of town. A pleasant-looking pink building six stories high, it housed an emergency room, surgeries, patient beds, and doctors' offices. Her dad's medical office was on the fourth floor. Ambulance arrivals were on ground level—where all the bloody, gory stuff happened.

With an Aluminum smelter and pulp mill being the two main employers in town, accidents happened. Balidova remembered her dad telling her about a man who had molten aluminum spilled on him while it was being poured into ingots. He got burned so severely that he lost the use of his arm. Another person had his fingers sliced off by one of the grinding machines at the pulp mill.

"*No wonder they painted it pink,*" Balidova thought as they drove into the parking lot, "*to disguise all the awful stuff you see inside.*"

Balidova sat sullenly in the stark white emergency waiting room. Fluorescent lights glared down at her as she stared at the makeshift poultice on her hand. Her mind retraced the events of the incident, looking for someone to blame. "*June shouldn't have made fun of me. She knows I hate that. She was bugging me on purpose—hmph.*"

She turned over her swollen hand and sighed. "*Well, at least it's my left hand, not my right. I can still punch. And I can still write.*" *Haha, the pen and the sword are in accord, just like Dad says they must be.* She let out a deep breath of relief, raised her head, and looked up. Scanning the room, she noticed other people waiting for the emergency doctor. Then she did a double-take. *Wait a sec, is that who I think it is? What's he doing here?*

The person she'd been looking at caught her eye, took a closer look and walked over. He was a fairly tall, middle-aged man with a clean-cut, oval face. He wore simple, clear-rimmed glasses. He had the medium build of someone who worked out, but not too much. The only thing that stood out from his otherwise unremarkable appearance was a slightly bulbous nose that did not match the rest of his face or his elegant-sounding name.

"What are you doing here, Balidova?" he said, standing a few feet in front of her.

"Hi, Mr. Winston. Oh, I cut my hand on some glass." She raised her bandaged hand as evidence. She didn't feel like getting into the details and hoped he wouldn't ask.

"Looks like you cut your sleeve too," he said, pointing to the tear on her jacket.

She turned her head to look at it. "Oh yeah, that." She said quietly. "That's something else."

"That's what?" He asked.

"Oh, nothing. What are *you* here for?" she said, changing the subject.

"Oh. I, uh, have a terrible case of reflux," he said, placing his hand on his throat, his tone promptly changing. He seemed uncomfortable. "Are you here by yourself?"

Balidova noticed that he was now changing the subject. *Oh well, I guess he doesn't wanna talk about it, just like me.* "No, my mom's here with me. She just went to the bathroom," Balidova answered politely.

Meeting her teacher in an unusual place like this was weird, but she knew she still had to be courteous.

"So, what happened?" Mr. Winston persisted.

"Oh yeah. I cut my hand on some glass," she repeated.

"No, I mean to your sleeve. How'd you get that big rip? I bet that used to be a nice red jacket," he chuckled. As a teacher, he was used to seeing kids abuse their stuff.

She looked at her sleeve again. *Should I tell him? Will he get it? Or laugh at me like June?* She studied him for a moment. *He does seem genuinely curious. And he is my science teacher, after all. If anyone can explain how this happened, maybe he can? Oh, what the heck? I'll just go for it.*

"I saw tracks in the woods behind our house and followed them 'til they led to a dead moose—its blood spilled all over the snow. The wolves that killed the moose attacked me, and I nearly died. But some kinda invisible wind spirit swooped down and saved me." She blurted it out as fast as she could, afraid that if she told the story slowly, it would sound made up.

He stepped back and put his hand to his mouth, his whole body stiffening in surprise. A moment later, regaining his composure except for his raised eyebrows, he leaned in closer and whispered to Balidova, "Who else have you told about this?"

"No one," she said. "Well, except for my sister, but she didn't believe me."

"Good. Don't tell anyone else," he continued in a whisper.

"Why?" she asked, puzzled, lowering the volume of her voice as she mirrored his tone.

"Because they won't understand."

"You mean you do? You believe me?" she asked, startled.

"Yes," he replied with a sly smile. "Yes, I do."

A wave of relief washed over Balidova. The degree to which she needed someone to believe her took her by surprise. She wanted to trust in the invisible energy more than she realized. She needed confirmation from another human being, preferably someone she trusted, that it was real.

"What did it say to you?" Mr. Winston inquired nonchalantly. He was trying his best to withhold his excitement.

Balidova didn't notice. She was so happy that someone believed her. *Yes, it was real! The wind spirit was real. I wasn't just imagining it.*

"Um, ah, it didn't say much. It sounded like the wind whispering. I couldn't tell." Her voice trailed off.

"Were there any words you thought you heard?" he pressed on.

"Well, there was something I thought I heard, '*You are the one.*'"

"Oh, wow." Mr. Winston's jaw dropped, and he stepped back again. A grin slid across his face, and he quickly asked another question. "And after that?"

"Yeah, the last thing I heard was '*Meet full moon.*' I don't have any idea what that means."

"Hmm," he put his finger to his lips, pausing for a moment,

repeating the words to himself. "Full moon... full moon. Meet... meet..."

Balidova shifted her feet expectantly, waiting for his response.

"Could it mean to meet at the next full moon?" his eyebrows raised in excitement.

"Yeah, maybe, but where?"

"I don't know," he looked puzzled. "But would you do it if you knew?"

"I'm not sure. This is all super weird. I mean, nothing like this has ever happened to me before. I don't even know if it's real! Except for one thing," she mused.

"What's that?"

"Well, I did get a feeling."

"Of what?" he asked curiously, leaning toward her.

"I did get a very calm feeling inside me when the wind was swirling around. Sort of a... wind of peace. If I could feel that again, that'd be pretty awesome."

"So, are you going to do it?"

"I dunno. I'm not even sure the whole thing was real," she repeated.

"What makes you think that? The tear on your sleeve sure is real. And so is the fact that you're alive, right?" People around them in the emergency room were starting to look at them now.

"Why do you care so much?" Balidova wondered aloud.

"Oh, no reason, just curious," he replied, backing away, realizing he had pressed her too much.

Balidova looked quizzically at him for a moment, then shrugged her shoulders. "What do you think I should do?"

Mr. Winston paused for a moment, then reached out and touched her hand—the one that was cut. He got a little streak of her blood on his finger. Balidova pulled her hand back slightly but also liked the comfort.

"I think you should go for it. This invisible wind spirit sounds pretty powerful. You wouldn't want to disobey it. Besides, didn't it tell you—*You are the one?*"

Balidova smiled. *Yes, it did.*

She liked that idea. It made her feel important—to be chosen for something. She was always trying to carve out her own space with her sisters. Trying to be better than them. Proving that she *was* better than them. As a middle child, she struggled to find her place. Neither the oldest nor the youngest, but in between. This would give her a leg up.

"You will meet it on the full moon, won't you?" he continued, looking at the little red smear of her blood on his finger.

So many questions ran through her mind. *Why is he being so demanding? Why is he so interested? How does he know so much about invisible creatures? Including my encounter with this wind spirit? And why is he inspecting my blood?*

She hesitated, then answered the only way she felt possible given the circumstances. "Yes, I'll do it."

Just then, her mom returned from the bathroom.

"Oh, hi Mr. Winston. How are you?" She asked politely.

"I'm well, Mrs. Forester. Very well," Mr. Winston said emphatically, his curly brown hair bobbing to and fro as he nodded.

"Balidova Forester," the nurse called. "The doctor will see you now."

The Mom got up and started walking toward the nurse's desk.

As Balidova stood up to follow her, she heard Mr. Winston whisper, "Don't forget Balidova, don't forget. You're a powerful being." He spoke quietly so only she could hear, and winked at her as she turned toward the emergency room.

"I won't," she replied.

She thought of how unusual his words were—*powerful being*. No one had ever called her that before, but it felt good. Cupping her bloody hand with her non-injured hand, she muttered, "I won't forget."

IN THE CAR, driving home after having twelve stitches, Balidova winced in pain. *Hmph, one stitch for every year of my life. Another birthday present.* She ran her fingertips gently across the top of her hand. She could feel sharp string edges poking out through her skin beneath the layers of bandage. The cut—where glass had penetrated the soft layer of skin—was semicircular, like a crescent moon. *Good thing I was wearing gloves or my hand mighta been cut even worse.*

As the car turned to leave the hospital parking lot, a sliver of moonlight shone through the windshield onto the skin of her other hand. She looked up and saw a white globe of light hanging in the dark sky, just above the line of trees.

"The moon's almost full. Just a couple more days," she whispered to herself. She thought back to what had happened in the lagoon.

I'm naming this one the Wolf Moon.

She remembered what the wind spirit had told her:

You—are—the—one. Meet—full—moon.

She smiled at the idea of experiencing that wonderful sense of calm again.

Almost immediately, a troubling thought passed through her mind, and she frowned.

Where exactly am I supposed to meet the spirit?

I have no idea.

CHAPTER 7
THE EMERALD GREEN LIGHT

Two days later, the full moon arrived, but Balidova didn't know where to meet the invisible wind spirit.

How am I supposed to find the meeting place if I don't know where to go? And how am I supposed to know I've come to the right place if I don't know where that is? This is impossible!

After what seemed like hours stewing in her room after school on a Thursday afternoon—pacing back and forth, doodling on scraps of paper, then lying on her bed staring up at the ceiling—Balidova was done. Wallowing in self-pity, nursing her bandaged hand and bruised pride, not knowing if she would ever feel that intense calm again, wasn't working for her. So, she decided to jump into action.

I've gotta do something. I just have to. But what? Maybe I could go into the lagoon again? And see if it's there? But what about the wolves? No, it's too dangerous. I can't go down there.

Slowly, she got up, dried her tears, went downstairs, put on her torn red jacket, and headed outside. She wondered why her mom had not asked her about the tear in her coat the other day at the hospital.

I guess she's so much in her own world that she didn't even notice? Or was she so concerned with my cut?

Sometimes she couldn't figure her mom out. In any case, Balidova had no idea where she was going. She just knew she had to go. She couldn't just sit in the house wondering about things, her mind going round in circles. She would self-destruct. She had to do something, and getting outside was the only thing she could think of—besides, it always made her feel better.

The Forester girls were given a lot of leeway to do their own thing on and around the three-acre family property, which went hand-in-hand with the high level of responsibility they carried with their farm chores. Even at a young age, it was not unusual for them to be gone for hours at a time, in the barn or out on a horseback ride. They didn't always tell their mom where they were going, and with four girls headed in different directions, a farm to manage, meals to cook, a house to clean, and animals to care for, she didn't always check.

BALIDOVA STOOD—CLAD once again in her red winter jacket, black and white snow boots, grey hat and gloves—at the edge of the property. A cold, January wind blew from the North and bristled across her face, making the hairs of her neck stand on end. She pulled up her jacket and sunk deeper into the plush fabric. Despite her layers, she felt a cold spot on the center of her chest, in the slight hollow between her collar bones—her necklace. She was wearing her favorite emerald green stone.

"Okay, now what, genius?" she asked herself aloud as she stared into the forest. It was still light out, but the sun was setting. "Which way do I go?" She let out a deep sigh and shrugged her shoulders, then took a breath and began putting one foot in front of the other, trudging through the snow. When she crossed the backyard and reached the forest's edge, she stopped. She saw a dead tree covered with a fungus that looked interesting, so she went over to it. Continuing through the woods, she walked an oddly familiar route—past old pine trees and groves of cedar, hemlock, and spruce.

She followed not only her eyes and ears but also her nose. Even in winter, the smell of decaying plant matter guided her to the densest groves of trees where fallen logs provided homes for countless forest creatures, both large and small. Fox, raccoon, marmot, and mouse made their homes in the rotting timber.

Trees are so cool. They provide shade, oxygen, and habitat—not to mention wood to heat our house! What would we do without trees? Plus, they're just plain beautiful. Balidova noticed a handful of pure white snow crystals hanging off the rounded edges of a green cedar branch. *I love being in the forest. Just being around trees lifts my spirits. Is it because they're a part of my name? Balidova Forester. I have a theory about how people live up to their names—thank goodness my last name's not Pain or Dupe!*

After walking for a while, Balidova noticed that she passed by the same gnarled, fungus-covered tree. *Uh-oh, that means I'm going in a circle! This isn't as easy as I thought it would be.*

Just then, a dragonfly alighted on her hand. Its iridescent blue body balanced two pairs of translucent wings in the shape of infinity loops. Large, bulbous eyes made it possible to see in all directions, while two small antennae curved out from its head, reminding Balidova of the shape of a heart.

Oh, wow! At 300 million years old, you're one of the first winged creatures on the planet, and one of the very few that can fly in all six directions—up, down, left, right, forward, back. Wait, she thought. *What're you doing here in winter? Things are getting weird.*

The dragonfly flew off. She followed it until she couldn't see it anymore, then worried. She was deep in the forest. It was getting dark, and she had no food or water. Plus, she didn't know how to get back.

This was such a dumb idea, you stupid girl. Why did you think you'd ever find the wind spirit? It probably doesn't even exist. The whole thing was just a figment of your imagination.

Balidova started to cry. The weight of everything bore down on her, and she became filled with a heaviness that cut into her shoulders like a backpack filled with bricks. The cut on her hand, the fights with everyone in her family, the spat with her best friend, not talking to her mom, and her near-death experience with the wolves all wore on her.

Her breath shortened, her eyes darted around, and the negative thoughts in her head seemed to attract more negative thoughts until her mind was sucked into a whirlpool of disaster, and she couldn't see a way out. Her whole body tensed, and she began breathing rapidly, in shallower and shallower spurts. The world seemed to spin, and she couldn't hold on. She was sinking.

All of a sudden, a little blue bird fluttered in front of her. She noticed it was blue with white wing tips. *Wait a sec, is that the same blue bird I saw in the lagoon after the wind spirit scared the wolves away?* She followed the bird with her eyes and heard a sound coming from the same direction. Walking that way, she noticed an opening in the woods and walked towards it.

More and more light filtered through the trees until, eventually, she saw the moon in full splendor, shining above the treetops, illuminating a meadow in the middle of the forest. A large open space filled with untouched, powdery snow greeted her. As she took in the wide expanse of the meadow in the silvery moonlight, her breath slowly returned to its normal pattern.

She looked around and thought she saw a long, flowing creature woven around the trees on the edge of the clearing. It seemed to be made of branches, as if it had emerged from the trees. As she watched the branches of the trees swaying and moving in synchronicity with each other, that same feeling of irrational calm came over her. A sense of sinking deep into herself in a good way. A tingly feeling as if someone had zapped her with a magic wand and then poured fairy dust on her. The same feeling she'd had with the wind spirit.

What's this thing in the forest? Some kinda tree spirit? Where'd you come from? How'd you get here? Were you here all along? Balidova's mind raced with a million questions.

As she watched, the tree branches got still, and something else moved in the woods. As if the energy of the trees had transformed into—*What is that?*

Without warning, a creature emerged from the tree branches and stood up on its hind legs, facing her. It had a huge body with four large legs and paws ending in sharp claws. Its round face was marked by alert eyes, short ears, and wide, flaring nostrils at the end of a powerful muzzle. It was an enormous white bear. Moonlight reflected off its cream-colored fur, creating a luminescent glow around the animal.

She had heard the legend of the white bears. Different from polar bears, they were called Kermode or Spirit bears and were very rare in these parts. Because they were so difficult to spot, they were also called Ghost bears.

In all the world, they could only be found here, in the Pacific Coast Rainforest of British Columbia, Canada. Black bears born with white fur. Not because they were albino—they had pigmentation, as evidenced by their dark eyes. But because they had the rare, recessive gene for white fur. Balidova remembered reading something about them from Indigenous legend. "Raven made one in every ten black bears white to remind the people of a time when glaciers covered the world, and to be thankful for the lush and bountiful land of today."

The bear was so beautiful in the moonlight, blending in with the snow—it took her breath away. *But wait, what's a bear doing out and about in the middle of winter? Shouldn't it be hibernating?*

Balidova started to retreat from the beast but heard a sound coming from about forty feet behind her. There was a rustling noise in the underbrush, then the unmistakable snap of a twig. Her whole body went on high alert. She froze in place—her muscles tensed, her ears listened intently, her eyes scanned for signs of movement, her nose smelled for hidden clues, and her skin tingled with anticipation.

Then she saw it.

The metal barrel of a gun pointing directly at the bear and her.

Yikes! I didn't even know anyone else was here! But it's illegal to hunt spirit bears! She peered closer and spotted the unmistakable camouflage outfit of a hunter, its sights set directly on its prize.

Balidova shouted at the top of her lungs. She wanted to alert the bear and startle the hunter enough for him to miss his shot—and it worked.

The bear seemed to know what was going on and disappeared into the underbrush just as an explosive gunshot went off, nicking a tree not far from Balidova's head.

The hunter looked up from his crouched position, straight at the girl. She was easy to spot in her bright red jacket.

They locked eyes for a brief second, and she saw who it was. She didn't recognize the face at first, but it all flooded back. She thought back to the time, years ago, when she saw him hit her friend Gus and how she had run away in fear.

Now he was standing in front of her with a gun pointed at her. If she got shot in the forest, no one would know. She was about to yell at him for nearly shooting her, but a wave of fear passed through her. She saw the look of hate in his eyes—a hatred so deep, it chilled her to the bone.

The person hunting the spirit bear was Mr. Polter—Gus's dad.

What Balidova did not know is that the hatred and anger he felt was not necessarily for her but for life in general. A life that had taken away his livelihood, his wife, his health, and his relationship with his only son. All that hate, at this moment, was aimed straight at her.

He stared, giving her a look that said, "I know you know I'm not supposed to be here. You'd better not tell anyone."

For a moment, he raised his rifle, aiming it directly at her.

For a few seconds that seemed like an eternity, Balidova saw her own life flash before her eyes.

Then a dragonfly swooped down and brushed him with its wings.

Distracted, he waved his arms furiously, and his gun sight shifted. Once he regained his composure, he seemed to have changed his mind.

He gave Balidova one last glance, tucked his rifle over his shoulder, and disappeared into the forest.

She listened for the sound of branches snapping until she couldn't hear them anymore, hoping she was now alone. Half a minute later, she gasped for air, not realizing she'd been holding her breath.

Out of the corner of her eye, Balidova caught a flash of white on her left. She saw the bear staring at her. Slowly, she turned toward it, squashing the temptation to run. She knew that running from a bear could trigger its predatory instinct and make it chase you. Although they looked like sluggish creatures, bears could run surprisingly fast. Climbing a tree was not an option either because they also climbed trees. Although spirit bears looked totally different from regular black bears, she knew they were surprisingly similar in their behavior. She had studied them in school.

What am I supposed to do? I don't have any bear spray on me.

She held her hand in front of herself protectively as she started backing away, but tripped on a log and landed flat on her butt.

She was on the ground, utterly vulnerable to the dangerous creature only a few horse lengths away.

If the bear charged her, there'd be nothing she could do, just hope for the best, play dead—by rolling into a tight ball—and cover her face.

But the white bear did not move. It just watched her, cocking its head sideways as if in amusement.

"Slow down, dear one, slow down. Where are you going?" the creature said.

"What? You can talk?" Balidova looked dumbfounded, her jaw agape as she stood up onto her feet again.

"Yes, I can speak your language and many other languages too. What do you want to ask me?" the bear said, its small ears perking up on its large round face.

"Okay," Balidova said, still on edge, unsure whether to believe her ears, "then why don't I start with my first question. Who are you?"

"I am a bear. A Kermode spirit bear," the animal said, lumbering closer to her.

"Yes, I can see that," Balidova said nervously, backing away. "You're unusually white, and most bears are black or brown."

"I'm not most bears," the beast chuckled.

"You came out of nowhere," Balidova continued, her fear now turning to curiosity as she watched the ghost-like creature with its fuzzy fur and raccoon eyes.

"Nowhere to you, but somewhere to me. I came from the trees."

"The what?"

"Don't worry," the bear laughed, "you will learn soon enough. The real question is, who are you?

Balidova looked sideways at the bear, puzzled. "What do you mean? I'm Balidova Forester."

"I didn't ask what your name was. I asked, who are you?"

"I'm a girl," she replied, puzzled.

"Yes, I know that, but *who are you?*"

"Oh," the answer clicked in Balidova's mind straight away. She slapped her mittened hand on her forehead. "I get it. I'm 'The One.'"

"Are you now?" the bear asked, its broad chest and long snout close to her.

"Why are you questioning me so much?" she said, drawing back slightly.

"I am merely reflecting what's going on inside of you. You are questioning yourself, are you not?" The bear looked her in the eyes, and she noticed a golden glow around its pupils. It reminded her of the owl.

"Well, yeah, but that's none of your business," Balidova said, slightly annoyed that the bear could see inside her thoughts.

For a moment, she forgot that this beast was at least five times her weight and happened to have razor-sharp claws and teeth, neither of which she possessed. She forgot that bears were notoriously dangerous and unpredictable in these parts. Every year there was a story of a child in her town who'd gotten mauled by a bear.

The bear placed one of its massive front paws near Balidova's foot. She could detect the fishy smell of salmon on its fur—a favorite food of bears. It was so close she could touch it. The bear splayed its claws out and opened its jaws wide as it tilted its head up and released a sort of growl. She felt fear surge in her body. *Oh no, did I misjudge this creature? Is it not my friend? Is it going to attack me?*

Suddenly, she doubted herself.

Doubted the feeling of calm.

Doubted the feeling of safety.

Doubted the feeling of curiosity she had felt moments earlier.

What a fool I am! Too trusting! Too gullible! She scolded herself. *What can I do now? I'm too close to run, but bears have sensitive noses. What if I hit it on the nose? Would that give me enough time to run?*

Just when she was about to strike out, the bear raised its paw in the air.

She thought it would swipe at her right then, but it opened its paw and handed her something.

A stone—a simple, plain-looking stone. Grey with white specks. A small stone, no bigger than a bird's egg.

"Do not fear me, Balidova. Do not be annoyed with me. I am not your enemy. I am your friend. For now, take this stone and know that I am real. *Know* that my presence is true. Keep it with you always, for it shall guide you when you need it most."

Balidova took the stone from the bear's paw and rolled it in her fingers. Its weight pressed onto the bandage of her left middle finger, over her stitches, but strangely enough, it didn't hurt. It felt comforting.

"You are the chosen one. You must learn the seven steps of the Dragon Tail Breath before it is too late."

"Wait, what? Chosen for what? What's the Dragon Tail

Breath? What do you mean by *before it's too late*? Too late for what?"

Balidova was full of questions. "It all sounds like gibberish. Can you help me understand? Can you teach me something to help me *believe in myself* and hang onto this calm feeling? Something that I can take back home with me? Something more than a stone?"

The bear brought its head down and looked deep into Balidova's eyes with a fire-like intensity. The golden-brown glow of the creature's eyes carried the reflection of Balidova's entire being in them. The ghost bear looked inside her as it stared into her chocolate brown eyes, reading her soul. After a long pause, it raised its head and spoke slowly, deliberately.

"Yes, I will teach you how to breathe in the light. I will teach you how to draw in the colors of the rainbow through the energy centers of your body. I will teach you the Dragon Tail Breath."

BALIDOVA'S EYES GREW WIDE. She perked her head up and stood straight and tall. "Wow, that sounds epic."

"But you must do something for me," the bear continued.

"What?"

"You must learn to control your anger." The bear said solemnly. "Anger is not bad, but it is a very powerful energy. You must control it. Not let your anger control you."

"Uh, okay, I can do that," she said hesitantly, not realizing that the bear could detect any seed of darkness or fear within her.

"Good. Then let's continue." The bear only wanted to know that Balidova was willing. The girl did not have to know how yet.

Balidova furrowed her brow inquisitively and changed the subject. "Why's it called the Dragon Tail Breath? Am I gonna grow a long tail if I do it?" She laughed nervously.

"No," the bear smiled, "but you will bring all the colors of the rainbow into your body. All the colors between black and white—between my white fur and a regular bear's black fur. It's called the Dragon Tail Breath because breathing is the backbone of you. Just as a dragon's tail gives it power and balance, the Dragon Tail Breath will give you power and balance. Dragons are extraordinary creatures that can create or destroy. Just like you."

"Oh, I like that!" Balidova grinned, nodding her head. She quickly forgot about all the angry things she had done.

"It will allow you to become the person you want to be. As you breathe the colors of light into your body, you will gain strength and clarity about yourself," the spirit bear continued steadily, ignoring her excitement.

"Wow! That's amazing. When can we start?" Balidova asked enthusiastically.

"Right now."

The bear walked over to a log and sat down on its haunches next to it, motioning with its head for the girl to join.

Balidova followed the bear and sat on the log, utterly fascinated by this creature. She didn't even notice that her butt was now covered in snow and was starting to get wet. She had forgotten to put her snow pants on.

"Let's start with the very first color—emerald green," the bear said.

"Like the stone on my necklace?" Balidova touched her hand to her chest. She could feel her necklace beneath her jacket. "And the trees?"

"Yes." The bear pulled on a branch from a nearby tree, and snow tumbled off it. "Like the underside of the needles in this forest."

Balidova looked around, taking in her surroundings, amazed at how much green was around her, even beneath the snow cover.

She hadn't paid attention to it before. *I guess these trees are called evergreen for a reason.*

"Imagine a stream of emerald green light coming through the forest and pouring into your heart. Breathe it in. Breathe it out. Feel the warmth as it passes through your entire body from front to back. Feel it opening and expanding your heart as the light enters and fills your heart space."

BALIDOVA CLOSED her eyes and imagined the light coming in. She was always good at visualizing things using her imagination—she did this in karate all the time. She could see tall, majestic evergreen trees in her mind's eye and feel a stream of energy passing into the front side of her body and exiting out her back.

The feeling wasn't that strong.

It was pretty subtle, but at least it was there.

A few breaths later, she shuddered and noticed goosebumps on her arms.

She breathed deeply, again.

Inhale.

Exhale.

"Good," the bear continued. "Now open up that stream of light. There's an energy center in your heart. Let the green light fill that space and grow wider and wider until it spreads through your entire body. Let it travel up into your head and neck, down your arms, and through your whole torso. Let it travel into your legs, all the way down to your feet, until your entire body is pulsing with light."

Balidova took another deep breath as she followed the bear's instructions. Her whole body was still and quiet as she focused on bringing in the light. She imagined the emerald green stone expanding like a ball of light within her.

"Oh, that feels amazing! I can feel the light moving through me. It feels kinda warm and tingly on my skin. It feels like rain."

"And while you do that," the bear smiled, "Say these words—*All is well.*"

"Why?" she asked, shifting her body weight from one foot to another.

"Because," the creature continued, shifting its own body from one paw to another until all four paws were planted firmly on the ground, "deep down, all *is* well. All the chaos in your life is merely an illusion. The physical reality of earth is not the only plane of existence you know."

"I was gonna ask you where you came from. Even though you look like a real bear, it doesn't seem like you're from here..." her voice trailed off.

"That's because I don't *only* live in this earthly realm. There are other realms, Balidova. You will get to know them in time. The key to accessing those other worlds is your feeling. *Feel the light, Balidova. Feel* it within you."

The bear lifted its furry, white forelegs high in the air and stood on its hind legs. It seemed to be emphasizing something.

"Breathe in deeply, silently counting four seconds as you pull air in."

Balidova took a deep breath, counting silently in her head.

1... 2... 3... 4.

"Now breathe out all the air from your lungs, drawing your belly button into your spine, silently counting to four as you push air out."

Balidova did as she was told, pulling her stomach in and counting to four in her head.

1... 2... 3... 4.

"Repeat this four times," the bear commanded from its elevated position. Still balancing on its hind legs, the creature counted as it watched Balidova's chest rise and fall through her thick down jacket.

Breath two.

Breath three.

Breath four.

When she finished, the creature lowered its front paws to the ground, landing with a soft thud on the snow. The spirit bear now stood quietly on all fours.

"That is the 4x4x4 breath. Breathe in 4 seconds. Breathe out 4 seconds. Repeat 4 times."

"Wow," she said, filled with awe at the calm feeling inside her.

"It goes with the Dragon Tail Breath," the bear continued. "Every time you breathe this color in and out, do it four times. Breathe deeply and know that *All is well*."

Balidova sucked in a breath as deeply as she could, taking in the mesmerizing tone of the bear's words.

She released the air inside her lungs in a long, slow exhale.

"That's it." The bear encouraged her. "Breathe, Balidova, breathe. Deeply and deliberately."

What's so special about breathing?" she asked. "I mean, I do it all the time without even thinking about it."

The ghost bear looked at her solemnly. "Breathing is the first thing you did when you were born, and the last thing you'll do when you die. Breathing gives your body more than oxygen. It brings you back *into* your body and clears your mind. It's like a pause button that lets you be less reactive to everything around you."

Balidova's eyes widened. She looked stunned. "You mean, if I do this breathing, everything will bother me less? I'll fight with everyone less?"

"In a way, yes. The Dragon Tail Breath will shift the energy within you and bring you into a different state of mind. But only if you want it to," the bear chuckled.

"Wow, that's amazing," Balidova exclaimed as her red jacket fluttered in the wind. "It's like a special power."

"Breathe in the light, Balidova. And repeat the words, *all is well*. This will ground you in the dragon magic."

"The what?"

"The dragon magic—what you asked for–the magic that will help you hang onto the feeling you so desperately want. Something more than a stone. The light, the breath, the words, and *you* combine to access the dragon magic."

Balidova looked down at the grey, speckled stone the Kermode bear had given her, feeling its smoothness in the palm of her hand. She turned it over and saw just how ordinary it was.

She looked up again at the white bear.

A feeling of wonder and magic filled her heart as she gripped the rock tightly in her mittened fist. Her whole body tingled with delight.

She breathed deeply as she stood in her snow boots and horse feed-stained sweatpants, almost in a trance. As her eyes closed, her whole body swayed from side to side. She heard the bear say something, but it didn't fully register as she wasn't fully paying attention.

"Do not speak of me to anyone. For they will not believe you."

When she opened her eyes again, the creature bowed its whole body toward the girl, then disappeared into the trees, returning to spirit form.

ALONE IN THE FOREST, Balidova began her walk home. The sun was setting, sending long, golden rays of light horizontally through the trees.

She noticed that the snow had formed a thin crust on top as

temperatures dropped. With each step, she pierced that crust, breaking new ground.

That's the cool thing about snow, she thought. *It's the same, AND it's always changing. Kinda like breathing.*

As she placed one foot in front of the other, Balidova couldn't help thinking one simple thought over and over again. A truth that resonated in every fiber of her being.

A breath changes everything.

ALL IS WELL

CHAPTER 8
A WEIGHT LIFTED

Balidova couldn't stop thinking about the white bear while at school the next day. As she placed her books from her locker into her backpack, she went over and over in her mind what the spirit bear had said—the same words she had heard from the wind in the lagoon.

"You are the chosen one...."

Well, almost the same words. The wind spirit whispered, "you—are—the—one." The bear added the word "chosen." Which I quite like, by the way. It just makes me feel a little bit more special.

Balidova had a wicked memory. She could remember small, seemingly insignificant details about things that others didn't notice. She had learned to use it to her advantage. On history tests, and when arguing with her sisters about whose turn it was to do the dishes. Now it was coming in handy in a way she'd never imagined.

She closed her locker door and heard the lock snap into place. Despite all the deep breathing she'd done with the bear yesterday, she still felt puzzled. All she knew was that learning Step One felt good inside of her. She took a deep breath, smiled, and thought of the emerald green light passing through her heart, warming her whole body. "All is well," she murmured as she placed the palm of her hand on the blue metal frame of her locker.

Her backpack full, she turned away from the privacy of her own space and faced the hallway. *Why's it so empty?* she wondered. The bell rang while she was daydreaming.

Balidova started walking quickly toward class. She was alone in the hallway, except for one other person walking in the same direction about twenty feet ahead of her. Both pairs of wet running shoes made 'squelch, squelch' sounds on the linoleum floor, which she could hear loud and clear. No other sounds were audible. That's how she knew they were alone.

All of a sudden, a figure came out of nowhere and sideswiped the person in front of her, just as they were passing the stairwell. Balidova saw a blur of orange and pink as the girl in front of her tumbled down the stairs.

For a moment, Balidova looked toward the girl who'd gotten shoved. The girl lay in a disheveled mess, face-up, at the bottom of the stairs. Balidova instantly recognized her. It was Jojo Beadle, a friend of Angel's. Not as close as she was to Angel, but close enough. Instinctively, Balidova swiveled around to see who had done it.

A tall boy clad in dark grey pants and a white t-shirt faced her. His dirty blonde hair waved carelessly around his face. He wore a gutsy expression on his face as if he were daring Balidova to challenge him.

Gus. Again.

She clenched her fists by her side, preparing to strike, but saw one of his friends behind him and knew a whole gang of groupies were ready to defend him. She wanted to deck him right then and there but stopped herself. There was no way she could take them all on at once. Instead, she glared at him and marched right past in search of help for Jojo from the nearest teacher.

"You're next," he whispered as she walked past. "You can't escape. I know where you live." She glared at him, noticing that one of his friends pointed his phone camera right at her.

As Balidova ran down the hall searching for a teacher, she thought back over the past several months. Everyone in the school was talking about it—the bullying was getting out of control. The authorities needed to do something. Someone needed to do something. Of course, Gus denied that he was part of any of it.

And now there was this incident. Balidova was the only one who had seen it, so her word was against his. He had his whole gang of friends to back him up.

She had nobody.

A few minutes later, as she neared the science wing, a commanding voice came over the loudspeaker for the whole school to hear.

"Gus Polter and Balidova Forester. Report to the office immediately."

That was fast. A teacher must've come by the stairs...

Together, Gus and Balidova sat silently in the principal's office. When she'd arrived at the office, he was already there, sticking his phone back in his pocket.

"You both know why you're here, don't you?" the principal, Mrs. Marsh, said in a booming voice. "You do know what happened to Jojo Beadle?"

Balidova looked up sheepishly. "Is she okay?"

"She broke her arm falling down the stairs," Mrs. Marsh replied with a stern look. The blood in the woman's cheeks matched her maroon-colored dress. She was *not* happy. "Would either of you happen to know anything about that? You were the only two people present that I know about."

Gus and Balidova turned and pointed at each other. "She did it," Gus said, while Balidova simultaneously said, "He did it."

Oh my goodness, Balidova realized. *Gus is trying to pin it on me.* She hadn't fully realized the depths to which he would go to frame her.

Balidova sighed and sunk a little deeper in her seat. She started pulling at her almost non-existent earlobe, something she did when nervous. Meanwhile, Gus was smirking, knowing he had trapped her.

"Let's hear from you first, Mr. Polter. What do you have to say for yourself? You don't exactly have a great record at this school."

Gus kept a poker face, even while lying through his teeth. "I was just walkin' down the hall, and I saw Balidova push this girl down the stairs. I ran over to help. One of my friends was nearby and took a picture of Balidova running from the scene."

Balidova dropped her jaw open, shocked by his made-up story. "I was going to get help!" she interjected. "I was running to find a teacher who could help Jojo!"

"Why didn't you help her yourself, Balidova?" the principal asked, curious to hear how the girl would respond to the inference that she had behaved improperly. The principal seemed to know something Balidova didn't.

"I—it all happened so fast. I wasn't thinking."

"Yeah, you weren't thinking all right." Gus continued. "You were just being mean."

"Oh yeah?" Balidova turned to face him. "Why would I do that? I don't exactly have a history of pushing people down the stairs," she said, defending herself.

"You're a martial artist, after all. And, I hear that Jojo is gettin' close with your best friend now that Angel's not talkin' to you," Gus retorted.

Balidova gasped. "How do you know that?"

The principal listened curiously, letting the drama play out between the two students.

"Well, ever since that thing happened with Angel where you didn't do nothin' to help her—I guess she's a little mad at you, isn't she?"

Balidova glared at him with steely eyes. "Yeah, you would know about that, wouldn't you?"

She looked at the principal. "You're looking at the school's number one bully here, Mrs. Marsh. And it's not me!"

She slumped back in her chair with her arms crossed, keeping her mouth shut. She was afraid that anything she said from here on in would dig a deeper hole for herself. She could feel anger rising in her body and remembered the hole she'd punched in her bedroom wall just a few days earlier.

"Ok, that's enough. Both of you." Mrs. Marsh announced, laying her pen down. "There are reasons why it could've been either of you. Gus, this isn't your first time in my office. Let's just put it that way." Mrs. Marsh turned to face Balidova. "And Balidova, I'm surprised that you're here. You're normally such a good student, but Gus has a point. You did have a motive. And you are stronger than the average kid. After all, you're a karate fighter, tougher and more aggressive than you think. Since I don't know who it was, and Gus has video evidence of you, Balidova, you'll have to wear it. I'm punishing both of you."

Balidova's head spun. *Gus has a video? Is that why his friend's phone was pointed at me? When did he have time to show Mrs. Marsh? In the few minutes he got to the office before me?*

"But... but... that's not fair!" she protested.

Mrs. Marsh ignored her and continued. "Both of you will write a note of apology to Jojo Beadle. Both of you will have detention after school every day this week. Both of you will be assigned twenty community service hours. You are both on thin ice. If anything like this happens again, where a student is injured, and you're involved, you could be expelled."

Balidova looked at Gus. He was smirking as if very pleased with himself. He didn't seem to care if he got expelled. It seemed to suit him just fine.

"Go. Get out of my office now—both of you. And don't get in any more trouble," Mrs. Marsh ordered.

They both marched out, glaring at each other as they went their separate ways down the hall.

BALIDOVA LOOKED AT HER WATCH. She had science class next. She headed in that direction, steaming mad.

The Principal's words reverberated in her head, "You're a karate fighter after all—tougher and more aggressive than you think."

Okay, so this is how it's gonna be. I'm being punished for being good at something. Where's Angel when I need her. I need to talk to someone.

Just then, by some remarkable coincidence, Angel passed her in the hallway. But Balidova's best friend looked straight ahead without connecting eyes.

Oh gosh, she's mad at me still for not standing up for her. Well, I guess she has a right to be. But I need someone I can talk to right now.

Walking down the hall, Balidova noticed everyone looking at her with strange, puzzled glances. Kids looked down at their phones, then looked up at her. *Had word spread that fast?*

She pulled her phone out from her backpack and saw it—a post from someone she didn't recognize. A video of her running from the scene. She had a frightened, slightly angry look on her face. The video panned to an image of Jojo crumpled at the bottom of the stairs. The caption read: "This is what happens when you get between BF and her BFF."

Balidova closed her eyes, wanting to shut out the whole world. She almost threw her phone down but stuffed it in her bag at the last second.

She walked into science class and sat down at her desk. A long black shelf bordered the room, filled with science textbooks and lab materials. Along the walls was a poster of the Periodic Table of the Elements, and a poster of Marie Curie, the only woman to have won the Nobel Prize twice—and in two different scientific fields, physics and chemistry. Above the door hung a poster of Albert Einstein saying,

> "Logic will get you from A to B.
> Imagination will take you everywhere."

Today, the class was scheduled to do a light wave experiment. She'd been looking forward to it for a while, but now she couldn't concentrate. When she got angry, she 'lost her head' and couldn't think straight.

"Okay, class, listen up!" Mr. Winston announced, getting everyone's attention. The blue and white polka dot bow tie at his throat wobbled when he spoke loudly. "Today, we're experimenting with light. We will see how light bends and how the different colors of light diffract when they are put through a prism. It's a straightforward experiment, so no one should have any trouble with it—as long as you're paying attention." Mr. Winston raised his eyebrows and tilted his head down, scanning the class over the rims of his spectacles. He looked from one side of the class to the other to make sure everyone was watching him.

"We will shine a flashlight through a prism and see what happens."

Balidova collected her lab book and all her gear. With a shuffling gait and downcast gaze, she walked over to one of the standing lab tables with a shiny black surface and laid down the items.

"Balidova, are you okay?" her lab partner, a nervous girl named Melissa, asked.

"No. And I don't wanna talk about it. Let's just do this."

The two girls set up the experiment and turned the flashlight on, shining the light through the prism. As if by magic, part of the light bent and became white. Another part of it bent the other way and turned into a rainbow of colors.

"Wow, that's cool," Balidova said as she held the glass pyramid and rotated it slightly. "The different wavelengths of light show up as different colors." Fascinated by the science behind the rainbow, she felt a brief respite from her sour mood.

"Yeah, that is cool," her lab partner echoed, holding the flashlight.

For a moment, Balidova forgot all about being in the principal's office, her detention, community service hours, and almost getting expelled from school. She forgot about the great injustice that had been thrust upon her. She was utterly transfixed by the rainbow of colors that appeared before her eyes, as if by magic.

Then she heard people talking in hushed tones, "Did Balidova push that girl down the stairs?" Rumors were spreading already. And she knew who was spreading them!

She dropped the prism.

It made a loud crashing sound as the glass hit the cement floor. She felt a sharp pain in her right hand. She looked down and saw a shard of glass sticking out from the top of her right hand, which wasn't cut before. She was bleeding.

She looked up and noticed everyone staring at her. Suddenly, she felt panic rising in her body. Her throat went dry, her hands began to shake, and her heart beat out of her chest. Everything seemed to blur together.

The flashlight was still on, its round frame gently rolling back and forth along the black tiles. As it shone, the light hit a prism piece and illuminated a ray of green on the floor, which also moved back and forth. Balidova caught a glimpse of the flashing green, and it snapped her out of her misery.

THE GREEN LIGHT—THAT'S *what the spirit bear showed me. What were those words?* She struggled to remember.

She took a deep inhale, breathing in as she counted to four.

1... 2... 3... 4...

Breathing out as she counted to four.

1... 2... 3... 4...

Repeating three more times:

Second breath...

Third breath...

Fourth breath.

4 seconds in. 4 seconds out. 4 times.

Thirty-two seconds later, she felt her whole body relax, like a shaken snow globe returning to its original, unshaken form.

As the words came to her, she smiled.

All is well.

All is well.

All is well.

She repeated the words three times in her mind while kneeling on the floor to get closer to the green light, and get away from the prodding eyes of all her classmates who had gathered around.

"Okay, everyone, get back to work!" Mr. Winston shouted. "Move away and give her some space." He knelt beside her, then looked up at the class again. "I said, get back to work!" Slowly, her classmates returned to their lab experiments.

Turning to her, he asked, "Are you okay?" He was rankled to see one of his students bleeding.

She noticed he had a patch on his throat. *That's weird,* she thought. *He must have gotten that from the hospital when I saw him there.*

"Yeah, I'm fine," she answered.

"You seem unusually calm for someone who just got into an accident," he said. Noticing she'd been whispering under her breath, he asked, "What were you saying to yourself?"

None of your business, she thought, looking at him with a blank stare.

She wondered whether she could trust him but realized she didn't have anyone else to tell. She also remembered that he was the one who had encouraged her to go back and meet the wind spirit, which ended up being a spirit bear. If it wasn't for him, she might not have met the white bear at all.

"*All is well.* That's what I was saying," she replied. "I learned it from the spirit bear."

"The spirit what?"

"The spirit bear."

Mr. Winston looked around and lowered his voice. "When did you meet this spirit bear?"

"Yesterday. On the full moon, just like you said I should when we met at the hospital."

Mr. Winston reached down and collected up the bits of broken glass, including one that had a drop of her blood on it. He held that piece separate from the others as if it were precious—as if it carried something special. Before he walked toward his desk, he turned and said, "I want to know more. I want to know what happened with the spirit bear. Stay after class."

THE REST of the period continued uneventfully until the bell rang. Everyone completed their experiment and cleaned up their materials. Mr. Winston helped Balidova bandage her hand and sweep up the glass. She felt gratitude toward him for keeping a first aid kit in class. She didn't have time to go to the nurse before her next class started and didn't think the cut was that serious.

She was walking out the door when Mr. Winston called, "Balidova, come over here." It was just the two of them in the classroom. He walked around and sat on his desk, facing her. "Tell me. What happened with the spirit bear?"

Why are you asking me so many questions? she wondered. She looked down at her bandaged hand and thought of how he'd helped her clean up the mess of the broken glass and guard her from the nosiness of her classmates.

She sighed. "Well, after you encouraged me to meet the spirit on the full moon, I did. I went into the forest, and I saw something there. It was like a tree spirit that seemed to turn into this white creature. Before I knew it, a Kermode bear came over to me." She omitted the part about the hunter.

"It said, 'You are the chosen one. You must learn the seven steps of the Dragon Tail Breath before it is too late.'"

Mr. Winston looked startled. He furrowed his brow, then rubbed his chin with his fingertips. "Is that it?" he queried. "Did it say anything else?"

"I asked the bear, 'Before it's too late for what?' but the bear never told me." Balidova shrugged her shoulders.

Mr. Winston relaxed his brow and smiled. "Did it teach you the first step?" He seemed quite interested now.

"Yes," she replied nonchalantly.

"What is it?" He seemed excited now, leaning towards her.

"Um," she took a step back, suddenly feeling like he was invading her space, even if it was nice to have a teacher so genuinely interested in what she was saying. At the same time, she took in a deep breath, preparing the words she was about to say.

"The first step of the Dragon Tail Breath is breathing the color green through my heart while saying the words *All is Well*. I calm down everything inside of me and come back to neutral. That's Step One."

"Okay, got it." Mr. Winston said. He seemed a little amazed at the simplicity of the steps, as if he were expecting something more. "So is that what you were doing just now, down on the floor after the prism broke?"

"Yeah," she replied, "I saw a spot of green light on the floor, and it reminded me that I didn't have to panic. I remembered that I could calm myself down by breathing and saying *All is well*.

"Good. That's really good." Mr. Winston nodded his head and turned back toward his desk.

"Can I go now?" She looked at the clock. She only had a couple of minutes to get to her next class.

"Yes," he said absent-mindedly, touching the patch on his throat. "Yes, you can go."

She walked toward the door, pausing to look back at him. *Hmm, maybe I can tell him more. He seems to be the only one I can trust with this info. He is my science teacher, after all. Maybe he does know about all this spirit stuff? Just like he knows about wavelengths of light. The bear was teaching me about light, and so is he. Are they connected?*

"Oh, and one more thing." Balidova paused. "Someone tried to kill the spirit bear."

"Who?" Mr. Winston leaned forward.

"Gus Polter's dad."

"Oh, wow."

Balidova walked out of the classroom with a lighter gait than she'd had coming in. She felt relieved not to carry the weight of being the chosen one—the weight of the secret steps—on her own.

CHAPTER 9
KARATE CONFUSION

Several weeks went by. Balidova told her parents about what had happened at school—getting blamed for Jojo's broken arm, being hauled into the principal's office, detention, and community service.

When she told them, she spoke mostly to her dad. He was not happy about the detention but understood when she explained that she didn't do it—she just happened to be in the wrong place at the wrong time. She served her detention and did her community service at the local soup kitchen begrudgingly.

She also got her stitches out—the cuts on both hands were healing nicely. However, the tear on her red jacket was not. Her mom had finally noticed it and was not happy. Balidova took the scolding silently. She was still not talking to her mom. And Angel was still not talking to her.

One morning, Balidova and her sisters had another workout with their dad in the basement, preparing for the regional karate competition. As usual, they lined up in age order from right to left, oldest to youngest, sitting in seiza with their legs tucked underneath them, backs straight, hands on their laps. Their dad was at the front of the dojo, facing them. Together, they all bowed in unison, showing respect to their Sensei. Turning and facing each other, they bowed again, showing respect to their fellow students.

After warming up, the older three practiced their team kata together. Actually, they practiced *bunkai*—the real-life application of the kata moves—against each other. Balidova paired up with her eldest sister.

"Kiotski. Rei. Shi-ho-hei!" her eldest sister April, and team kata leader, commanded. *Stand at attention. Bow. Name the kata.* Then, they began. Turn, step, punch. Turn, step, punch. Turn, step, punch. Turn, step, punch. Look right, block, sidekick. Look left, block, sidekick. Turn backward, step, backfist, double punch. Turn forward, step, backfist, double punch. Finish and bow.

When her sister punched, Balidova blocked, and vice versa. They executed the movements close up and in sync with each other, as if they were fighting real opponents with the pre-arranged moves.

After a couple of rounds of this, the sisters started to get snarky. When they performed one particularly rapid series of blocks and punches, April's fist came down hard on Balidova's forearm, near her hand.

"Ouch, that hurt!" Balidova shouted, holding her arm. Her cuts had almost healed over since the stitches had been removed, but there was a scar on the middle finger of her left hand and the back of her right hand. And now there would be a big bruise on her arm.

"Pay attention, Balidova," April growled. "You keep messing up."

"You didn't have to whack me," Balidova protested. She looked down at her hand and noticed that it was throbbing in the spot where her stitches had been.

"Balidova, your timing is a little off," her dad commented. "Visualize how you want to perform the kata in your mind before doing it with your body."

"Oh yeah, sorry," Balidova said sarcastically, annoyed that he was siding with April.

The eldest sibling continued her bossy tone, directing it toward another sister. "The turn isn't to the left, May. It's like this." April demonstrated the kata movement exactly as their dad had shown them.

"Who's the favorite daughter now? Huh? Do it exactly like dad says," May taunted the eldest one. "Visualize perfection."

"Oh, shut up. You're just jealous coz I can do it better," April hit back.

"No, I'm not. You'll see. I'll smoke your butt at the tournament," May said, giving April a death stare.

"Okay, you're on," April replied, glaring at May. The competition in the household was in full swing, even though the tournament was a month away.

"No one asked my opinion." Balidova chimed in.

"Who cares what you think? You're not that good anyway." May retorted.

"Just follow along and don't mess up," April added.

Great. Just what I need. Everyone is telling me what to do. Again. Little Balidova, she can't do anything right.

Balidova tightened her green belt around her waist to protect herself, fiddling nervously and adjusting the ends, so they were evenly matched.

She paused for a moment.

What about me?

Just asking the question made her feel in control again, even when she knew she wasn't.

I'm furious that my sisters are in charge and I'm supposed to listen to them. And that all of us have to listen to my Dad! What about what I think? Doesn't it matter? To anyone? It's all just so unfair.*

She looked over at her two older sisters, still arguing away, seemingly oblivious to her existence.

All I know is that I'm not supposed to be mad. I got in big trouble for punching a hole in my wall. Not only did I have to repair it, but I had to do all the fence repairs for the horse paddocks too. Everyone thinks I'm crazy when I'm mad, and they listen to me even less. I'm supposed to be okay with my older sisters leading team kata and deciding how to do it. Okay with my dad deciding we're going to this tournament. Okay with all of it. Do I even deserve to be mad? No. There's nothing to be mad about. I shouldn't even be upset.

By now, Balidova wasn't angry anymore. She was resigned. Subdued. Sad. She hung her head and shuffled to the side of the dojo, plunking herself down on the floor with her back resting on the wall. She couldn't deal with it all. Her sisters. Her dad. Her mom. Angel. Jojo. Gus. The cuts on her hands, not one but two. Everyone unhappy with her. Blamed for something she didn't do at school. Ignored for something she wanted at home.

It was all just too much. Too many things had eroded her self-confidence and made her question herself.

Her heart rate quickened, and her breath grew shallow as her body tensed. She felt a blanket of doubt and worry close in around her. Confused, she didn't know whether to trust herself. She didn't have the will to fight anymore.

She turned to her sister, "Okay, I'll do it as you say. I'll do the kata your way—you win."

She sighed and shook her head, feeling completely deflated. *Oh well... at least we'll win the tournament. No one can beat the Forester sisters in team kata.*

Then she got up, clenched her jaw, swallowed her pride and anger, and lined up with the team. *No one cares what I think anyway. I hardly even care anymore.*

All the stuff the spirit bear had taught her about the Dragon Tail Breath seemed so far away that she could barely remember it.

CHAPTER 10
THE RIDDLE

Balidova fidgeted incessantly at school the next day, a bandage still wrapped around the middle finger of her left hand where she'd had her stitches removed. It looked hideous and throbbed like crazy. The whack from April had re-injured the cut.

Right when everything's getting better, something comes along and sets me right back, like what happened after I met the spirit bear. Things were going so well, and now they suck again. Feels like my heart's in my finger and is gonna pulse right outta there any minute. Is that what happens when you focus on something, she thought as she looked at her finger. *Do you get more of it?*

The more she focused on the pain, the worse it became. She'd read about that kind of power in one of her favorite books and decided to try it out. In her least favorite classes, English and drama, she focused on the pain in her finger a lot, and it seemed to get worse. But in her favorite classes—math and science, she could hardly feel it when she was happily preoccupied.

Could she regulate her pain?

Balidova loved playing these little mind games with herself. *If this, then that. If that, then what?* Words were like numbers to her. She could add and subtract letters or spaces to make new words with different meanings, just like a new equation. For example, *no where* becomes *now here* when you change where the space goes. *Impossible* becomes *I'm possible* when you add an apostrophe and a space. *Disease* becomes *dis-ease*, which shows you the real meaning of the word. *Responsible* becomes *response-able*. She busied herself with her mind puzzles, keeping her thoughts off her pain.

Despite her facility with words, Balidova didn't like English class because she was forced to read books not of her choosing. However, she loved to write. She always kept a journal where she jotted down little ideas and notes about her thoughts and feelings. She found it comforting to write down her thoughts, as if she were paying extra attention to a part of herself that didn't usually get much attention.

She found that over time, as she went back and re-read her journals, patterns and connections showed up between things that happened in her head and things that happened in real life. Writing stuff down brought a clarity she didn't have with just thinking. It connected the dots in a way she couldn't otherwise see. Simply put, keeping a journal helped Balidova sort out her life.

She also loved numbers. Math was her favorite subject, followed closely by science, which was the application of numbers and rules in the real world. She liked the predictability of numbers and rules you could trust. *Once you know the rule, you can change the variable and still know the answer. Apply the formula and get the correct answer. For example—shining a light through a prism reveals a rainbow.* She found security in knowing that certain processes would yield predictable results.

"Balidova, are you daydreaming again?" Her biology teacher said, tapping her desk with a ruler. "Who are you nodding at?"

She snapped back to attention, "Oh, uh, just remembering something," she replied sheepishly.

"Okay, class, quiz on recessive and dominant genes next week. Make sure you review," her teacher announced. "Also, make sure you know the difference between an albino and a recessive gene."

Balidova cocked her head sideways as if recalling something. *The white bear. It's not albino because its eyes have color. The white fur is from a recessive gene that both parents must carry, even if they have dark fur. That's why it's so rare.*

She stuck her hand in her pocket and noticed something there. After pulling it out, she looked at it—a simple, grey stone. She didn't think anything of it until she glanced at the white speckles.

"Hey, isn't that the stone the spirit bear gave me?" She turned it over in her hand and felt a shiver run down her spine. "I must've left it in my pant pocket all this time. I gotta find that bear again. Everything's gotten so crazy."

WHEN SHE GOT HOME that afternoon, Balidova dropped her school bag, grabbed an apple strudel and a banana from the kitchen, and went straight out the side door. She ran toward the edge of the forest, panting.

She looked around, not sure if this was the right spot. Then she let out a big sigh of disgust as her head sank. *Why didn't I pay more attention to where the meadow was? The most important thing that's ever happened to me, and I don't even know how to get back there.*

Inhale.

Exhale.

With each deep breath, she slowly released her frustrations. And after an extra-long exhale that seemed to go on forever, she remembered the truth she had felt before—*a breath changes everything*. She flung her head back and smiled up at the sky.

"Show me the meadow."

"Show me the meadow!"

"SHOW ME THE MEADOW!"

She didn't know if shouting to the sky would make any difference but had no other ideas at that moment.

She paused and looked around again. All of a sudden, a bird fluttered by and landed on a branch next to her, just inside the forest. After a few chirps, it got her attention. *Hey, isn't that the same bird that guided me to the meadow last time? It sure looks the same.*

As she got closer, the bird flew off and landed on another branch, waiting for her to catch up. She noticed white specks on its wing tips. Balidova smiled, "Yes, it IS the same bird!" As she walked closer, she felt a surge of happiness. A doorway had opened inside her. A doorway to possibility. A doorway to feeling calm again. She didn't realize how much she looked forward to seeing the white bear—how desperate she was to feel better. Her exuberance surprised her.

Balidova picked up her pace through the trees, breaking into a trot as she followed the little blue bird to the meadow.

When she got to the edge of the clearing, she stopped and gasped at the beauty of the open space. Light danced off the snow cover like crystalline fairies performing a ballet. The afternoon light was still low in the sky, filtering through the trees, coming straight toward her. Golden rays simultaneously cast long shadows behind her and greeted her, illuminating her face and making everything invisible as they shone straight into her eyes.

No bear was present in the meadow. There was nothing except snow and the little blue bird chirping.

"Spirit bear, where are you?" she cried desperately. "I need you."

When nothing happened, she called the bear by another name. "Tree spirit, come out," she demanded. "I'm here, and I need to talk to you."

Nothing happened. No leaves rustled, no wind blew, and no snowflakes floated up.

"Tree spirit, I need you!" she called even louder.

Still nothing.

She questioned herself. Something that had been so real a short time ago had faded into the back of her mind.

"TREE SPIRIT, WHERE ARE YOU!" she shouted at the top of her lungs—a hint of desperation evident in her voice.

Suddenly, she *remembered*.

She paused.

Collected herself.

And took a deep breath.

With the power of her thought, she said calmly, steadily, and firmly in her mind, "Tree Spirit, please come to me *now*."

She called the spirit bear with her mind, heart, and spirit. Not her mouth. As if talking to the bear on another plane of existence.

Calm, yet commanding.

A BREEZE PICKED UP. Snowflakes swirled in the air, and tree branches swayed together, forming a pathway illuminated by a stream of light. As the light reflected off the underbellies of the evergreen needles, it cast a green glow all around. Out of this light path, the magnificent white face and wide, piercing eyes of the spirit bear appeared. Small ears protruded from the crown of its head, leading down its thick neck to a solid shaggy body.

"Am I ever glad to see you," Balidova announced with great relief.

"You called me?" the bear asked, stepping toward the girl.

"Yes," Balidova smiled cheekily. "How'd you know? I didn't say a thing."

"I can hear your thoughts," the bear said without any fanfare, as if it were a regular thing. "That is how we speak to one another. That is how we communicate," the bear spoke slowly, emphasizing each word as if the words themselves were little bits of energy passing between them.

"Hmm," Balidova pondered, "you mean telepathy?"

"If you want, you can call it that. I call it the *Knowing*." The spirit bear paused to let those words sink in as it rotated its head in a big circle, encompassing everything around it.

"When you know what you want—and you feel it with your body, mind, and soul—I feel it too, and I respond. When you speak with your inner voice and speak your truth, I hear it too." The bear picked up one paw and touched its own heart.

"Wow, that's cool. That's very cool. I've never spoken with anyone else like that," Balidova announced. She placed a hand on her heart, mimicking the bear.

"Oh yes, you have." the bear said in a deadpan voice.

"With who?" Balidova asked, upturning her mittens.

"Your horse. Your dog. Your cat. They all speak this language. All animals do, humans included. It's just that humans like to pretend they've forgotten," the bear smiled.

"Oh yeah, you're right. I talk out loud to the animals in the barn all the time, but I also speak to them silently, in my head," Balidova grinned. "It's like they can feel my energy. They know when I'm sad, when I'm happy, when I'm in a rush, and when I'm relaxed. My mood affects them. Animals are smart that way."

"Yes, they are," the bear nodded with its snout.

"Can I speak that way with other humans?" Balidova wondered aloud.

"You will, in time," the bear said, shifting its weight to its hind legs, sitting upright, facing the girl head-on. "So, Balidova, why did you call me?"

The girl looked down at the snow and made a figure-eight track with her boots. "I had a hard time over the past few weeks. I was doing a science experiment at school—diffracting light through a prism. But I dropped the prism, and there were shards of glass everywhere. My hand got cut and was bleeding all over the floor. Everyone in the class was staring at me, my teacher was annoyed, and I was in pain. Plus, the same day, I got blamed for a bad thing someone else did at school." Balidova let out a long sigh. "And I fought with my sisters during karate practice, again. I feel like no one listens to me. No one understands me."

"So, what did you do?" the bear asked unsympathetically.

Balidova looked up, staring straight into the bear's eyes. "Well, I listened to you. I used the Dragon Tail Breath."

"Excellent," the bear said, somewhat surprised. "What was that like?"

Balidova shrugged, "I dunno, it was okay." She paused. "Actually, it was pretty cool." She paused again. "Amazing. It changed everything." A grin slid across her face. "I paused. I breathed. I stopped focusing on all the staring and screaming, even while it was still happening, and I tuned into myself."

"What did that feel like?" the bear said, bringing its head so close to Balidova that she could see the long row of white teeth in its jaw and touch its steely whiskers.

"It felt like angry octopus tentacles gradually releasing their tight grip around my core. A yucky feeling detached from my body and got further and further away. There was space where I could breathe without being wrapped up in all that craziness."

"Wow, that's amazing!" the bear confirmed. The creature pulled its head back and sat upright once again.

"So, I breathed some more," Balidova continued, adjusting her toque down on her head, getting ready for what came next, "and then I breathed in the green light." Her face beamed with pride.

"Very good!" the bear clapped its front paws together. "What did *that* feel like? Do you know that light is a vibrational frequency? You breathed in the green frequency, a lovely vibration!"

"Yeah, I learned about all that in science class," Balidova smiled. "As I breathed in the green light, I could feel it filling my body. At first, it started with a little ball right in the center of my heart."

Balidova placed a hand on her heart, then lifted it off her body, mimicking the rise and fall of her chest with the breathing motion. "With each breath in and out, the ball of light grew bigger and bigger until my entire body felt like it was pulsing with green light. I saw that everyone was freaking out, but I wasn't a part of that, at least not for long. The more I breathed, the more I felt protected by a light shield. I felt different, surrounded by that light. Really different. I've never felt that before."

The bear nodded its head gently, in sync with the swaying trees on the meadow's edge, listening intently and encouraging her to continue.

"When my teacher came up to me and started talking, the green light faded. So, I used the words you taught me. I kept saying them over and over in my head as everyone in the class stared at me. I started saying *all is well*."

"Very good."

"Those words carried me through the day. As soon as I said them, I calmed right down."

"Well done!" the spirit bear said, holding its front paws out wide. "Well done, Balidova! That is the Dragon Tail Breath. The first part of it anyway."

Balidova gasped, "You mean there's more?"

"Would you like to learn Step Two?" the bear inquired, clasping its front paws together.

"Oh yes! I didn't know there was more."

"Because you had the compassion to help me escape from the hunter who tried to shoot me, even when I was a total stranger to you, I will show you." Without missing a beat, the bear gave the girl the following instructions:

"Meet me on the next full moon when the sun is low in the sky, and you are way up high with the light shining straight into your eyes."

With those final words, the spirit bear winked at the girl in her red coat, lay its front paws back onto the snow, and lumbered off into the trees.

BALIDOVA, startled to be alone in the forest once again, turned to head home. With each step she took, she repeated the phrase as the bear had spoken it, word for word. She wanted to anchor each phrase into her body so she would remember it. As she navigated the dense underbrush, she slowed the bear's sentence down and turned it into a poem:

> *Meet me*
> *on the next full moon*
> *when the sun is low in the sky*
> *and you are way up high*
> *with the light*
> *shining straight into your eyes.*

She had no idea what the words meant, but she knew she had to figure them out quickly. The riddle was the key to her learning Step Two of the Dragon Tail Breath.

CHAPTER II
GOLDEN LIGHT STREAM

In her room after school the next day, Balidova felt cooped up in the house—irritated like a caged animal—not sure what to do. *Ugh, I need to get outside. Get some fresh air and open sky. I need to get out to the barn.*

She put on her red jacket, white & black snow boots and trudged out through the snow to the big red building at the back of the property. It was still bitterly cold and getting dark early in February. But she wanted to go for a quick horseback ride before the sun went down.

THE BARN WAS Balidova's refuge. She loved being with the animals. Their energy was pure. They didn't fight with her, argue with her, complain, or judge her. They were there for her. Always.

Melody whinnied when she heard footsteps, and Balidova responded by heading to the feed room to get a handful of grain for her favorite horse. The other horses whinnied too, but she treated Melody first before going to them.

Balidova brought her horse out of the stall, rubbing the white star and stripe down Melody's face. Tenderly, she brushed her horse down, picked the dirt out of her hooves, and threw a bridle over her head. She decided to ride bareback—no saddle—because she loved the feeling of Melody's body right next to hers, with nothing in between. She loved feeling the warm embrace of a creature who just accepted her as she was, no questions asked.

Together, girl and horse clip-clopped out the driveway and turned left, along the gravel shoulder next to the paved road. They took another left turn down another street and picked up the pace to a trot. Melody sniffed the cold air, snorting with glee. She was happy to be outside too.

"We both love the outdoors, eh Melody?" The earthy smell of fresh evergreen trees—a mix of pine, cedar, spruce, and hemlock—filled the air. A deep layer of snow framed the roadside, part of the white winter wonderland stretching in every direction.

Together, they reached the end of the paved road and turned down the forest path toward the Kitimat River. Yesterday's fresh snow had already been packed on the trail by hikers. A thick canopy of trees overhanging the path blocked some snowfall, so it wasn't impassably deep. Still, Melody's hooves sunk several inches, making a muffled sound on the snow.

Picking up the pace again to a canter—a much more comfortable gait to ride bareback—they sped down the path. Balidova sat up tall, gripping Melody's mane between her fingers, soaking in the beautiful feeling of being alive with her horse beneath her. She closed her eyes for a split second, letting her other senses take over. The cold wind touched her face, the taste of snowflakes blanketed her tongue, the smell of pine needles engulfed her nostrils, and the sound of hooves pounding filled her ears. She loved the feeling of riding through the forest. Two of her favorite things—trees and horses—together.

Just as she opened her eyes from this blissful reverie, a low-hanging branch smacked her in the face. She tumbled to the ground.

Immediately, Melody slowed and came to a halt. The young mare turned around and looked back at her rider, sprawled on the ground. Melody's ears twitched back and forth, listening for the girl.

Luckily, the snow had cushioned the girl's fall. Yet Balidova held her forehead where the branch had hit her, moaning out loud.

She took a deep breath, walked over to Melody, and jumped back on. Her Mom's words echoed in her head: "If you fall off your horse, just get right back on—that's how you deal with it."

By now, the sun was setting, resting low in the sky, casting long streams of light through the trees. Both horse and rider faced the sunset, with golden light shining into their eyes, illuminating their faces. They stood still as Balidova regained her balance, taking four deep breaths in and out.

All of a sudden, she squealed, "That's it! The riddle! The answer to the riddle! What were the words again?"

Meet me when the sun is low in the sky, and you are way up high with the light shining straight into your eyes.

She flung her head back and hollered, "I got it! I figured it out! It's right here, right now, where I am! I'm way up high on Melody, and the sun is low in the sky—that's the sunset—and the light is shining straight in my eyes. This is where I learn Step Two of the Dragon Tail Breath!"

She looked around excitedly, expecting the spirit bear to appear, but didn't see anything. *Maybe I need to go more toward the light.* Lightly tapping Melody's sides with her heels, they walked forward toward the river.

Still nothing.

They continued walking down the winding path. The stillness of the forest was calming and a bit spooky at this time—dusk. The day creatures were preparing for sleep, and the night creatures had not yet emerged.

But Balidova didn't want to go home yet. She felt a deep sense of peace here—a beautiful, irrational, calm.

Wow, there's that feeling again. The same feeling I had with the spirit bear in the meadow. The same feeling I had with the wind in the lagoon.

She desperately wanted to learn Step Two of the Dragon Tail Breath.

As the sun disappeared and the moon rose, Balidova did not see the bear anywhere. Doubt started to set in. But just as she was about to turn back toward home, she noticed the river in front of her swirl strangely.

The water formed into a whirlpool, swirling faster and faster. It formed a deep eddy in front of her, then abruptly switched directions, releasing a spray of foam that rose up and took on a life of its own. All of a sudden, the rush of water droplets shifted dramatically.

For a second, Balidova felt afraid. She noticed that Melody did too. The horse's ears lay flat back, a sign of fear or aggression. But as the water droplets formed into an oversized shape, both girl and horse changed from feeling fear to sensing wonder. Melody's ears perked forward, and Balidova's eyes softened.

Light, reflecting off the water molecules, gave the distinct appearance of... the head, body, and tail of a gigantic fish! Balidova noticed from the streamlined body and fin markings that it was a salmon. Crystallizing in full silver scaled splendor, the aquatic creature appeared.

Her jaw dropped. *Is this real?*

She glanced at Melody, who was reacting to it too.

Yup, it's real.

She held the reins tightly in her hand in case Melody balked and tried to run away.

"Hello, dear one," the fish said, looking straight at her with golden eyes. It seemed to be hovering above the river, with only its tail submerged in the water.

"How'd you do that?" Balidova said, startled.

"Do what?" The fish wiggled its slippery body.

"Appear out of the water like that!"

"I have power over the water. And you will too, in time."

"Really? Will I ever be that powerful?" she said with a sly grin.

"Yes, but before you can master the earth elements, you must gain mastery over yourself. You must master the elements within YOU," the fish turned and pointed its dorsal fin toward her.

"What are the *elements within me*?"

"Your body, mind, and spirit." The fish said quietly, just above the sound of the rushing water.

Balidova paused for a moment. She almost didn't hear what the fish had said. "Will Step Two allow me to master myself?"

"There are many steps," the fish laughed, "many steps. And Step Two will move you along the path. Because you have demonstrated that you can connect deeply with another creature—your horse—enough for her to want to stop and help you when you've fallen, I will teach you."

Balidova looked at Melody, who was standing patiently, enjoying the respite before she would carry her rider again.

The fish rocked its strong tail back and forth in the water as it spoke.

"Step Two is breathing golden light into the solar plexus."

The fish's rhythmic motion almost lulled Balidova into a trance. "The what?" she said, snapping back to attention.

"The solar plexus. Do you know where that is?"

"I learned that in karate." It's at the base of the chest bone, above my belly button. There's a spot where all the abdominal muscles come together and form a small hole. That's the solar plexus." She looked down at her stomach and put her finger on the spot.

"Yes, that's right." The fish nodded its silver head. "There's an energy center there—a very important one representing your internal strength. Breathe in and fill yourself with light. Rise to a new level of power—not a fear-based power, but a love-based power."

"What's the difference?" Balidova asked, scrunching up her face in confusion.

"One is power over others. The other is power within yourself."

"Which one's which? Balidova smiled cheekily.

"I think you know," the fish winked, its black pupil floating in a golden eyeball. "Become *Lovingly Powerful*."

"Or powerfully loving?" Balidova asked.

"Lovingly powerful." The fish repeated, clapping its pectoral fins for emphasis. The noise startled Melody, and she backed away from the water for a moment.

"What's the difference?" Balidova asked, reassuring her horse with a gentle pat on the neck.

"You tell me," the fish replied.

Balidova pondered the words. "Well, *powerfully loving* seems super, super loving. Whereas *lovingly powerful* sounds like a power that comes from a loving place?"

"Yes, exactly. Bring in the power that comes from a loving place. Breathe it into your solar plexus and breathe it out your mid-back. Let it travel through you and fill you up."

BALIDOVA HELD the leather reins in her hands as she stood next to Melody. She breathed in the light as if she were breathing in warm golden rays of morning sun straight into her body. Standing in this stream of light, she let it pass through her, soaking in the glow.

"That's it, Balidova, repeat these words as you breathe in the light—*here now*. They will help you draw even more light into you."

Slowly, she let the words *here now* roll off her tongue. Her spine shuddered as something released from the back of her neck. The energy in her body shifted, and she suddenly felt more present, as if a bundle of her worries had sloughed off.

"Just let all that stuff go," the fish reassured her. "All your fears and worries, all your 'have to's and 'should do's, just let them go. Stop. Detach and disconnect. Remove your commitment to all that stuff. Wrap it with love and let it go." The fish paused. "Stop. Detach. Remove. Wrap. **S.D.R.W.**"

The fish shook out its fins and tail, sending silvery sparks of light and water into the air. "Right now, just be present with your breath, your body, yourself, and me."

BALIDOVA CLOSED HER EYES AGAIN. She breathed in the light, the water spirit, and herself. With her feet firmly planted on the ground, she felt the pebbles below her and the fish's presence before her. She heard the gushing sound of the stream and saw the moonlight reflecting off the water's surface. Everything seemed to come alive at a new level. Her whole body shuddered.

Whoosh.

Inhale.

Exhale.

She breathed in for four seconds, breathed out for four seconds, and repeated four times.

Half a minute later, as she opened her eyes, everything

seemed brighter. Sounds seemed louder, her breath deeper, the colors of the forest, stream, and sky more vivid.

"What happened?" she asked. "Everything's different."

"That's what happens when you pay attention. When you allow your senses to become fully present—here now—you can truly hear, taste, touch, see, and smell."

"Wow, that's amazing." Balidova bent down, touched the water, and felt its cold, silky smoothness on her hand.

"Remember Step Two of the Dragon Tail Breath, Balidova. Breathe in the golden light. Bring it with you into your daily life."

And with that, the fish held its shape for a second, then transformed into water once again, merging with the river in a plunging splash.

"But, wait! Where are you going?" Balidova cried out. "When will I see you next?"

The river spoke to her in whooshing tones:

"When you see a fiery mane,
on a face as bright and beautiful as the sun,
you will know you have become one
with the fourth element—the opposite of water.
Seek it in your name."

All she could hear now was the rushing sound of the river. A few whitecaps rose in the distance as if the water spirit were waving goodbye, and then the whitewater turned and flowed around the bend.

She looked down at the stream. A small brown pine cone was in the spot where the fish had disappeared. Rough ridges jutted out from its oval shape, creating a fan-like effect. She picked it up and showed it to her horse.

"Interesting, huh, girl?"

All of a sudden, she noticed how dark it had become. Slivers of moonlight through the trees illuminated the forest path. She looked up toward the full moon.

The Fish Moon.

Mounting her horse again, she rode back home as the torn sleeve on her red jacket flapped in the wind.

So many strange things have happened lately... the wind spirit that turned into an owl... that little blue bird... the tree spirit that turned into a bear and left me a stone... and now the water spirit that turned into a fish and left me this pine cone.

The whole time, I've had the same feeling of deep calm. But it doesn't make sense with everything going on. How can I feel this good with so much craziness in my life?

As they trotted home, Balidova reached down and petted Melody on the neck. She needed to feel the solidity of her horse at that moment, to make sure she wasn't making up her equine friend. Somehow, with all that had transpired over the last month since her birthday, the line between real and imagined was blurring.

Together, girl and horse made their way home through the moonlit night—the stone in one pocket, the pine cone in the other. Carrying a sense of magic home with her, she wondered, *How long will the feeling last this time?*

Once she'd put Melody safely back in her stall and returned to her room, she found her journal and scribbled the riddle as quickly as possible. She was desperate for anything that would enable her to hang onto the calm, joyful energy inside.

CHAPTER 12
BALIDOVA OSTRACIZED

Sitting at her desk the next day, Balidova couldn't stop thinking about the fish. *How did a giant fish appear out of the Kitimat River?* She reached into her pocket and pulled out the pine cone. Feeling the roughness of the seed between her fingers, she nodded her head. *Yes, it's real.*

As she walked down the hallway, breathing deeply, saying *here now*, she felt so excited, her whole body tingling and alive. What she had learned from the fish, the bear, and the wind, had completely blown her mind. A simple thing we do every day—breathing—can be so transformative!

She ducked into the bathroom before class. Pushing open the blue door, she stopped in her tracks. Right before her, Angel was washing her hands at the sink. She and Angel hadn't spoken much for the past month since Angel had gotten bullied by Gus, and Balidova was too proud to apologize. Their friendship slowed down to a trickle of gestures without any real connection between them. They hadn't hung out for weeks. By now, Balidova was *really* missing her best friend. She wanted to share her revelation with someone.

"Hey Angel," Balidova tried to sound calm, even though she was nervous and excited at the same time. She coiled the green cord of her hoodie around her fingers, then released it and started rubbing her earlobe.

Angel glanced over, widened her eyes in surprise, then turned back to the sink, continuing to wash her hands.

"I, uh, I'm sorry I didn't stand up for you before," Balidova said, her hands trembling.

Angel moved over to wipe her hands on the towel. "Well, that's nice, but it's kinda late now, Balidova."

"What do you mean?"

Angel sighed. "It's complicated."

"Well, I have some cool stuff I wanna tell you," Balidova continued, stepping closer. But Angel reached down to grab her backpack.

Sensing that she didn't have much time before her friend took off, Balidova blurted out, "I've been learning this dragon tail breathing technique, and I wanna share it with you."

Angel turned to look at her.

Oh, it worked. I got her attention... I'd better continue. "You breathe in the light, into different parts of your body. I've been meeting these spirits—wind, tree, and water—that turn into animals. So far, I've met an owl, a spirit bear, and a fish."

"What are you talking about?" Angel cut her off. "Are you sure you're okay, Balidova?"

"Yeah, I'm good. And this breathing thing... it's amazing." Balidova stepped closer to emphasize her point, hoping that Angel would get it if she were just more enthusiastic.

"Well, that's cool, Balidova, but it's kinda late, like I said. Lots of things have changed." Angel said as she stepped back.

"Huh?" Balidova said, puzzled.

Angel dropped her voice to a whisper. "I'm not supposed to tell you." She sighed, but she continued. "Gus threatened Jojo and me not to talk to you again. He said if we go near you, they're gonna destroy us."

"What? He can't do that. He can't tell you who to be friends with," Balidova protested.

"Look. I'm just sharing with you what's going on. And honestly, I'm still mad at you for what you did. That's where it's at Balidova. See ya later." Angel put her other backpack strap on and walked out of the bathroom before Balidova could get in another word.

Balidova stood in shock, leaning against the wall. She started talking to herself to sort out her jumbled thoughts. "I can't believe Angel, my best friend—well, former BFF, apparently—would give up that easily on me. And what about Gus and his gang? They can't go around threatening people!"

"Well, they just did." Jojo Beadle stepped out of one of the stalls and walked toward the sink. Her arm was still in a sling where it had been broken from her fall down the stairs. She glared at Balidova, her pointy nose directed at the girl in the green hoodie, as she turned on the faucet and washed her one good hand. "Serves you right, pushing me down the stairs like that because you're jealous of me being friends with Angel. You deserve whatever you get. I hope Angel never talks to you again in your life!"

"Look, I didn't do it," Balidova retorted. "I didn't push you down the stairs. Gus did! How could you not know that?"

"Hey, I didn't see who attacked me. One minute I'm looking down at my phone, another minute, I'm at the bottom of the stairs, and you're standing near the top. Plus, that video that got sent around— how could I *not* think it was you?"

Balidova looked dumbfounded—stunned into silence.

"Well, that's very convenient then, isn't it?" Jojo continued. "Blaming him. You were there, Balidova. And whether you did it or not—as you say—you were part of it... you didn't even come and help me up! You just left! And I got hurt!" Jojo turned off the faucet abruptly and tore a paper towel from the dispenser.

Jojo walked up close to Balidova and pointed her finger in her face. "You'd better watch out. Gus and his friends they're out to get you. I dunno what you did, but they're going after you, big time."

As Jojo walked out of the bathroom, she turned back to say one last thing before the door slammed shut. "Oh, and by the way, Angel and I are BFFs now."

Jojo's last words stung Balidova the most. Being hated by the school bully was one thing, but being rejected and replaced by her own best friend? That was something else entirely.

BALIDOVA HUNG her head in shame. Her hands dropped listlessly to her sides, and her whole body felt small. No one believed her. She felt powerless to win Angel back, powerless to convince Jojo of what had actually happened, and powerless to stop Gus from hurting her friends. A wave of helplessness descended upon her as if a dark cloak was wrapping itself around her, enveloping her in its grasp.

Feeling dejected, she stuck her hands in her pockets.

Something was there.

The stone... from the spirit bear.

As her fingers rubbed the rock, she suddenly remembered back to first grade when she and Gus hung out together. He cared about those butterflies they used to catch in the meadow, watch intently, and release into the afternoon sun.

Balidova was the only one who knew the truth—underneath that tough exterior was a sensitive boy who cared deeply. Perhaps so deeply, he had to hide it from everyone by being a bully. *Is this how he's making himself feel powerful? By bullying other people?*

Suddenly, Balidova felt indignant. She didn't mind paying for her own mistakes, but for someone else's? That was unfair. She straightened her back. *Well, I'm strong too. You're not gonna get me, Gus. I know who you really are.*

OVER THE NEXT couple of weeks, she kept to herself, going through the motions at school and doing her school work. At home, she did her farm chores, karate, and piano practice. She stuck to her routine. When she was frustrated, she took out her anger on the punching bag. When she was sad, she went to the piano to drown her sorrows on the keyboard. She learned to allow martial arts and music to complement each other. She felt lonely at times, but she also had Melody and Nutmeg. When she was bored, she shot rocks at the pine cones hanging from trees with her slingshot.

Glancing around her room, she returned to the stone and the pine cone sitting on the desk—the one the fish had given her—coming back to *here now*.

She breathed the green light in and out through her heart.

She breathed the golden light through her solar plexus.

Despite her efforts, with each passing day, the positive effect of the breathing seemed to become less and less as the realization of how alone she was grew more and more.

AT SCHOOL ONE DAY, she noticed red everywhere. Students were carrying cards and candies in the hallway. She looked at her phone; it was February 14, Valentine's Day—one of the most anticipated school days of the year—filled with oodles of joy for some and crushing disappointment for others. And queasy anticipation for all, not knowing what side of that equation they'd be on.

Balidova and her friends always shared Valentine's grams—little notes with candies attached that you could deposit at the office to be handed out to the recipient. It was a tradition. She and Angel had been best friends for years. Throughout elementary school and now in high school, they'd been there for each other. She looked forward to getting something today, but at the same time, she wasn't sure what would happen. As she headed to class that day, a nervous feeling filled the pit of her stomach.

Valentine's grams were given out in the third period after teachers received and sorted them in the morning. For Balidova, this happened to be in English class. She sat expectantly as names were called—each one resulting in a smile or flicker of glee from the recipient. Pretty soon, the whole class was reading notes and eating chocolates, except for her and one other girl. Everyone had received some gram, some message, some candy, some sign that they weren't a complete outcast.

Balidova felt embarrassed, lonely, and angry all at the same time. She left the class, noticing that people were looking at her. Gritting her teeth, she stuffed her books in her backpack and stormed out of the room into the hallway. *Everyone in this school hates me. I don't have a single friend.*

Balidova could feel everyone's eyes on her. She didn't know what to do, so she went to the safety of her locker. But as she neared, she could see a group of people standing around it. They were whispering and laughing. She pushed her way through to her locker and saw what they were snickering at. A picture of a dragon, breathing, with a long tail wrapped around in a circle and a big X through the entire thing. The words underneath said, "BF is a weirdo."

At that moment, May walked by, staring at the poster. Balidova saw the look on her sister's face. She could see May thinking, *What's that all about? What's my little sis not telling me?* Then she kept on walking with her friends.

Balidova ripped the sign down, opened her locker, crumpled the paper, and shoved it inside. It was all too much for her. She had no one she could confide in. All the dragon stuff wasn't making her life better. It was making it worse. *I'm the chosen one, huh? Yeah, chosen for what? Chosen to be a weirdo and a loser.*

The bell rang, and the crowd dissipated. Facing the privacy of her compartment, a single tear rolled down her cheek. She wiped it away quickly. *I can't let them see that they've gotten to me.* She slammed the metal door shut and headed to her next class.

As she walked by the doors where Gus and his gang normally hung out, they taunted her, "Hey Balidova, where are all your friends? You don't have any, do you?"

She stared at the floor, clutched her books to her chest, and walked faster.

As she neared her science classroom, she spotted Gus talking to Mr. Winston. *Hmm, that's weird. Why are they talking to each other? I didn't know he had Mr. Winston for science too.* She had an uneasy feeling about it but shrugged it off and continued walking down the hall. Both Gus and Mr. Winston looked up and stopped talking as she came closer.

Gus whispered in her ear as he walked by, "Watch out, Balidova, I'm gonna get you. I know who you really are."

BALIDOVA HAD a hard time concentrating in class. She was thinking about Gus's threat and all the strange things that had transpired since her birthday. A whole new world was opening up to her on the inside—the breathing, the light, the words.

At the same time, it seemed like her outside world was shutting down. She was still not talking to her mom, had no friends at school, and had no hope of getting them back anytime soon. Plus, she was the number one target of the school bully. The only beings on her side were Melody, Nutmeg, and Mr. Winston. And two of them weren't even human.

Sighing, she shook her head, got out her notebook, and scribbled down the lab procedure for the day—an experiment about kinetic and potential energy. Energy that moves now and energy that's stored for later. *All this dragon tail breathing stuff might feel good to me in the moment, but it's making my life worse.*

I don't think I can do it anymore.

Maybe if I drop it, things will change for the better.

CHAPTER 13
THE FORESTER SISTERS

The weekend after Valentine's Day, Balidova had bigger worries than riddles and bullies. The regional karate championship was held in Kitimat, with clubs from several nearby towns participating. Of course, 'nearby' was a relative term—it meant several hours drive because human habitation was scarce in the province's northern regions. Clubs from Terrace, Prince Rupert, Smithers, and Hazelton drove the desolate highway to Kitimat, which was literally at the end of the road. Since the town was at the tip of the Douglas Channel, a deep inlet along the western Canadian coastline that emptied into the Pacific Ocean, driving any further than Kitimat was simply not possible.

Balidova would be competing in two different events—kata and kumite. Together with her two older sisters, she'd compete in team kata. She would also be competing in individual kumite—sparring with a real opponent, with just two thin gloves and a mouthguard for protection.

Karate is touch contact to the face and full contact to the body, which requires a tremendous amount of control. Punches to the face must be pulled at the last second, but punches to the body can be delivered full force. Sensitive areas like the back, joints, and groin are off target—fighters will get a penalty if they hit someone there. The goal, unlike boxing, is *not* to knock someone out—if a fighter does that, they'll be disqualified.

Quite the contrary, the goal in karate is to show that you have the *potential* to knock your opponent out and the *control* to hold yourself back, even while attacking at full speed and power. Sometimes people get hurt because the difference between a broken nose and not is often a matter of a single inch. If your opponent thinks you will move back, and you move forward instead—watch out. You could easily end up with a broken nose and a sea of blood.

The tournament was being held at the Kitimat Community Center, a beautiful, brand-new building built with the support of the local Aluminum Smelter, which employed most of the people in town. Its unique shape and style blended in with the local mountains. Pine floors, large glass windows, high ceilings, river rock walls, and spacious gyms gave a sense of prosperity to the whole community, even when the economy was down.

Balidova and her sisters carried their gym bags into the well-lit locker rooms and changed into their white karate uniforms. Lots of other girls were changing too, eyeing the sisters warily. Everyone knew the Forester sisters trained a ton and couldn't be touched in team kata. Huddling their raven-haired heads together, the four sisters talked in hushed tones.

"Let's win this," April said, putting her arms around her younger siblings.

"Yeah, no problem," May chimed in, tightening her blue belt in a samurai knot.

"Okay, let's do it," Balidova agreed, enthusiastically placing her hand in the middle of the circle. After being rejected by her friends, it felt good to be in solidarity with her sisters.

"Everyone in," June said excitedly, putting her hand on top of Balidova's. They all quickly placed their hands on top of each other and did a private cheer.

Balidova and her sisters entered the gym and sat on the wood floor by the edge of the competition ring. The ring was a six-by-six-meter square of blue interlocking mats, framed by a two-meter wide square of red mats, for a total of eight-by-eight meters.

Other kata teams flanked them on the left and right, but that didn't faze Balidova because this was one of the few times she competed *with* her sisters instead of against them. It was one of the few times when she felt the safety and protection of her sisters as a single unit vs. the outside world.

Despite the comforting feeling of safety with her siblings, Balidova felt torn. She didn't like that her winning caused someone else to lose. Although she'd promised herself to win at karate no matter what, deep down inside, something about it didn't feel right. Part of her wondered if she had to be someone different from who she was to win? There was only one gold medalist.

But team kata was different. She and her sisters were a team. Win or lose, they did it together. It was one of the few times she felt united and in sync with the people she shared her home with. Because they practiced karate in their basement dojo and the club dojo, the Forester sisters were excellent—head and shoulders above the rest. They'd have to seriously mess up to *not* win team kata. Balidova liked the certainty of knowing they would do well. She could almost always count on feeling good after competing in team kata. Who needs the Dragon Tail Breath when you're winning?

When they were called to perform, the three girls looked at each other, stood up, and fanned out a couple of meters apart, standing in a line on the edge of the mat. They bowed, then took three big steps forward together. Their bare feet hardly made a sound on the floor. Balidova's older sister, positioned in the middle, continued another three steps ahead so the girls formed a triangle in the center of the ring. One in front. Two behind. Their crisp, white uniforms stood out against the blue tatami background.

Although they had rehearsed this opening so many times that it was second nature to them, Balidova had a nervous twitch in her cheek. Five referees surrounded them, one on each of the four corners of the ring, plus one front and center. Each referee held scorecards—white placards with two sets of large black numbers that flipped over to reveal different combinations of scores.

As soon as April announced the kata—"Basadai!"—the three girls began a series of kicks, punches, and blocks. With perfect synchronicity, they executed a variety of techniques: open hand, knife hand, spinning moves, even a part where they jumped up high in the air and landed on the floor crouching like tigers, looked left and right in a cat-like stance, then came up to finish with a loud, synchronized "Kiai!" at the end.

Partway through the kata, Balidova suddenly felt like she was losing focus. She remembered what had happened in their home dojo—she'd gotten in trouble for being out of sync and messing up the timing of the kata sequence. For a split second, she panicked.

I don't wanna be the outcast again—not here, not now, with everyone watching me. What about the promise I made to myself, to be perfect?

Instantly, her self-preservation instinct kicked in. She remembered what the fish had taught her—*here now*. Saying the words in her mind, she took a deep breath and felt focus return to her body. She went deeper inside, to the calm, untroubled region within. Another breath later, she felt something fire up on the inside. Suddenly, she was able to access all her previous training. For the remainder of the kata, she kept breathing steadily.

The shift was dramatic. She finished that kata not as the weakest team member but as the strongest. Blood pulsed in her veins as she remembered the vow she'd made to herself weeks earlier—*if I'm gonna do karate, I'm gonna win, no matter what it takes.*

Balidova had entered the ring with a nervous twitch in her cheek. But by the time she was ready to leave, she felt the tremendous power of her body, mind, and spirit activated within herself and with her sisters. She gritted her teeth with determined satisfaction.

AFTER THE GIRLS finished their kata, all three stood in the middle of the ring, breathing heavily. The kata had demanded their full focus and attention, their full speed and power through several minutes of strong, dynamic movements. It was a tremendous output of energy. Now they needed to catch their breath.

The head referee blew his whistle, and all five referees held up their scoreboards simultaneously, rotating them in all directions for everyone to see. An official at the front table called the numbers out loud while another person quickly scribbled them down. "5.9, 5.8, 5.6, 5.7, 6.0." Six was considered a perfect score. The highest and lowest scores were subtracted, and the remaining scores added up, giving a total of 17.4.

A gasp went through the crowd as the total was called out. The Forester sisters had done it again. It would take a miracle to beat them. The three sisters bowed, stepped back in unison, and lined up at the edge of the ring. Sitting cross-legged, they smiled at each other.

"Good job," April whispered.

"Yeah, we killed it," May added.

"Not bad," Balidova finished.

Other teams performed after them but didn't come anywhere close to their score. The Forester sisters had won team kata again.

A few moments later, their dad came over wearing a navy blue referee's suit and a white collared shirt. A red whistle hung on a string hung around his neck. He beamed from ear to ear, patting each of them on the back.

"Well done," he said, obviously pleased with his daughters' performance.

Balidova smiled, too, soaking in the glow of her father's approval. She felt the adrenaline rush of being the best. And more importantly, having everyone—including her dad—*look* at her and her sisters as if they were the best.

Her mind flashed back to the scene at school earlier that week, where she'd ripped down the embarrassing poster on her locker making fun of her. *This sure beats everyone looking at me like I'm a reject... I feel amazing!*

The pull of competition was intoxicating to Balidova. The nervousness of being pitted against one another... the surge of excitement from fighting and competing... the thrill of victory... and the rush of being viewed as the champ. It was all-encompassing. Whether others liked or disliked the Forester sisters, they respected them for rising to the top.

The idea that she and her sisters were better than others gave Balidova a boost from the murky depths of her low self-esteem. For a brief moment—the time between one tournament and the next—she rode the wave of victory.

The only problem with this type of thinking was that someone else had to lose for her to win. When she was the winner, everything was fine. But when she was the loser, that thrilling ride became a devastating trench of sorrow, disgust, self-hatred, and shame. There was no middle ground between the two extremes of victory and defeat.

Balidova would do anything to avoid going to that place. This meant she had to continue to win. Because not competing at all was simply not an option.

She didn't realize it, but she was slowly getting habituated to competing for *everything*. Her entire self-worth was getting wrapped up in winning. She began to believe that her value as a human being was tied *only* to the result of the match in the ring. If she won, she would be on top of the world. If she lost, she was worthless.

This <u>black-and-white thinking</u> filled her mind until there was no room for other thoughts. There were no shades of grey, and there was certainly no room for other colors. Yet, for Balidova, this type of thinking grew normal.

A FEW HOURS LATER, it was time for the kumite events. Balidova would be competing individually—against her sisters and other fighters. She couldn't rely on her sisters to carry her. She had to do it entirely by herself.

Kumite events are single elimination matches of two minutes each. The person with the most points at the end of time, or the person with an eight-point lead, wins. Different techniques are awarded different numbers of points. A punch to the body or face is one point. A punch to the back of the head or a kick to the body is worth two points. A kick to the head or foot sweep followed by a punch while the person is on the ground is worth three points. Any technique that has the potential of injuring your opponent to a higher degree, or is more complex, is awarded a higher number of points.

When her name was called, Balidova stood at the edge of the

ring, facing her opponent. Both bowed and stepped onto their marks in the center of the ring, about three meters apart. The referee signaled them to bow to each other, which they did, then bowed to the referee.

In a kumite match, the head referee is in the ring at all times, ready to stop the match when someone scores, if things get too heated, or if someone gets hurt. The head referee moves with the fighters so they can see what's happening. Four additional referees sit on chairs in the corners of the ring, holding red and blue flags, which are used to signal who's scored.

Balidova wore a red belt and red gloves. Her opponent wore a blue belt and blue gloves. A red flag raised by a corner judge would indicate a point for her. A blue flag would indicate a point for her opponent.

The two girls stood there, feet splayed wide apart, hands in fists by their sides, staring intently into each other's eyes. They both knew that when the referee said "Hajime!" they would lunge at each other and exchange blows.

Despite her fears, Balidova loved kumite. It terrified her and ignited courage within her at the same time. She was always riding that thin line between fear and excitement. Sometimes she would tip one way and sometimes the other. Today, coming off the team kata win, she was feeling excited. But the girl she faced was big and looked tough. Balidova nodded her head, thinking to herself—*this is gonna be a good match.*

"Hajime!" The referee shouted, signaling for them to begin. Immediately, both girls stepped forward, moving around cautiously, feeling out the distance between them. The other girl attacked first, lunging forward with a kick-punch combination. But Balidova saw it coming and stepped out of the way, just in time.

Part of the fighting skill is controlling the space between you and your opponent. Whoever controls that space controls the energy of the match.

Balidova quickly responded with an attack of her own—a punch to the body followed by a roundhouse kick to the head. Both were slightly out of reach as the girl moved back. Still, she'd let her opponent know they were on equal footing.

Just then, Balidova got distracted by a loud noise on the sidelines. For a brief moment, she lost her focus. Her opponent spotted it instantly and lunged in for a quick, sharp jab to the head. Score! The referee immediately stopped the match and awarded the point to her opponent. 0-1.

Balidova was down a point.

That's okay. I got this, she reassured herself. *There are still one and a half minutes left.*

Balidova's specialty was timing punch. She liked to draw people in by backing up and then spring on them when they least expected it, assuming she was on the defensive.

When the timing was right, she attacked with one of her favorite techniques—front hand punch to the face, followed by a backhand punch to the body. *Double up*—a two-punch combo in rapid succession. The front hand fake to the face was meant to get your opponent to block upward, exposing their chest for the real attack. Full contact is allowed to the body, so Balidova sank her second punch deep into her opponent's solar plexus—that small unprotected hole below the breast bone where all the abdominal muscles join together.

Wham!

Here now.

As she nailed the double up, her focus and breath brought even more power to her technique. For Balidova, there was nothing quite as satisfying as delivering a good solid punch to your opponent's gut.

Inhale.

Exhale.

"Yame!" The referee stopped the match and awarded a point to Balidova.

Now the match was tied, 1-1.

This time the other girl upped the ante. She faked, caught Balidova off guard, then executed a kick to the head. The blow caused Balidova's braces to graze against the inside of her mouth. Three points for her opponent. 4-1.

Balidova touched her hand to her mouth to see if it was bleeding, but nothing red showed up on her fingertips. Without missing a beat, she turned the blow into fuel and responded with a foot sweep followed by a punch. Wham!

The other girl landed hard on the ground. Three points for Balidova. 4-4.

Game on.

Both of them did another series of moves that earned them two points each. 6-6. Time was almost up. Whoever earned the next point would win.

Balidova knew she had to be careful. If she went in too early, she could be picked off. If she went in too late, she could miss her opportunity and lose the match. The next attack had to be just right.

But as she danced around her opponent, Balidova's back foot caught on the edge of the mat. She stumbled and lost focus for a split second. Her opponent wasted no time taking advantage of her misstep, landing a solid punch in Balidova's gut. Balidova went flying backward, landing on her butt.

A few seconds later, she stood up slowly, more humiliated than hurt. She felt sick to her stomach—not because of the punch, but because she knew she'd lost.

The two fighters bowed to each other, the referee signaling her opponent's win by raising his arm toward that side.

Balidova could barely look up. Ashamed of her mistake, she

stepped back and sat down on the edge of the mat. The good feeling she'd had from the team kata win had evaporated. A dawning panic rose in her. *If I don't win, nobody will like me. Second place means nothing.*

Balidova looked around to see if anyone noticed her internal crisis. From across the hall, she caught her dad's eyes. He frowned at her, then upturned his palms to say, 'what happened?' The sting of his disapproval hurt her just as much as that last punch to the gut.

Her breath shortened, and the muscles on her hands started to twitch. She felt beads of sweat roll down her temples. She loosened her belt a little and tried to take short breaths, but hardly any air entered her lungs. She was hyperventilating. A feeling of complete worthlessness swamped her body and overwhelmed her senses. She couldn't see any good in herself. An invisible Cloak of Fear seemed to be closing in on her, sending her into a full-on panic attack.

Right there, on the edge of the competition ring, she disintegrated inside. She looked for a place to hide, but competitors and spectators were everywhere. Besides, she had to stay by the ring until everyone in her division had finished competing.

Quietly looking down, Balidova pulled her gi over her face to hide her tears, anger, and confusion. With the sweaty uniform pressed against her eyes, she clenched her teeth and decided.

I am going to figure out the riddle the fish told me.
I will figure out where to go on the next full moon.
I have to learn Step Three of the Dragon Tail Breath.

CHAPTER 14
BLUE LIGHT BREATH

Back home that night, Balidova desperately searched for the words she had written in her journal, trying to find the riddle the fish had spoken. She knew they held the key to her learning Step Three of the Dragon Tail Breath. But when she found them, as hard as she tried, she couldn't figure out what they meant:

When you see a fiery mane,
on a face as bright and beautiful as the sun,
you will know you have become one
with the fourth element—the opposite of water.
Seek it in your name.

'The fourth element—the opposite of water.'
What's the opposite of water?

A siren sounded in the distance. Balidova listened with intense awareness.

Is that a fire truck?

She wondered if someone's barn was going up in flames from the heat caused by wet, moldy, fermenting hay.

Wait a minute... fire!

Fire trucks carry water!

Water puts out fire!

Water is the opposite of fire!

Yes, that's it.

She pumped her arms in the air triumphantly, then quickly frowned again.

'Seek it in your name.'

What the heck does that mean?

My name is Balidova Forester.

How's that related to anything?

Balidova... that doesn't sound like any place.

As she shifted uncomfortably on her bedroom floor, she noticed the pine cone the fish had given her. She'd forgotten all about it the last couple of weeks, with all the focus on the tournament and the drama at school.

Wait a second—a pine cone is the seed of a tree.

A giant tree can grow out of this tiny cone—it's waiting there to come out. She thought of the hundreds of pine cones she'd seen scattered outside.

What if each one of those grows into a tree?

Lots of trees together make a forest.

What about my last name?

Forester...

Forest.

I got it!

The place where we next meet is the forest!

Balidova did a little twirl on her butt, gleefully spinning around in a circle.

Then stopped.

But where in the forest? The woods are huge. They go on for hundreds of miles behind our house.

It could be anywhere.

She quickly went through the places she'd already been.

The lagoon, where I don't want to go again, not after nearly getting eaten by wolves.

The meadow, where I met the spirit bear.

The forest path by the river, where I met the fish—flooded now by rain and snow melt.

So that leaves the meadow.

But I have to wait for the full moon.

So far, I've only met the spirit elements on the full moon—the Wolf Moon in January, and the Fish Moon in February.

Balidova looked outside her window and saw a white orb in the clear night sky, surrounded by twinkling stars. It looked pretty big, but she could see a small piece missing.

She looked up 'next full moon' on her phone.

March 2nd. Two days away.

TWO LONG DAYS LATER, on a Thursday afternoon, Balidova put on her warmest pants, red winter jacket, and snow boots and hurried out the side door of the house. She ran into the forest, eager to see the spirit creature again. How would it show up this time?

There was no water nearby, so it couldn't be a fish.

She wanted to share her discovery about coming into *here now* during the tournament, and winning. She had experienced the shift while she and her sisters performed team kata. She had traveled from *there then* to *here now*. On her own.

There and back again.

She could do it—bring her focus back to what she was actually doing (the kata) rather than daydream about other stuff. In the few days since the tournament, she had already forgotten about her kumite loss, choosing to focus on her team kata win.

Nearing the edge of the wood, Balidova made a high-pitched chirping sound and looked for the little blue bird. A few seconds later, a small beak poked out from behind a branch. The bird tilted its head inquisitively, looking at the girl as if it knew she'd be coming.

"Can you show me the way through the forest?" she asked. "I promise I'll pay attention this time." *I want to be able to find the meadow on my own,* she thought. *I need to. I'm going to pay closer attention to everything from now on. Especially things I want. I'm gonna pay attention to them with my eyes, ears, nose, and all my senses.*

SHE FOLLOWED the bird as it flitted from branch to branch. Together, they skipped through the forest, reaching the clearing quickly.

Standing in the center of the meadow with her arms by her side, she called out, "Wind spirit, tree spirit, water spirit, I'm here now. Come to me."

A flash of light caught her eye, and she noticed something shining on top of the melting snow—a piece of glass. She picked it up and turned it in her hands, noticing how the light reflected off the sharp edges. Holding it still for a moment, she looked at her reflection. What was that behind her? She gasped when she saw a flicker of orange growing bigger and bigger.

A fire? In winter?

She looked around, wondering what to do when a voice sounded.

"Don't fear. It's me."

She spun back toward the fire, but there was no one there—

only flames rising several feet in the air. The fire was close to the edge of the meadow. Soon it would spread to the trees and light up the forest. Despite the snow cover, flames could catch the underside of the branches and burn from the bottom up. Her beloved forest would be destroyed, and there was nothing she could do about it. Balidova started to weep.

"Don't fear, it's me." the voice repeated.

"What? Who? Where are you?" Balidova asked frantically.

"The fire, look into the flames. What do you see?"

Balidova did as she was told, staring into the frightening orange and yellow heat. At first, her eyes focused on the movement of the flames. But as she held her gaze, she noticed something beyond the fire. Something lying deeper within.

Is that a pair of eyes? A fire spirit?

She shook her head and blinked vigorously, thinking it couldn't possibly be true.

Before deciding whether it was real or not, the fire changed shape and became a tall, thin flame extending up to her height. She gasped, fearful that she would get burned, but something remarkable happened.

The wild flames died of their own accord and left a beautiful, tall sunflower in their place. Its thick green stem and leaves were as tall as her. Balidova found herself staring into the very eyes she'd seen in the fire, except that now they were the eyes of a golden sunflower! Bright yellow petals fanned out like a lion's mane around the wide-open face of the plant.

All of a sudden, Balidova was reminded of the words from the riddle—"When you see a fiery mane, on a face as bright and beautiful as the sun." Although her head was spinning with questions, Balidova was overwhelmed by the sunflower's presence.

"Whoa! Cool! How'd you do that—transform from fire to flower?"

"Well, I am the sun-flower after all," the plant laughed.

Balidova shuddered. "And you can talk? Talking to animals is one thing, but talking to plants? So, the magic *is* real?"

"Why wouldn't it be? Don't you trust your eyes? Am I not here before you?" the sunflower beamed.

"Yeah, but it's just so weird. You keep... changing. I mean, if you're the same creature, that is?"

"What if I am? What if I'm not? Would it make a difference as to whether you listened to me?" the sunflower asked. "Does the form I show up in matter that much to you?"

"Well, we humans care about that stuff," she chuckled. "But I guess it doesn't matter that much because the feeling I have is the same."

"And what feeling is that?"

"Calm, good, peaceful, happy." Balidova paused. "There is something that happened since I learned from the water spirit. You won't believe what happened."

Balidova grinned with excitement. "When I was competing in team kata with my sisters, I was drifting off, daydreaming, and then I used *here now* to bring me back. My intention and focus got stronger and stronger as we did the kata so that by the time we completed it, I felt like I was flying. I was so strong and sharp—the movements just came alive."

"Well done, well done," said the plant, raising its flowery face. "That is the power of *here now* coming into the present moment."

The sunflower looked straight into Balidova's eyes, searching her soul before uttering its next words. "Only in the *now* are you able to access the magic. Only then are you able to access *all* your powers. Otherwise, they remain distant from you because you remain distant from yourself."

"So *here now* is like the base—the foundation of the house we're building? The foundation of the magic house?"

"Yes, you could say that. Being present, being in this moment, is the foundation of the *House of Balidova*. Everything rests on this foundation. Without it, there is no house. There's no place for you to call home." The sunflower smiled warmly at her, appreciating Balidova's quick mind.

Balidova placed the tips of her fingers together and pressed them into each other, bending and straightening them repeatedly, giving herself time to think. "But I have a few questions—how do I know I'm in the present rather than in the past or future? I mean, how do I *really* know?"

"Well, you tell me," said the fire spirit as it bent down into a patch of purple fireweed growing near Balidova. "What happens in your own experience? How does it feel?"

"When my head was in the past, my kata wasn't good. My energy and focus weren't really on it. I was worried I was gonna make the same mistake I made in practice." Balidova paused and looked up to the right as if recalling something more. "And when my head was in the future, I was thinking about the trophy we would take home afterward. It was like my energy was split. Part of it was in my body, doing the kata. And part of it was getting a medal placed around my neck. So, I couldn't enjoy either one. I wasn't fully there for either one of those things."

"Exactly," said the sunflower. "Not being present splits your energy. Divides it. Shatters it, like a broken prism, shards going in all directions." The sunflower splayed out its petals as wide as they would go. "But when you focus your energy into one place, it's as if all those shards collect and become a shiny, glistening mirror again, where you can see yourself so clearly." The sunflower retracted its petals, curling each one into a tight, fist-like ball.

Balidova sighed, then continued somewhat sheepishly. "Um, there's another thing I want to ask you about."

"What is it?" The sunflower replied.

"After we won team kata, I lost my individual kumite match. I felt terrible afterward. All that focused, good feeling from the team kata win vanished instantly." Balidova looked down as her voice dropped. "I felt as if I was sinking into a dark pit—as if a cloak of fear was wrapping itself around me, and I couldn't see any good anywhere. Not in me or anyone else." Tears welled in her eyes just thinking about that moment.

THE SUNFLOWER PAUSED FOR A MOMENT, straightened its stem, and slowly uncurled its leaves. As it did so, it spoke softly and cautiously to Balidova. "Dear girl, there is something you must know. This Cloak of Fear you felt? It's real."

Balidova looked up. "Really? It wasn't just my imagination?"

"No. Have you felt it before?" The sunflower looked concerned.

"Yeah, a few times." Balidova paused to think. "First was at home in my room, when I felt trapped and hating on everyone, including me. Then I felt it with my sisters in the dojo when I realized they didn't care what I thought. I felt so worried, and I doubted myself a lot."

"Yes, when else?" the sunflower prodded her.

"In the bathroom at school, when Angel and Jojo dissed me. And then, when Jojo said Angel was her BFF. I felt helpless to do anything about that. The dark cloak...." Balidova's voice cracked, just remembering how awful it felt.

"There's an invisible Cloak of Fear surrounding the planet," the sunflower explained.

"It's not just me?" Balidova sounded relieved.

"No. It affects all humans." The sunflower's voice dropped to a deeper, more serious tone. "The Cloak of Fear amplifies the fears of individual humans by reflecting them back, so that's all you see. There are many forms of fear, including anger, worry, hatred, helplessness, shame, jealousy, revenge, sadness, and worst of all, doubt."

"I had no idea," Balidova gasped. "You mean it affected my sisters when they didn't listen to me? And my friends, when they rejected me?"

"Yes. The Cloak of Fear exaggerates your fears. It makes them bigger and more powerful. And it joins your fears with everyone else's fears, forming a layer of dark energy around the planet. But since it's invisible, you don't know this. People feel intense negative emotions, not only because of what's inside them, but also because of the energy around them. And then they behave very badly."

"That's awful." Balidova puckered her face in horror. "The Cloak of Fear turns everyone into their worst self. That's nasty."

"Yes, it is. It must be stopped before it seals over the earth and traps all humans in fear forever. If that happens, all that humans will know is fear."

"You mean, once the Cloak of Fear seals, no one will ever feel good again?"

"That's right. No one will know love, peace, harmony, joy, happiness, laughter, or fun. Hope for a brighter future will be lost."

"That's terrible. That can't happen! How do we stop it?"

"Only light and love can stop it." The sunflower paused as if it were about to say more but then decided not to. All its petals were unfurled now, forming a beautiful gold mane around its face. "Are you ready to learn Step Three of the Dragon Tail Breath?"

"Yes, I am." Balidova had a new tone of resolve in her voice. She found a log and sat down, then picked up a handful of snow and started mushing it between her fingers, squeezing the white crystals until they melted in her hand and dripped out. She seemed oblivious to the cold... because an inner fire had lit.

The sunflower bent down with her toward the remaining snow, hard-crusted due to a recent rainfall followed by another freeze. Its brilliant gold petals glistened in the sun. "Because you have shown consistency in your ability to learn the steps, solving the first two riddles and coming to the meadow again, I will teach you." The sunflower paused. "But first of all, do you remember the initial steps?"

"Yes, I do," Balidova said deliberately.

"Tell me what they are," the sunflower smiled.

"Step One is breathing green light in and out through the heart." Balidova picked up a stone and rubbed it in her palm, remembering the rock the bear had given her.

"Good."

"Step Two is breathing gold light in and out through the solar plexus." She picked up another stone and rubbed the two rocks together in the palm of her hand.

"Excellent. Step Three involves the throat and the color blue—the brilliant hue of the blue sky that all plants reach toward as they grow. Step Three is breathing blue light in and out through the throat."

BALIDOVA LOOKED up at the open, blue sky, taking in its vast expanse. After a while, her gaze returned to the meadow and the sunflower. She looked at the ground and picked up a third stone. "What do all the different colors mean?"

"They are different frequencies. They represent the whole range of light frequency."

"Really? What's frequency?" Balidova asked, feeling the smoothness of the three rocks in her hand.

"How quickly a wave particle rises up and down. Imagine a roller coaster with long, low rises and dips. That's a slow frequency. Now imagine a roller coaster with high peaks that occur in rapid succession. That's a high frequency."

"Our bodies are light conductors. Humans require all the frequencies of light to function at our full potential. As we breathe in all the different colors of light, we raise our vibration and increase our energy. We expand the range of frequencies that we can hold."

"Really? But why does it matter?" Balidova wondered aloud.

"Everything is made of energy. Every. Thing." The sunflower looked at the stones in the girl's hand. "From hard rock to fluid water, invisible air to brilliant sunlight... everything on this planet is made of energy, including yourself. And guess what?" The sunflower lowered its voice as if it were sharing a long-lost secret. "Even invisible things like your thoughts and feelings are an energy frequency. Just like radio waves and cell phone waves. You can't see them, but they still exist."

"I don't know what that means, but I'll just take your word for it."

"No, don't do that." The sunflower shook its golden mane, frowning. "Experiment. Be curious. Ask questions. That is how you will know what is true and what is not true—for *you*. Don't just think about this idea. Experience it. By asking the universe to show you its meaning."

"Ok, but how do I get to know about frequency?"

"Watch and *feel*." The sunflower gestured beside Balidova, pointing out a bee hovering near her.

"Can you feel the buzzing and lightness in your body? What does it feel like right now?"

"It feels tingly. It feels good."

"Yes. That's a light frequency—a high vibration. And what words would you use to describe how you feel right now?"

"Happy. Relaxed."

"What does it feel like when you're fighting with your sisters and when everyone at school rejects you? When you're not talking with your mother?" the sunflower continued.

Balidova frowned and cast her eyes down. She was embarrassed that the sunflower could detect the things that were wrong with her. The mere thought of being angry created a reaction in her body—she tensed up. Choosing her words carefully, she spoke slowly, answering the sunflower's question.

"When I'm angry, my body feels small, tight, like I'm trapped in sludge and can't move."

"That's a heavy frequency—a low vibration." The plant continued. "High and low vibrations within you reflect your emotions. **Emotions aren't good or bad. They just are.** What you do with them can land you in trouble or not," the fire spirit chuckled.

"That's sure not what I learned at home," Balidova cried out. "Everyone blames their bad feelings on everyone else like they're a nasty contagious virus or something." her voice trailed off as she looked down at her scarred finger.

"Can someone insert a feeling in your heart? Or place a thought into your head?" The sunflower challenged her, pointing its broad leaves toward her chest.

"Well, no. But they sure try." Balidova retorted.

"Yes. Others can *influence* you. But at the end of the day, no one can insert a feeling into your heart. No one can *make* you feel anything. Only you decide how you feel."

"Instead of blaming everyone else for how you feel, now *you're* in charge. You are response-able. Blame is false, Balidova. The only one ever really in charge of you is you."

"So what do I do now?" Balidova asked.

"Pay attention to how you *feel,* dear girl. Not how you should feel. But how you *actually* feel. This is your *internal GPS*. Do not run from your fears, Balidova. Turn and face them. Otherwise, they will only grow stronger."

THE SUNFLOWER PAUSED, allowing the words to sink in. "Your emotions will tell you what's happening with your vibration. Your emotions will tell you which frequency you are tuned into—high or low. You can change it at any time, like changing a radio station. It does take some practice, though. Keep these two questions close to you, and ask them often of yourself:

How do I feel now?
How do I want to feel?"

"I don't get it. It doesn't seem like I have a choice about how I feel."

"That's ok. You will get it in time." The sun spirit spoke with a booming voice now. As if speaking to all the creatures in the meadow and Mother Nature herself.

"For now, just breathe. Breathe in the blue light," the sunflower reminded her, pointing its leaves to the sky. "Remember Step Three of the Dragon Tail Breath. Ask yourself, 'What do *I* want'? To say yes to yourself, you must be able to say no to others. Honoring what *you* want means not always pleasing others."

Balidova took in a deep breath.

The sunflower seemed to know what she was going through. It seemed to know that Balidova was trying to please everyone but herself. The girl wanted to slow everything down again.

Inhale.

Exhale.

She took four slow, deep breaths.

Slowly, Balidova stood up. She placed both hands by her side, put her feet shoulder-width apart, and tucked her hips in. She swayed gently from side to side in a sort of wave motion. The tone of her voice changed as she became more focused. It was calmer and clearer.

"When I breathe in the blue light, I feel like I'm breathing in water—I feel like I'm breathing in the open sky. I feel like I'm flowing." Balidova closed her eyes, nodding her head up and down, relishing the sensation inside.

Although she didn't know it, as she breathed deliberately in and out, she allowed the energetic elements of water, air, earth, and fire to strengthen inside her body, mind, and spirit.

Slowly but surely, like a blossoming flower, the dragon magic was coming alive within her. As Balidova opened her eyes, the sunflower's golden presence faded, and its last words echoed in her ears.

"Remember, dear one, what you want may not be the same as what others want. Always be true to you."

Balidova smiled. She looked up at the full moon in the waning daylight and immediately thought of the sunflower's bright face.

The Flower Moon.

As she turned from the center of the meadow to head home to the Forester family farm, a question arose within her—a query she could no longer ignore.

What do I want?

CHAPTER 15
THE HORSE BARN

Thank goodness it's Friday, Balidova thought.

Almost a month had elapsed, yet Balidova barely had time to think about the sunflower or the Dragon Tail Breath amidst her farm chores, school work, karate practices, piano practice, and horseback riding. The wonderful feeling of open blue sky that she'd felt with the sunflower didn't last.

One day after school, she'd had enough of the endless busyness. The pressure of all the demands on her triggered a flood of bad feelings—being misunderstood by her mom, frustrated with her dad, annoyed with her sisters, rejected by her best friend, threatened by Gus, and down on herself.

She jumped off the bus, ran up the long semi-circular driveway of the Forester home, and entered through the brown front door, which stood out beside the green siding and white trim of the rest of the house. She put her backpack down and headed straight for the side door, deliberately leaving her phone inside her bag.

As she stepped outside, free of her school books, everything she was leaving behind flashed through her mind—the indoor world of fluorescent school lights, loud hallway chatter, and her electronic devices. She was sick of paying attention to everything and everyone other than herself.

She stepped happily into another world—the outdoor world of blue sky, fresh air, chirping birds, and tall trees. A world with no expectations, no demands, and most of all—no social media. With each crunch of her steps on the gravel path in the backyard, she left the human world behind and entered the natural world.

SLIDING the big red door aside, she stepped inside the musty air of the barn and breathed a deep sigh of relief.

All the gucky clutter of the day seemed to clear off as she entered the building. The stable was a refuge for Balidova. She loved the sound of gravel, mixed with dirt, crunching under her black gumboots with every step. She loved the smell of dry hay blended with horse pellets. She loved the low, muffled neighs of the horses as they heard the tin lids of grain bins opening up. She loved the touch of wind on her cheek as it blew through the hallway, and the tweeting of baby swallows in their nests in the rafters. Most of all, she loved the sight of the old red building with white trim, dirty from years of mud, manure, dust, and use.

As she walked into this faraway land in her own backyard, a familiar face greeted her—Melody poked her fuzzy head over the stall door. Balidova opened the stall door to get closer to her horse. She stroked the mare's neck as they greeted each other without words. There was an unspoken link between them as if their souls overlapped. They communicated in a language all their own—energy, feeling, and gestures.

Melody understood Balidova's body language, tone of voice, lilt and rhythm of speech, the tilt of her head, arm gestures, and facial expressions. They could feel each other's vibe. How else could Balidova explain her feelings to a horse? Words didn't do the feelings justice. At least not her words, not yet.

Maybe when she got older, she would find the right language to clearly express what she felt? Right now, she just couldn't. But Melody understood anyway—the little horse sensed that the girl was feeling down and nuzzled her, pressing her hairy cheek onto the girl's head. Balidova wrapped her arms around Melody's shaggy neck, still thick with winter fur.

"You're the best, Melody. Always there for me when I need you most."

Balidova fetched Melody's grain and dumped it in the black rubber bucket inside Melody's stall. Once she knew her horse was taken care of, she grabbed a wheelbarrow and a pitchfork, and got busy mucking stalls. As she worked, she started to feel better.

While heaving a wheelbarrow out of one of the stalls, she spotted something lying on a hay bale in the barn hallway. One of her sisters must have put it there as a quick snack—a bag of sunflower seeds with a picture of a golden sunflower on the front.

She stopped in her tracks. And all of a sudden, Step Three of the Dragon Tail Breath rushed back to her. She thought of the question the sunflower had asked her.

"How do I feel now? How do I feel right now?" she asked herself.

Balidova paused, leaning on her pitchfork, scanning inside herself with her mind. She wanted to clear off all the frustration, fatigue, and stress of her day—tests, school gossip, and arguments at home. All the have to's and should do's of homework, chores, and karate practice. She wanted to wash that off and come out feeling good on the other side.

She felt the swirl of emotion around her—the confusing energy soup of interacting with hundreds of people in a day. It overwhelmed her sensitive system.

What do I want?

She repeated the question in her mind. *I know I don't want this. But what do I want?*

She took a deep breath in. She let a deep breath out—allowing airflow to pass through her.

It took so much to ask that simple question. Placing her hand on her heart, she paused.

In the quiet stillness, right there in the middle of the barn hallway, just for a moment, she could feel her heartbeat pumping in her chest. She placed her hands on the wheelbarrow's two wooden handlebars, hauled her load out to the large sprawling manure pile behind the barn, and dumped it. Simply asking herself the question made her feel better, and she hadn't even answered it yet.

Now she didn't mind the smell of the manure. She didn't mind balancing the wheelbarrow on the thin board that led up to the top of the pile—she was an expert at it. She'd done it so many times before.

Balidova finished mucking Melody's stall. As she started the next stall, the same question popped up in her mind again.

"What do *I* want?"

She repeated the question out loud, emphasizing the word *I*. "Not, what does Mom or Dad want. Or my *sisters*, or even the horses. But what do *I* want?"

Balidova closed her eyes, leaned on her pitchfork, and took a deep breath. Everything stopped spinning and began to settle down like snowflakes on a moonlit night, slowly drifting down from the sky back to earth. She gasped as the answer came to her, and her eyes popped open.

Suddenly, she knew what she wanted. "I wanna feel clear of everyone else's crap. I wanna feel connected to all the good stuff —connected to nature, the horses, and myself. I wanna feel *good*."

Balidova finished mucking Gypsy's stall with a few more big shovelfuls, walked out back, and dumped her load onto the manure pile. With each wheelbarrow she offloaded, she could feel the weight on her shoulders lightening and lifting. As this happened, she noticed that all the horses were in their paddocks doing their own thing, heads down, eating, tails swishing. They glanced over at her now and then but, for the most part, left her alone.

When she got to the last stall, she honed her answer a little more. "Oh, and I want the horses to come and say hello to me," she thought. "Yeah. That would be cool. They come to me instead of me always going to them. I wonder if I can draw them to me? Just by feeling good. By shifting my energy and sending out good vibes. Can they feel it?"

Balidova lifted her full wheelbarrow out of the stall, locked the black cast-iron latch behind her, and prepared to dump the last load of the day on the manure pile. But she was so busy thinking about what she wanted that she ignored where the front wheel was situated on the 2x6 board going up the pile. Halfway up, the wheel slipped off, and both she and the wheelbarrow went tumbling into the pile of excrement.

"Ew, gross!" she shouted as she stood up, looking at her dung-covered jeans, gumboots, and hands. With a disgusted look on her face, she picked herself up, shook her hands, and attempted to brush herself off. She was covered, from head to toe, in manure. Her new red jacket was now brown. *Yikes, Mom's gonna kill me.*

She looked around, thought of calling for help, and then realized no one was there except for the horses. She was about to cry in exasperation when she heard a buzzing sound. She recognized the tone. Not the high-pitched buzz of a mosquito, but the low-pitched buzz of a bigger insect, a bee. *Oh great, just when I'm stuck in the mud, I'm gonna get stung by a bee!* It landed on her gloved hand.

Instinctively she went to smack it, but something held her back. She looked closer and noticed it had a bent antenna. The bee didn't fly off when she bent down towards it. It stayed still on her hand as if it wanted to communicate with her. It seemed to be looking at her!

"Hey, little bee." The bee moved around clumsily on her glove. "You're a clumsy little one, aren't ya? Kinda like me," she laughed, looking at her situation. "I'm gonna name you Bumby." And with that, the bee flew off.

As her eyes followed the bee's flight, Balidova caught a glimpse of Melody watching her. She remembered what she had asked for—to draw the horse to her—and wondered if it was still possible.

"Well, I smell like her now," Balidova laughed.

She took a deep breath and focused on what it would feel like in her body to *be* relaxed and calm. Just thinking about being calm had an effect on her.

Her breathing slowed, and she began to feel a warmth in her heart. All the highs and lows of the day, week, month, and last several months—kumite loss, valentine rejection, dad disappointment, friend fights—started slowing down, becoming less intense and less volatile. Instead of a swirling whirlpool of thoughts, the space around her began to feel clearer. The space in her head started to feel less cluttered and more open.

After a few more deep breaths... she looked up at the sky, which was a little overcast. A patch of blue appeared, with sunlight shining through. *That's how I want my mind to feel. Like an open, blue sky—just like the blue light breath."*

Just then, she heard a bee buzzing around her. *Is that you, Bumby?*

She felt good now—her legs pulling her up and out of the pile, arms outstretched for balance. All her limbs worked in synchronicity. She felt strength in them—firing up, getting her out of the manure pit—yet without anger or frustration.

Instead—she felt joy.

Giggling, she walked back toward the barn. But before stepping into the building, something touched her shoulder. She turned around into Melody's soft muzzle nosing its way through her hair.

Balidova placed her head on Melody's warm body. "Oh, I love you, girl. Thanks for coming to say hello."

Melody looked at the girl, a twinkle in the mare's big brown eye. The little horse stamped her hooves and blew her nose.

"Looking for a treat again, are ya?" Balidova chuckled. She patted her horse again, rubbing her hand down Melody's face and reveling in the soft touch of the horse's skin against her hand.

Balidova looked down at her muck-covered arms, hands, and legs. *So, it is possible—I can bring in what I want by shifting my mood. That's where it starts—letting go of all my worries, madness, and sadness and just appreciating what's right in front of me.*

She felt a surge of light within her. As she patted her horse, she felt deeply connected to this creature who had filled her up with love. She felt connected to the land on which they stood. She felt connected with herself. *The sunflower was right. Breathing in blue light and asking myself, 'what do I want?' works. I can create a feeling inside me. There is a way to feel good that has nothing to do with winning.*

Scooping dung out of the stalls, even falling into the manure pile, had left her with an unusual feeling. She felt full—of love, of joy, of life. She felt **G.R.C.H.** Good. Relaxed. Calm. Happy. She wasn't used to feeling this way. Bumby flew around and landed on her shoulder. She just watched the bee curiously, not the least bit afraid of being stung.

"You know, I kinda feel like you," she said to the tiny creature. "I'm buzzing."

As Bumby zoomed off, Balidova caught a whiff of the stench coming off her body. "I know what else I want." She marched over to the wash rack to hose herself off. "I want a shower!"

CHAPTER 16
A POWERFUL DECISION

The weekend flew by, March turned to April, and winter officially turned to spring. When Balidova woke up on Monday morning, the sunflower's words *"What do you want?"* still swirled inside her. Every time she looked up at the blue sky over the weekend, she was reminded of those words. She breathed them in through her throat, along with a stream of blue light. She thought it was the most important question in the world and wondered why she had waited so long to ask it.

Balidova wanted to marinate in that yummy vibe forever but knew she couldn't. It was a school day—the weekend was over. Lying in bed, she shook her head vigorously and blinked repeatedly to get the woozy feeling out of her brain and wake up fully. Monday morning reality hit her—karate practice, then school.

"What do I want?" she asked aloud, matter-of-factly this time.

Almost immediately, a thought popped into her mind in response to her question.

The answer was crystal clear.

I want Angel to talk to me again.

Having no friends sucks.

She listened for sounds of her sisters getting ready for the morning workout or her dad's call to them from downstairs, but all she heard was silence, so she snuck some extra minutes in bed.

When it truly was time to get up, she slid out of her comfy, warm bed into the cool air of her room—the wood stove had slowed down overnight. She put on a pair of blue jeans and a green sweater from the top of her clean clothes pile.

A hot bowl of oatmeal porridge later, Balidova nodded goodbye to her mom and ran out to catch the bus, just as it was rumbling down the street. On the twenty-minute ride to school, she sat by herself, staring out the window at the wide open expanse of wilderness. Spotting an eagle, she watched it soar effortlessly yet powerfully up high, its lone, dark silhouette in stark contrast to a blue sky streaked with white clouds.

She wondered what it would feel like to be that powerful, yet move with such grace. Her shoulders and jaw relaxed as she took a deep breath. Just thinking about the eagle calmed her down. She was in awe of its beauty and solitude. *Look at how that magnificent bird moves in the sky without even flapping its wings. It's just riding a current of air.*

She remembered what the sunflower told her about energy waves—sunlight and all the colors of the rainbow travel in invisible waves.

I wonder if I can ride those energy waves too.

As the bus lurched to a stop in front of her school, Balidova snapped back to reality. Everyone climbed down, chatting and laughing, their backpacks bumping into each other. Still daydreaming of the eagle, Balidova was the last person to leave the bus. She'd only taken a few steps on solid ground when she felt a tap on her shoulder.

"Hey, Dova."

It was Angel.

Angel was the only person, other than Balidova's sisters, who called her by that nickname. Yet she was surprised to hear Angel talking to her. The two friends hadn't spoken since Valentine's Day. Remembering the question she'd asked herself that morning, Balidova thought, *Wow, asking for what I want does work.*

"Hey Angel," Balidova answered. Was Angel back? Should she tell her friend about all that had happened? *The spirit elements warned me not to speak about them because others won't believe me. But this is my best friend, shouldn't I tell her?*

"Looks like you're lost in thought," Angel said.

"Yeah, I was just, uh, thinking about some things that've been happening lately in the woods behind my house."

The two girls started walking toward the school. As they entered the building by the side door, Balidova realized she'd been swimming in her thoughts and had not said much to her friend.

"Anything interesting?" Angel asked.

"Yeah, real interesting." Balidova wanted to tell Angel all about the amazing Dragon Tail Breath she'd been learning. She wanted to tell her about the wind spirit, the spirit bear, the fish, and the sunflower in a way that Angel could understand. She wanted to tell her about the green, gold, and blue light. Most of all, she wanted to tell her about the insanely calm way it all made her feel. She wanted to share her incredible experiences with her BFF. But now was not the time. The bell rang, and they couldn't be late for class. Explaining the Dragon Tail Breath was not a two-minute conversation.

"I'll tell you all about it later, Angel. Gotta go to class now." She smiled at her friend, started walking away, then turned back and said, "See ya."

"Okay, whatever. See ya, Dova," Angel replied with a shrug.

Well, I messed that up, didn't I? Balidova thought as she strode to class. *First time Angel's spoken to me in weeks, and all I can say is, 'Hey Angel.' Good one Dova, good one.*

SHE HEADED to her locker to drop off her jacket and pick up her notebook. As she placed some books in and took other ones out, she felt a push from behind and slammed face-first into the cold, metal locker.

"Ow!" she yelled.

She turned to see who had done this and saw a boy behind her, smirking, a pair of scissors in his hand. His disheveled, dirty blonde hair fell over his face, and stood out against a black hoodie.

It was Gus.

Her palms still on the blue metal, she felt her fingers curl into fists almost reflexively—her body gearing up into fight mode.

As her body posture changed, so did her mind.

He picked the wrong person to shove this morning. Even if I'm a lot smaller, size doesn't mean everything. I've seen plenty of karate fighters beat bigger opponents using their skill, timing, and technique. Good strategy outweighs brute force any day.

She was about to hit him back, but something stopped her.

She knew she wasn't supposed to use her karate at school. And Gus had been her friend once, even if it was a long time ago. She'd been warned by her Sensei—her dad—not to stoop to the level of those who resort to violence to get their way in the world. *I'm better than that.* She felt the pull of conflicting ideas within her.

Angel, standing nearby, saw the look of shock and anger on Balidova's face when she first got shoved and was hopeful that Balidova would retaliate against the same guy who had deliberately attacked her. But Angel saw confusion in Balidova's eyes and mistook it for fear. Angel's face creased with a look of pity and then disgust for her friend. She shook her head and was about to walk away, when she saw Balidova turn and catch her eye.

For a moment, Balidova wanted to disappear. She couldn't figure out what to do. Should she fight back or not? Several seconds had already gone by, and she'd done nothing. Was it too late?

Then she saw Angel's face—a look of pity mixed with disgust. It sparked something in her...

Balidova placed one hand over the other, something she did instinctively when she felt vulnerable as if protecting herself. With the fingertips of her left hand, she could feel the callouses on her right knuckles. Thick layers of skin had developed from years of hitting the leather punching bag. She remembered the first time they bled from just a few dozen punches on the bag. Now they were tough and hardened from years of use. She could trust that they would not bleed, even if she punched a hundred times.

Angel's look sparked something deep inside her.

Can I trust myself to know what to do? Isn't that what the Dragon Tail Breath is all about?

Am I a coward? Or am I the One?

She thought of the wind spirit, who had first uttered those words in the lagoon—the powerful and magical wind spirit that had scared away the wolves and saved her life.

Pausing, she sucked in a big breath, letting her belly and chest rise. She exhaled vigorously with a whoosh, creating her own burst of wind.

Instantly, all three steps of the Dragon Tail Breath that she'd learned thus far merged within her. As she stood there, breathing green, gold, and blue light through her body, her breath formed a rhythm with her heart. Her posture became more erect, and her feet splayed apart in a firm, grounded stance. She thought of the bear, the fish, and the sunflower and the affirmations they had taught her:

All is well.

Here now.

What do I want?

In her mind's eye, she saw the sunflower in the meadow, its green stem and golden face standing tall and proud. And made a decision.

Removing her hands from the locker, she turned around and said, "Hey, Gus."

He was giving sly glances and nods to his friends and the gathering crowd.

"Yeah?" he spun around also.

HER FOOT WAS ALREADY on his chest. Within a split second, she had changed her focus, taken one step toward him, and executed a perfect sidekick right to the center of his torso. The full power of her body movement hit him straight on, and he flew backward, landing on his butt.

It happened instinctively. Once she decided to act, her karate training emerged—a tremendously strong, perfectly placed sidekick.

The speed at which she had reacted shocked even her.

Gus sat on the floor, gasping for air. She hit him right in the center of his chest—the solar plexus.

The kick caught Gus by surprise. He had assumed Balidova wouldn't do anything and he was already claiming victory.

Now, he was laid out on his butt, sucking wind.

For a moment, he thought of getting up. But he couldn't breathe. Without oxygen for his muscles, he couldn't *move*.

Masses of kids gathered around in the hallway.

No one could believe Balidova Forester had just laid Gus Polter out on the floor!

She glanced around the crowd of kids—all ages, all sizes, all colors—and noticed that Angel was staring at her, smiling from ear to ear. Balidova could almost hear the thoughts running through Angel's head—*glad you found your courage, better late than never, Dova.*

Balidova smiled back at her friend without saying a single word. Her actions spoke louder than words.

For a split second, Gus wanted to get revenge right then and there. She could tell by the flicker in his eye. She had been trained to see it. Even though she was only a green belt, she'd been trained to look people in the eye without wavering her gaze. So she just kept looking at him without flinching—speaking to him with her stare.

Balidova's eyes were on fire. She was glaring at him so intently that she could have burned a hole right through him. He was no emotional genius, but he knew something had shifted inside her. Just when he thought he had her, when he thought her courage had died, it had come alive as he'd never seen before. The flicker of revenge in his eyes passed as quickly as it had appeared.

"Don't ever do that again," she said with a slow, steely tone as she leaned toward him. "To me or anyone else."

There was a hush in the crowd as Balidova spoke her final words to Gus. For a few seconds, no one flinched.

ONLY AFTER GUS GOT UP, brushed himself off, and walked back to the safety of his gang of friends by the east side doors, did Balidova turn back toward her locker to collect her things. In the safety of numbers, they would undoubtedly be laughing at her for some reason or another. But she didn't care. She had stood up for herself.

"You don't learn karate, never to use it. You learn martial arts to know *when* to use it," her dad had taught her. "If your physical safety is threatened or someone attacks you physically, you have the right to defend yourself. Physically. With the appropriate amount of force."

"If someone attacks you verbally, with words, then a higher standard is expected of you as a martial artist. You are expected to have more resilience, inner strength, and self-control. You are expected not to let those words get under your skin."

Her Dad's words reverberated in her head as she mulled over her thoughts. *He shoved me, physically, face first, into a metal locker. I could've gotten badly hurt! And those scissors? What was he gonna do with those? Someone has to stand up to him.*

Her heart was still beating fast. She could feel adrenaline coursing through her body like it did whenever she was in a kumite match.

To give herself time to calm down, she dug through the pile of notebooks in her locker and slowly pulled out her green science binder. At the same time, she confirmed the correctness of her actions. Rubbing her forehead, she could feel a small lump forming.

As if to reinforce her own decision, Balidova forcefully shut her locker, picked up her backpack, and headed off to science class. As she walked down the hallway, her breath and heartbeat returned to normal, and she noticed other kids staring at her with a look of wonder on their faces. A few gave her high fives, and others just grinned. Some looked the other way. She searched for Angel but couldn't find her. *She must have gone to class already.*

Fifteen minutes later, during science, a voice came over the loudspeaker. "Balidova Forester and Gus Polter, please come to the principal's office immediately."

"Oh great, here we go again." Balidova groaned as she put her pen down. She remembered what had happened the last time she was in that office. *This time's different. Gus was clearly in the wrong. He shoved me. And I had a right to protect myself.* She steeled herself with righteous indignation as she walked down the hall. At the office, Gus was not there, so she entered Mrs. Marsh's chambers alone.

"Have a seat, Balidova." Mrs. Marsh pointed to a chair facing her desk. She looked at the girl for a few seconds without saying anything, no doubt having heard what had happened only minutes earlier. "Tell me what happened."

"Gus shoved me into my locker and nearly cut my face on the metal." Balidova kept it short and to the point. "So, I kicked him and told him not to do that ever again—to me or anyone else." Her last three words reminded the principal that she still believed she'd been wrongly blamed for what happened to Jojo.

Mrs. Marsh paused as Balidova's words sunk in. Alone in the office with just one student and no one else to create a distraction, the principal sensed that the girl was telling the truth. The thought flashed through the woman's mind that perhaps she'd gotten it wrong last time and had blamed the girl for something she hadn't done. An uncomfortable feeling of guilt began to grow in the woman. But she shook it off. She was the principal, and there were rules to uphold.

"You know you're not supposed to kick people?" The principal spoke her words calmly and evenly, masking any underlying emotion.

Balidova looked straight at her and spoke calmly back. She still had adrenaline flowing in her veins, so she was bolder than usual. "Yes, I know. But it was self-defense. He attacked me first. That means I have a right to fight back." She sat back in her chair and crossed her arms.

Mrs. Marsh leaned forward. "Technically, that's not true. Students are never authorized to hit each other. Fighting in school is *not* allowed, for any reason."

Then the principal paused, leaned back, let out a sigh, and said something Balidova was not expecting. "But, given the unusual circumstances and what you've already been through with this particular student, I will make an exception."

Balidova's eyes opened wide, but she knew to keep silent. Mrs. Marsh wasn't finished yet.

"In this case," the principal continued, "I believe you were justified hitting him back. So there will be no punishment for you."

Balidova couldn't believe her ears. A wide grin spread across her face as she stood up to leave. "Thank you, Mrs. Marsh. You won't regret this." Instinctively, she nodded her head toward the woman as a sign of appreciation.

As Balidova turned to walk out, Mrs. Marsh lowered her voice and said, "Oh, and one more thing, I'm glad you took care of this yourself." She winked at the girl, then turned her eyes downward and read the papers on her desk.

Balidova chuckled to herself as she walked out of the office. *The principal's got my back.* She passed Gus sitting in the waiting room, ready to go in. *I wonder what's gonna happen to him? Oh well, that's none of my business. MYOB—mind your own business—as Grandpa used to say.*

BACK IN SCIENCE CLASS, Balidova stood by a smooth black lab table and caught up with the experiment the rest of the students were doing, mixing chemicals of various colors—blue, red, yellow—in a glass jar. The glass stir stick made clinking sounds on the edge of the container as she moved it round and round. The brew in the beaker mirrored the mix of emotions that were swirling inside her. She watched as the colors blended together, forming a different color—brown.

A new idea entered her mind.

I've got my own back. I can trust myself.

All of a sudden, it hit her. She knew she was strong and could create the kind of reputation she wanted. Her whole body shuddered, not with the cold but with a shift in her energy.

She inhaled deeply and imagined a stream of sky blue light washing through her entire being, cleansing her mind and body, just as the sunflower had shown her.

Feeling a surge of strength within, her confidence rose, and she smiled on the inside. For the first time since she'd lost the kumite match at the tournament, she felt vindicated in her fighting skills. She'd beaten the toughest guy in the whole school. And the principal had supported her.

Balidova took a deep breath in, filling her lungs with as much air as possible.

Held it for a few seconds.

Then exhaled very slowly, letting her shoulders fall as the tension of the fight released from her body.

Instinctively, she shook out her arms and legs and let her whole body shudder.

One more quick shake of her whole body, and it was done.

She was back. Not excited. Not upset. But right in the middle —neutral.

She looked at the glass beaker, now filled with brown liquid, and started writing the results of the chemical experiment in her notebook. A minute later, she stopped and reflected.

I wonder what Gus is gonna do now? He's not gonna like the fact that he got humiliated in public by a girl. I'm gonna need to watch my back.

CHAPTER 17
FAMILY DINNER

That evening, Balidova quickly washed her hands in the bathroom while staring at herself in the mirror. A purplish bruise adorned her forehead. She swished her bangs across her face to cover the evidence of the altercation at school earlier that day. Part of her hoped no one would notice, but another part wanted to tell what happened. Wouldn't her family be proud of her for standing up to the school bully?

She splashed a little water on her face, straightened her hair, and gave herself a once over in the mirror. After nodding in satisfaction, she headed downstairs.

The entire family gathered in the kitchen minutes after her mom rang the dinner bell. Moonlight shone through the big window above the sink, streaking its way across beige cupboards, cream-colored walls, and a grey linoleum floor.

A flurry of dishes ensued as Balidova and her sisters laid out plates, cups, and cutlery around the oval table, which was just the right size for the six of them. Red and gold ceramic, dragon decorated plates formed the center of each table setting. Cups in various colors—orange, green, yellow, blue—and simple metal cutlery completed the set.

The whole clan sat around the oak dinner table—two kids on either side and a parent on each end. Everyone sat in their usual places. Dad at the head of the table, closest to the back wall. Mom at the foot of the table, near the center of the kitchen, so she could get up and down easily to fetch stuff from the stove. The two older girls on the far side of the table, close to the doorway leading to the living room. The two younger ones on the near side, closer to the opening between the kitchen and the front door.

As Balidova looked down at her plate, she saw a dragon's face staring back at her. Its serpent-like body snaked around the center of the plate. Dragons seemed to be everywhere now that she was learning the Dragon Tail Breath.

Everyone sat down and closed their eyes while her dad gave thanks. "Thank you for this day, for each other, and for this food. Let us use it to nourish our bodies and do good in the world."

The family dug into the evening meal, with the clatter of utensils filling the air. Serving spoons scooped hot, steaming rice and spicy stir-fried veggies with chicken onto plates. For a while, everyone fell silent, concentrating on placing large spoonfuls of hot, yummy food into their mouths.

"So, what's everyone's rose and thorn?" her mom said. "Who would like to go first?"

This was something they did every dinner—a chance to share a highlight and a lowlight from your day.

"I'll go," Balidova's eldest sister, April, responded. "I got an 'A' on my history test. That's a pretty big rose, considering I wasn't doing very well before."

"Well done. Congratulations," both parents said simultaneously.

Academics were important in their house—*very* important. To be acknowledged for an 'A' on a test was a big deal.

"How about you?" Her mom said, pointing to Balidova's second sister, May.

"I didn't get to sit next to my best friend during reading time today. That's my thorn. The teacher separated us for talking too much," May grumbled.

"I guess you need to pay more attention in class," her dad said, raising his eyebrows.

"And you?" her mom nodded towards Balidova's little sister, June.

"We got extra recess today!" she said excitedly. "So, I got to play on the monkey bars for an extra ten minutes!"

Her mom smiled tiredly, feigning excitement, but Balidova could tell she was not interested or paying attention.

"What about you?" her dad asked her mom curtly. "What happened in your day? Anything interesting?"

"Nope. Nothing at all. And you?" Her mom redirected the question quickly, obviously not feeling like talking.

"Well," her dad said grimly, "we had someone in the emergency room today who had their arm sliced by a saw at the aluminum smelter. Pretty gruesome, with blood pouring everywhere. I was able to operate on him right away. We cauterized the blood flow and got him in stable condition—saved his life."

Everyone ate in silence for a few moments, pondering the image. It wasn't very appetizing.

APRIL BROKE THE SILENCE. "How 'bout you, Balidova? Is that a bruise on your forehead?" she smiled slyly. Balidova had seen her in the crowd after the fight with Gus at school. The oldest three girls attended the same high school.

Balidova put her fork down. She didn't want to say anything, but she'd been put on the spot. "Something very unusual happened at school today. Something that's never happened before. It's a rose and a thorn—I got shoved into a locker, face first."

She had caught their attention—all of them. Four pairs of dark brown eyes and one pair of green eyes stared at her, looking with such intensity, it felt as if they were boring a hole into her.

"And I did something about it," she continued matter-of-factly, responding to their stares by sitting upright in her chair. There wasn't a hint of victim in her voice. "I wasn't sure I was gonna do anything at first, but then I decided I couldn't just let him get away with it. So, I nailed the guy who did it with a full-on side kick, straight in the chest."

"Excuse me? You did what?" her dad nearly choked on his food.

"I kicked him," Balidova continued, expecting to be applauded for her skill and courage just as her sister was for her grades. "He went flying and landed on his butt. It was Gus Polter, the school bully. I just stared at him and didn't say a word. I thought he was gonna get up and come after me, but he didn't. He just brushed himself off, gave me a look, and went back to his wormy gang of friends."

She got the words out as fast as possible, not leaving any time for family members to interrupt her in between sentences. The last thing she wanted was to go over the whole thing in excruciating detail.

"Yeah, everyone at school was talking about it today," April piped in between sips of water. "Balidova's a big hero."

"That's a lot to take in, Balidova," her dad said. He was not in the Balidova-is-a-hero camp. "You know you're not supposed to get into fights at school, right?"

"Yeah, I know. I didn't get into a fight, though. I just defended myself," she said calmly, masking her surprise at his response. *Why isn't he proud of me?*

"Well, you know you're not supposed to use your karate

outside the dojo," her dad said sternly, "except in very extenuating circumstances." His eyes were fixed on her, watching and reading her movements.

"I know, Dad," she said slowly, slightly perturbed, looking straight back at him. "But this *was* an extenuating circumstance. I got shoved into a metal locker face first. I could've gotten badly injured. And he had a pair of scissors in his hand...." She hung onto the last word for effect, to make sure her father understood the danger she was in.

"Balidova," her dad sat up straight and tall now, imposing his presence onto everyone at the table. "You can't just go around kicking people."

She let out a sigh of frustration, her chest collapsing slightly. "I know, Dad! I didn't just go around kicking people. He pushed me on purpose. And he's done it before, to others."

"How do you know it wasn't an accident?" her dad asked, placing one hand on the table.

"Because of the look on his face. I just knew."

"Hmph," her dad said, obviously not convinced.

"Everything happened in a split second," she continued, visibly frustrated now. "And I just knew it was the right thing to do."

"Hmph," her dad said again. He picked up his fork, took another mouthful of veggies, and let out a deep breath. "Well, if you say so. But are we going to get a call from the school? Are you suspended?" His alarm had turned to annoyance now. He was not going to let this go, as Balidova hoped.

"No. I got sent to the principal's office and told there's no fighting in school. Nothing else." Balidova didn't think she should tell her parents about the principal winking at her. Somehow, her father's disapproval didn't warrant gloating over the principal's support. She looked down at her plate and pushed the food around with her spoon until the dragon's face was peeking out underneath white rice.

"You know you have support from the teachers and staff," her dad continued, as if reading her mind. "You don't have to take care of everything yourself."

Yeah, sure... but there were no teachers around.

"You sound upset that I used my karate at school," Balidova said, her frustration rising. "It's not like this happens every day. And I told you, I *knew* it was the right thing to do." She clenched her fork in one hand and her knife in the other, tightening her grip into a fist, turning both utensils upright, defiantly.

"I heard you the first time." Her dad did not like the tone of her voice, challenging his authority.

"Can't you just believe me?" she seemed desperate. "Can't you trust me on that?"

Her dad paused, glaring at her. "You're still learning when to use force and how much force. There is such a thing as the escalation of force. If someone does something small to you, do you pound them in return?"

"No. But I didn't—I used the right amount of force. He pushed me. He had scissors!" she said emphatically, tossing her knife and fork onto the table. "Why don't you believe me?"

She was livid now.

Everyone else at the table was silent, letting Balidova and her dad have at it—not daring to get involved. They could all feel the conversation heating up to the boiling point. Even her mother didn't intervene. She had her own battles to fight with him and needed to be selective about which ones she chose. She didn't have enough energy to fight them all, so she remained silent this time.

"I thought maybe you'd be proud of me." Balidova was shouting now, leaning forward over the table as if putting her body weight into her words. "Proud that I stood up for myself."

Tears welled in her eyes—her father's disapproval of her was almost too much for her to bear.

"Don't get me wrong, Balidova," her dad chose his words carefully, leaning back, moving his chair away from the table. He realized he had pushed his daughter too far, and now she was on the edge of an emotional cliff, about to go over. "I'm very proud of you and of how tough you are. But, *you* don't know yet how strong you are. You have to be careful not to use too much force. Your karate training is no small deal. That's all I'm talking about."

Balidova slid her wooden chair out from the table in a huff and stood up. "You just don't get it, do you? I *knew* it was the right thing to do, and I *didn't* use too much force! I just *knew*—from the look on Gus's face, from the feeling I had, from everything that was happening right at that moment. I just *knew*. Why can't you just trust me?"

BALIDOVA LOOKED FRANTICALLY around the table for support, but her sisters stared blankly at her. She couldn't tell if they felt sorry for her or were just glad their dad's disapproval was not directed at them. For a brief moment, she thought she detected a hint of support from her eldest sister, but wasn't sure. Or was it a look of guilt because April had spurred this whole argument with her comment about Balidova's bruise in the first place? The two older girls, April and May, looked at each other with eyebrows raised as if to say, "Who does she think she is, going off like this?" When Balidova glanced at her mom, however, she found a softened, knowing gaze that said, *I believe you. And I believe in you. I know you did the right thing in the situation.*

Her Mom's face was lined and worn down from taking care of four children and dealing with the demands, scrutiny, and questioning of Balidova's father, herself. She knew that Balidova had to fight this battle on her own. Even though she didn't utter a word out loud, she spoke volumes with the glint in her eye. She wanted to support her daughter in getting through this argument. She sensed how important it was. Balidova needed to learn that she didn't have to take in everything her dad said as given—the girl could deflect it. In that moment, her small indication of solidarity with Balidova was all the girl needed to continue.

Balidova used her mother's silent encouragement to catapult herself to a new level of acceptance of herself. She turned toward her dad one final time, squeezing her fists by her side. "I can't explain it to you. It doesn't make sense in words. I just *knew* it was the right thing to do," she finished in triumph, her voice reaching a peak.

"Were you mad like you are now?" her dad said in a low, steady, commanding voice. "Because sometimes when we're angry, we use more force than is necessary. We use excessive force. And when we do that, we're just as bad as the other person. We lower ourselves to their level."

Yeah, you would know... wouldn't you? Wasn't chopping the dishwasher cord excessive force?

Her father's unrelenting questioning, combined with his specific query about 'whether she had used too much force because she was mad,' made her doubt herself. Instinctively, she covered up her weakness with bravado.

She shouted even louder, "Of course I was mad. I was shocked! I don't get pushed into lockers every day." She had worked herself up into such a degree of exasperation that she was losing control now. "It's not like this is the first time this guy has done it, Dad. He's a bully. Get it? B-U-L-L-Y. He's done this before. He pushed Angel, shoved Jojo down the stairs, and broke her arm—something I got blamed for, remember? I told you about it months ago. He likes tormenting people. I wasn't just standing up for me. I was standing up for everyone. He has to stop."

"You're right. He does have to stop," her dad said, repeating her last words, trying to appease her. But it was too late. She had already gone over the edge of the emotional cliff. As he stood up from his chair—

"I'm done with this conversation," Balidova shouted. She stormed out of the kitchen, tears streaming down her face. "Just leave me alone."

SHE STOMPED up to her room and slammed the door. *Why can't they just believe me? Why can't they just trust me? Why do I have to explain?* She paced back and forth like a tiger in a cage, lumping almost everyone in her family in with her dad since no one had ushered a single word of support for her. *April said I'm a hero at school—did anybody even notice that? Does April really think I'm a hero, or is she being sarcastic? Mom's the only one who believes me.*

Balidova couldn't stand her dad's disapproval of her—even if she detected the hypocrisy in his comments. The feeling sat on her skin like an itchy blanket—very uncomfortable. His doubt in her made her question herself now—even though she had felt so sure before.

Did I use too much force? Did I do the right thing? Should I have kicked him at all?

She went over the sequence of events in her head: the push, turning around, seeing the smirk, feeling unsure about what to do, the disgusted look on Angel's face, her question to herself, and finally, her decision to kick him back. In hindsight, she could see the whole thing in slow motion.

Was it too much? Was it too hard?

She went round in circles in her head.

Especially in the solar plexus?

She rewound and thought about all the moments that had happened, replaying the whole scene in her mind.

More doubt crept in.

And then shame.

As she started to sink into self-judgment, her body followed her mind and fell to the floor of her room. But as she hit the carpet with a jolt, she remembered her mom's look—*I believe you.*

It stopped her in her tracks.

Instead of crumpling into a heap, she sat up, inhaled sharply, then let out a long, slow breath. Her mom's look gave her the spark she needed to snap out of her downward spiral. As she became aware of herself again, she remembered the question, *How do you feel now?*

She scanned inside herself and realized she felt awful. Immediately, she wanted to run away from her bad feelings, or do anything to get rid of them. But the sunflower's words rang in her ears: *Do not run from your fears. Turn and face them. Otherwise, they will only grow stronger.*

Instinctively, she knew this was true. Not only had she heard it from the spirit elements, but she'd also experienced it in the karate ring. *If you're afraid when you step into the ring, you've already lost, even before the match has begun.*

Then she remembered what the sunflower had told her about the Cloak of Fear—how it magnified negative feelings—and wondered, *Is this just me? Or is it also the Cloak of Fear?*

She paused with the idea that it might not be entirely her fault. Breathing consciously, she relaxed her shoulders and shook out her body.

After another big breath, she decided.

∼

For the first time in her life, she did not do what she usually did. She did not run away from her bad feelings by distracting herself with her phone. She did not try to get rid of them on the punching bag. She did not stuff them down with an apple strudel.

She just let them be.

It sounds so simple, but it was a revolutionary idea.

Just let it be.

Don't fight it.

Don't flee from it.

Don't freeze in the face of it.

Just keep breathing and let it be.

And then slowly, investigate the feeling.

What does confusion, anger, self-doubt, and fear of losing her dad's approval *feel* like in the body?

Balidova noticed that she felt heavy. Her body felt weighed down. She also noticed a knot in her stomach— she felt tight and constricted. Finally, she noticed that she felt the churn of her mind going round and round in circles, searching for a way out.

She simply sat with these feelings, as if they were small creatures vying for her attention. Instead of shooing them away, she knelt down inside and imagined herself extending her hand to them, caressing them, holding them. She brought her full attention and presence to them. She placed her hand around the emerald green stone at her neck and breathed quietly in and out as she sat still on the light green carpet of her room, closing her eyes and releasing a sigh of relief.

She didn't have to run anymore—getting busy with chores that only delayed having to deal with her genuine emotions.

As all these thoughts ran through her head, Balidova sat there, gripped the stone, and breathed.

She breathed into her anger and her sadness.

She breathed into her smadness.

She didn't try to get rid of it.

She just let it be.

And as she turned her attention toward that sensation, she noticed something.

She didn't feel bad anymore.

She released the jade stone, stretched out her arms, and opened her chest. She stood up and felt the bottoms of her feet pressing on the floor.

She felt pretty good.

It worked.

Balidova stood up and reached her arms to the ceiling, making herself tall, like the sunflower. She felt she'd passed through a dark tunnel and come out the other side, with light now shining on her face. All at once, she had a revelation.

The same energy that causes bad feelings can change into good feelings. If you just sit with it and let it be, it will eventually move on and maybe even transform...

WITHOUT KNOWING IT, Balidova's breakdown became a breakthrough. She had her first big experience of energy transformation, otherwise known as **dragon magic**.

'The light, the breath, the words, and you combine to access the dragon magic,' the white bear told me.

She shook her head. Shook out her arms, her torso, and her legs. She shook all that frustration, rage, and anger out of her body. And as she did that, she glanced at the stone and pine cone on her desk. She remembered what she'd learned from the bear and the fish—the creatures that had given her those items. She picked them up and held them, one in each hand. She felt the contrast between the jagged edges of the pine cone and the smoothness of the rock. She looked closely. One was a dark color, and the other light.

She paused.

And breathed.

She thought of the dragon's face on her dinner plate. If she'd learned anything from the Dragon Tail Breath, she'd learned how to breathe deeply and deliberately.

A couple of breaths later, after her anger and indignation had completely worn off, she felt something still lingering underneath. As if the anger had been a mask, hiding the real issue—her insecurity and self-doubt.

She stopped pacing, wiped her tears, and stood up straight. She was talking to herself out loud now.

What do I think?

"What was it the fire spirit said about my truth? My truth might not necessarily be other people's truth, but it's still my truth." As the image of the sunflower grew more prominent in her mind, the image of her father grew smaller. A few deep breaths later, and he had shrunk from giant to human.

She looked around her room and noticed a poster on the wall that said *Run like a girl*.

"Why am I spending so much time and energy worrying about what everyone else thinks? I don't have to get the okay from anyone else to know it was the right thing, especially when *they* don't always do the right thing. *I* know it was the right thing, and that's enough for me." All at once, she realized her father was not as powerful as she'd thought he was.

In a flash of insight, Balidova suddenly understood why Angel was so upset with her for not doing anything when Gus attacked. She had abandoned Angel in her time of need. Balidova rubbed the stone and pine cone in her hands and thought of all she'd learned from the spirit elements—about light, energy, and feelings. They were all connected by one thing—her. Ultimately what she did with all that was *her choice*. Only *she* got to decide.

She jumped on her bed, buried her head in her pillow, and let out a muffled scream. After a few more screams and some punches into the pillow, she released the whirlpool of emotions within her and sat up, a look of determination spreading across her face.

"I don't care what anyone else thinks. I know what I did was right for me. Everyone can just get lost. I'll probably get in trouble for storming off from the dinner table, but so what."

Balidova sat down at her desk and pulled out her journal. Putting pen to paper always helped clear her head. She wrote:

What do I want?
What do I WANT?
WHAT DO I WANT?
I want to trust myself.
I want to believe in me.
I want to KNOW that I'm the one.

She sat, quiet and still, pen in hand, breathing for some time—reflecting on what had happened.

T<small>UNING INWARD</small>, she noticed her emotions still changing within her, like a river flowing downstream. The whitewater rapids of anger had transformed into swirling eddies of doubt, and now emerged as a steady current of determination.

Gradually, like a dawning sunrise, Balidova became aware, for the first time in her life, that there was a part of her that was deeper than her emotions—different from them. A part of her that didn't go up and down with the waves of anger, sadness, jealousy, or shame she felt on the surface, no matter how intense those feelings were. A part of her that could simply watch. A part of her that was still, steady, and secure. A part of her that wasn't good or bad—it just was.

She put her pen down and smiled, catching a glimpse of

herself in the mirror along her bedroom wall. Her oval, bruised face stared back at her.

"You're alright, Balidova," she said aloud, looking straight into her own eyes. For a brief second, the thought that she might actually *like* herself crossed her mind.

"You're alright grrl," she growled slightly.

CHAPTER 18
THE FOUR ELEMENTS

That night, as Balidova lay in bed, she dialed down her thoughts and began to tune into what was going on inside her. She wanted to explore the part of her that was deeper than her emotions. She noticed how the quiet *felt*.

Calm and peaceful—so I can finally hear myself.

Alone in her room, she heard the steady tick-tock of her alarm clock. And what was that outside her window?

A raven's caw?

A wolf's howl?

A dog's bark?

All the sounds she wouldn't have noticed before now seemed loud against the backdrop of stillness.

She also noticed the sounds *she* was making. Her breath made a subtle swoosh as it flowed in and out of her nostrils. She could hear her heart beating in her chest. And when she focused her attention on it, she could feel its rhythmic pulse in other parts of her body—her throat, lips, thumbs, feet.

Why didn't I notice this before?

Because I was too busy doing stuff, including thinking, she chuckled.

This is pretty cool.

Placing one hand on her belly and one hand on her heart, she felt the gentle, steady rise and fall of her abdomen and chest. Air moved in and out of her body, ebbing and flowing like ocean waves lapping on a beach. Tuning in to the rhythm of those waves felt incredibly calming.

She stared out her window and saw the moon big and round —a giant orb, glowing like the eye of the sky, looking down upon her. The tide of moonlit night streaming through her window seemed brighter and clearer than before. More than ever, she noticed the moon's unspeakable beauty; it was tranquil, harmonious, and quiet. She simply lay there for some time, staring at its white light in a sea of darkness. *I feel as if the moon is guiding me. Protecting me from evil spirits—-the Cloak of Fear. Amazing things have been happening on the full moon.*

She thought about all the creatures she had learned from so far. The owl, bear, fish, and sunflower. They had appeared during the Wolf Moon, the Fish Moon, and the Flower Moon. Those were the names she'd given her ever-changing friend in the sky.

Pausing, she turned her head away from the window and looked up at the ceiling of her room. *Is there something that combines all that stuff? A creature that flies like an owl, is strong like a bear, has scales like a fish, and a bright mane like a sunflower?*

Is there something that can manipulate all the elements—wind, earth, water, and fire?

It seems impossible.

But what if things that I never imagined are possible?

Balidova curled her body into a cozy fetal position, pondering possibility as she drifted off to sleep.

∼

THE NEXT MORNING as she entered the kitchen, she spotted a note from her dad on her lunch bag. In black ink, the message said:

Balidova,
　You will wash all the dishes for the next week since you left the dinner table early last night and missed cleanup. If you don't do it for any reason, you will get more chores.
　— Dad

She turned the paper over to see if anything was written on the other side.
There wasn't.
Hmph. Ok, he's not happy I spoke my mind.
Fine. Good morning to you too.
I'm still not sorry I said what I did.

LATER THAT DAY, after school, she hopped on the bus home. Although it was early April and the beginning of the spring season, it was still cold out. She wore her red winter jacket but kept it unzipped as temperatures were now above freezing.

In addition to getting warmer, the days were also getting longer. Sunrise was now at 7:00 a.m., with sunset just after 8:00 p.m. In Kitimat, only 865 miles from the Arctic Circle, the towns-people would gain two hours of daylight in a single month as the year moved toward summer.

After getting off the bus, Balidova didn't even go inside the house to drop off her backpack. She ran straight to the edge of the forest. It would be light out till quite late, and her mom would think she'd just gone out to the barn for the afternoon. She wanted—no—*needed* to connect with the spirit creature, in whatever form it showed up. She felt a pulsing desire within her—a beat that got louder and louder, pulling her toward the meadow. The draw of that good feeling was so strong that it overcame her. She simply couldn't ignore it.

When she reached the trees, her school books bobbing up and down against her back as she ran, she slowed down and searched for the little blue bird that had guided her, every single time, to the place of her dreams. But it was nowhere to be seen.

For a second, she felt a stab of panic.

Then she took a deep breath and remembered how she had tuned in to the signs of the forest last time, using her five physical senses—sight, smell, sound, taste, touch—and her sixth sense, intuition.

Carefully examining the foliage around her, she spotted evidence of a slightly worn path through the trees where she had tread before—broken twigs, footsteps in the mud, branches turned aside. The way seemed obvious when she looked closely, as if the forest was guiding her.

She took a few tentative steps forward. And a few more. At that point, the bird appeared. But this time, her winged friend was not in front of her. It was beside her. She waited for it to fly ahead of her, but it didn't move.

"Well, aren't you gonna show me the way?" she asked.

The little blue bird chirped in response, looking at her with a sideways glance, its white-tipped tail feathers twitching intermittently.

"Well, come on then, we don't have all day."

It chirped again, still looking at her.

She paused, then realized the bird wasn't going anywhere. "Okay, I'll find the meadow myself then."

Balidova took a single step forward.

Then another.

And another.

With each step, she gained a little more momentum and

became a bit surer of herself. Naturally, she slowed her breathing down to match the forest's rhythm, so she could take in all the subtle signs it was giving her. Each time she paused, the bird was there, next to her. Together, they repeated this process, heading deeper and deeper into the woods until she concluded that the bird wasn't guiding her. The bird was accompanying her.

She was guiding herself.

All of a sudden, she looked up and saw an opening in the trees. The wide-open expanse of the meadow lay ahead. She broke into a jog, followed by a run, as she burst out from the brush into the green grass, yellow wildflowers, and blue sky of spring. Snow had melted, and new buds were emerging.

The turning of the seasons marked a transformation in her. She had come a long way since first finding this place in the depths of winter. So much had happened in the last few months since she'd encountered the wind spirit. Standing in the center of the clearing, Balidova could see where she had been and where she was now. She remembered the first time she came to this meadow—what seemed like a lifetime ago.

"I made it! I can't believe I made it!" Balidova shouted.

She threw off her backpack and danced for joy in the afternoon sun. First, stretching one arm high and one arm to the side like a 'J,' then lifting both arms above her head with elbows bent and fingers touching like an 'O', and finally, spinning around in a full circle and landing with both arms outstretched wide above her head like a 'Y.'

A J-O-Y turn!

Balidova closed her eyes, spread her arms as wide as possible, and stood in the open meadow, head upturned toward the sky. Rotating slowly in circles, she reveled in her newly discovered power—her ability to stand up to her dad and find her way to the meadow.

She had arrived at a place inside herself that felt comfortable and good. Her confidence in herself and her decision-making abilities was expanding.

She lay down on the grass, stretched out her arms and legs in a star shape, closed her eyes, and drank in the open sky.

"Creature of wind, earth, water, and fire... creature of the four elements... come to me. I have something to share with you," she whispered.

Lying on the earth and breathing deeply, she lost track of how much time had passed. In that state of bliss, it felt like only a few seconds has gone by before she felt something silky to the touch. Thinking it was the creature in another mysterious form, she rolled over excitedly, opened her eyes, and sat up.

Instead, it was a clump of wet leaves.

Scowling, Balidova looked around.

"Spirit creature, where are you?"

Nothing happened.

"Creature!" Balidova shouted at the top of her lungs. She stood up and searched the entire meadow with her eyes, scanning inside the trees, above the treetops, and high in the sky.

Nothing.

"You can't just come into my life and disappear like this. You're making me crazy! I never know when and how I'm gonna see you again. The uncertainty almost makes me wish I never met you."

She caught the words in her mouth and gasped. "No, no, no, no, no... I take that back. That's not true at all. I'm so glad I met you."

Balidova clenched her fists in frustration.

Inhale.

Exhale.

"Creaturrrrrrrre!" she shouted again.

The sound of her voice echoed in the wind.

Still, nothing appeared.

Just as she turned around and prepared to trudge back home, she noticed a tiny white flicker out of the corner of her eye. A little piece of paper was stuck on a branch about twenty feet away. She ran over to grab it, but it caught the wind and blew away. She ran after it, and it blew away again. Determined not to let it escape her grasp a third time, she dashed after it. This time she grabbed it before the wind did.

Looking at the paper, she noticed something written on it in beautiful flowing handwriting. Squinting to read, she wished she had her golden glasses with her. She could just make out the words. A message from the creature? The thought sent shivers down her spine as she read the words aloud:

> *Meet me where earth joins sky,*
> *and majestic birds soar up high.*
> *Beware of wolf and bear,*
> *for danger lurks everywhere.*

She reread the note, pondering the words '*meet me where earth joins sky*'.

That could be anywhere.

She looked around, noticing that the meadow was not perfectly flat. There were crests and dips in the ground.

As she examined the bumps, she wondered where the earth pushes up and meets the sky?

A fat blackfly buzzed around her, and she immediately thought of Bumby, the bee. It was just enough distraction for her to have an 'aha' moment.

A mountain!

'*Where majestic birds soar up high.*'

She started talking to herself, thinking that hearing her voice would help her solve the riddle.

"Eagles! Eagles are majestic birds. But they fly everywhere

around here. Where could the creature be talking about? What's the next line? *'Beware of wolf and bear, for danger lurks everywhere.'* I've seen both wolves and bears in this forest. Could it be somewhere nearby?"

"Well, there aren't any hills or mountains right here, so that must not be it," she reasoned. "But maybe the creature wasn't trying to say where wolves and bears live? Maybe it was referring to something different?"

Balidova paused for a moment, scanning her surroundings, allowing the riddle to seep into her mind.

She looked up and saw the moon's shadow visible in the afternoon sky. A lone eagle soared effortlessly across its greyish-white face. She noticed that the moon had the same shadowy white color as a wolf.

All at once, it hit her.

"Wolf Mountain! I've seen eagles circling up there!" she exclaimed excitedly. She could feel the idea resonate in her body. "Yes! That's it! I need to climb to the top of Wolf Mountain."

She paused, mulling over the last words of the riddle, *'danger lurks everywhere.'* Her whole body shuddered at the memory of her encounter with the pack of wolves.

As she walked over to pick up her school bag, an idea came to her, *How about Nutmeg? He's big. He could protect me if a wolf or bear came around. At least he'd bark and give me time to run away.*

Balidova clasped the paper in her hand, grinning at her own cleverness.

But first I have to go home and get Nutmeg.

She stuffed the paper into her pocket and sprinted through the woods, retracing her steps. As she made it to the backyard, she ran up to the house where the dog was tied. For a second, she thought of packing some snacks but decided against it, not wanting to attract attention and possibly get stuck at home doing chores. She did, however, set her backpack down beside the doghouse.

"You ready to come with me, Nutmeg?"

His brown eyes looked into hers as he wagged his tail heartily, happy to see her and to be off-leash.

"Okay then, let's go," she announced.

They set off together toward Wolf Mountain. She felt much lighter without her school books on her back. It wasn't a short trip, but they had several hours of daylight left since it wouldn't be dark until after 8:00 p.m. Still, they'd have to hustle. Over a mile there, and then another half mile up. When they reached the base of the hill, Balidova steeled herself for the climb. She would do anything to see the creature again. She looked at the steep ascent. *This is where all my training comes in handy.*

She found the well-worn trail up the mountain and started the climb with a surge of determination. Up and up they went, through the trees, scaling fallen logs, making their way through the dense underbrush. Over an hour later, they scrambled up the last ridge as the trail narrowed and trees became scrawny and wind-bent. The forested path opened to a rocky ledge at the mountain's crest. Standing near the edge of a steep drop-off, she could see for miles as the stony summit overlooked the entire valley.

The creature was nowhere to be seen.

In an act of both desperation and victory, she tilted her head up into the sky, calling to the wind, earth, water, and sun.

"Spirits!" she yelled as loudly and forcefully as she could. Nutmeg barked beside her in unison with her call.

Nothing happened.

Balidova stood still, catching her breath, taking in the beautiful scenery for a few minutes.

By the time her breathing returned to normal, a huge gust of wind had kicked up, and a cloud of dust, leaves, and sticks swooshed into the air. To her surprise, a mini-tornado formed, spiraling higher and higher, morphing into a shape.

Balidova gasped—it was the owl!

As she stood there staring at the miracle before her eyes, the wind gusted again, changing the mass of leaves and sticks into another shape with paws and a head.

"The bear!"

Balidova could hardly believe it, but more was coming. Nutmeg was going wild, running in circles at the sight of a bear, even if it was made of wind.

But as soon as the bear formed, it began to transform into yet another shape, this time with a smooth scaly body and fins.

"The fish!" Balidova shouted in wonder.

The wind kept blowing, transforming all the debris into the shape of a tall sunflower.

She grabbed Nutmeg by the collar and held the dog close to her, not sure whether to be excited or scared of what was coming next.

The girl stood in awe as the wind blew again, nearly knocking her over with its force in one final gust. Swiftly, key parts of the previous four shapes came together—the vast wings of the owl, the strong body of the bear, the glistening scales of the fish, and the wild mane of the sunflower. The dust, leaves, and sticks kicked up into the air and solidified into a single beast. Brown and green forest debris transformed into a full-color spectrum of skin and scales. A massive creature had formed from the wind, earth, water, and sun itself. A rare, triphibious creature equipped with the parts necessary to live in the air, in water, and on land.

What is it?

She blinked her eyes and looked again. *Is this real? Is this really happening?*

Nutmeg whimpered and stuck his tail between his legs, backing onto his haunches.

All at once, a pillar of white light burst forth—plunging into the earth and rising into the sky—illuminating everything in a stream of vivid light.

An incredibly calm feeling came over her, carried by a wind of peace—an unruffled feeling that was now familiar to her. A stillness so deep, it didn't make sense with all the chaos swirling around. An irrational calm resting in the center of her being. The same feeling she experienced when she first saw the owl, the bear, the fish, and the sunflower.

But this time, the feeling was even stronger.

It inhabited her whole body, right down to her bones.

CHAPTER 19
ARMED WITH ORANGE LIGHT

An enormous beast stood before Balidova. It had a gigantic snout, spectacular golden mane, robust legs, a long tail, and gorgeous rainbow-colored wings. The creature's skin was a shimmering emerald green that changed hue into a darker jade green or lighter bamboo green, depending on how the light shone. She blinked her eyes, taking in its full form.

Suddenly, her heart stopped.

She looked at its massive jaws and sharp talons. Nutmeg was puny in comparison. She wanted to turn and run when she noticed something—the creature's eyes.

They were a fiery yellow-orange, with a pitch-black, oval pupil resting deep in the center. At first glance, they looked menacing, but Balidova noticed that they had another quality to them. Something she couldn't quite explain, except that she *knew*.

The creature's fierce gaze softened, and Balidova's muscles relaxed.

At that moment, she no longer felt afraid. This wasn't a destroyer of things, an evil being. She could feel in her heart that this beast meant her no harm. Something in her just *knew*.

Quite the contrary, she sensed it was there to protect her.

As she lowered her guard, Nutmeg sat down without whimpering or growling, just watching. She held onto his collar, comforted by the touch of something familiar.

She looked at the beast and saw kind, loving, powerful eyes gazing back at her. Through her. Beyond her.

Involuntarily, she gasped.

All the spirit creatures I met before—owl, bear, fish—all had yellow eyes, and the sunflower had a yellow mane. That's the one thing they had in common. This is the same being.

What do those magical eyes see?

The same thing I see or something different?

The creature spoke in a low voice—commanding yet kind at the same time. "Hello, dear one, I have been waiting for you. And I see you've brought a friend."

She looked at Nutmeg, then shifted her gaze back to the beast. Her jaw dropped, and her eyes grew wide. "You can speak!? Like the bear and the fish?!"

After staring for a while, she mustered up the courage to ask, "Who are you? What are you?"

The creature replied in a steady, deep voice, "I am a dragon. I am *your* dragon."

Sensing that she could not yet speak further, the dragon continued, "I am the creator of all things. I am the power that creates worlds. I am the power that creates *your* world."

Balidova stood in awe, blinking her eyes, her hand gripping Nutmeg's collar.

"Finally. Finally, I get to meet you. I wondered why dragons were showing up everywhere—on my locker, the Dragon Tail Breath, and even on my dinner plate. I wondered what the owl, bear, fish, and sunflower had in common. They were all part of you, weren't they?"

The dragon smiled. "Yes. I come in many forms. I represent

your inner spirit, your inner strength, and your imagination. I am here to help you become who you can be. I am your guardian." The dragon bowed its head low toward the girl, its long whiskers touching the ground.

Balidova shook herself out of her stupor, gently releasing her grip on Nutmeg's collar. "I...I didn't even know I had a guardian," she replied, dumbfounded. "I mean, other than you, Nutmeg." She patted her trusty companion on the head, and the dog immediately inched closer toward her.

The dragon smiled. "Yes, you do. Every human does. But most cannot hear or see theirs."

A dragon as guardian? That's unusual. Are dragons good or bad?

Hesitating, she spoke again, "What does a guardian do?"

"A guardian helps you hold onto your dreams, navigate the world, and understand what's below the surface. A guardian gives you a map for the road ahead—a map to navigate your world when it turns upside down and nothing seems to make sense."

"Is that what the Dragon Tail Breath is? A map?" Balidova said, her courage slowly returning.

"Yes, it's a map for the *inside* of you. As you breathe each color of light into the energy centers of your body, you illuminate and connect parts of yourself that were covered in shadow and separated from each other."

"Wow. That's amazing," Balidova sighed. "I didn't know simply breathing could do that. I wish I could learn more of it."

"You can. I'm here now, in my true form, because you are ready to learn Step Four of the Dragon Tail Breath. You have passed a big test and reached the halfway point."

"You mean beating Gus?"

"Partly. But even more than that—standing up to your father and standing up for yourself. You now have the clarity of mind and power of heart to <u>stand in your truth</u>."

"Is that what that was?" The anger, rage, and frustration she had felt less than 24 hours earlier at the dinner table seemed like a distant memory. She shook out her whole body, letting go of that energy. "How did you know about that anyway?"

"I see many things," the dragon smiled knowingly.

Balidova looked at the creature, cocking her head sideways. "By the way, how'd you do that?"

"Do what?" the dragon replied.

"Change your shape. All of those other animals were you, right?"

"Yes," the dragon chuckled. "All those creatures were me. You, too, can shape shift, Balidova, even though you do not believe it yet. I will teach you in time. But first, tell me, what's going on with you?"

"I have so much to tell you!" Balidova laughed, remembering how comfortable she had felt confiding in the bear, fish, and sunflower. "You wouldn't believe what happened at school yesterday."

"Really? Try me," the dragon grinned.

"Okay," Balidova continued, adjusting the balance of weight on her feet. "I got shoved into a locker, and before I knew it, I side-kicked the guy who pushed me. He went flying in the air and landed on his butt. I thought he was gonna get up and come after me right then and there, but I just stared him down. I spoke to him with my eyes and with my body. Not with words."

"Good," the dragon said. "You spoke to him with your energy."

"Yeah," Balidova continued. "And afterward, I barely said anything to him, but my actions spoke loud and clear. He went off to his friends, and I went off to my science class. It felt so good. I felt like I could take care of myself and watch my own back. I felt like... *don't mess with me.*"

"Wonderful!" the dragon said. "What happened next?"

"I was all fired up and surging with adrenaline after being in a fight, so I had to calm down before I could do my schoolwork. I used what you taught me last time. I mean, what the sunflower taught me."

"You used your ability to create a different state," The dragon nodded its head. "You went from an elevated state back down to neutral. Well done. You are learning how to control your anger—something you must master to be able to use the dragon magic."

"Yeah, I guess you could say that. I did get hauled in front of the principal's office. Mrs. Marsh scolded me but didn't punish me. She winked at me. I think she was secretly glad that I took care of business and didn't wait for the adults to step in—because there were none there."

"A wise principal you have. There is much support for you in this world, Balidova, including much support that you don't even know about."

"There are so many things I don't know about. Every time I come and talk to you, I realize how little I know! I didn't know I could change my state. Is that what you call it? But I'm still here in Canada," she chuckled.

"Not your external state, your internal state."

"You mean my feeling?"

"Yes."

Well, why don't you just say that? she thought.

Because you are expanding your vocabulary of the internal world, the dragon responded silently.

What? You heard that?

The dragon looked at her and smiled.

"I didn't know I could call you with my vision, with my feeling," she continued aloud.

"Feeling is a very powerful thing," the dragon said, lifting its head to full height. "Trust your feeling."

The dragon paused for a moment, allowing Balidova time to breathe this idea into her body. Then the beast continued, speaking deliberately as if marking a turning point.

"So, young one, are you ready to learn Step Four of the Dragon Tail Breath?"

"Uh, no. I don't think so." Balidova looked sheepish. "I mean, I want to, but I just don't know if I'm good enough...." her voice trailed off as she stepped back to the safety of Nutmeg.

The dragon held its fierce yet loving gaze on her.

Several seconds later, sensing that the dragon had detected her half-truth, Balidova's frown morphed into a smile. "Just kidding. Yes, absolutely!" She laughed off any insecurity she had felt about continuing her study of the Dragon Tail Breath.

"Good. Then remind me of the first three steps," the dragon replied matter-of-factly.

Balidova planted her feet firmly on the wet grass, standing as tall as she could while remaining relaxed in her body. She looked up and to the left, recalling an image from her memory bank. "Step One is breathing the emerald green light into my heart. Knowing that *all is well*." She closed her eyes and imagined a green light as deep as the trees filling her inner canvas.

"Yes," the dragon nodded.

"Step Two is breathing the golden light in through my solar plexus. Coming into the present moment with *here now*." She imagined a sunrise illuminating her face with golden rays.

"Good."

"Step Three is breathing the blue light in through my throat. Asking myself, *what do I want?*" She leaned back and pointed to the vast sky, stretching beyond a chain of mountain peaks.

"Very good, Balidova, very good. You're becoming quite skilled at the Dragon Tail Breath."

"So, what's Step Four?" Balidova asked curiously, leaving the safety of Nutmeg and taking a step toward the dragon.

The dragon shifted its weight, sending a huge boulder clattering off the cliff's edge like a small stone, reminding Balidova how powerful this creature was. And how puny she was. For a moment, she wondered how she could master a technique taught by such a magnificent beast.

"Step Four of the Dragon Tail breath is breathing orange light through the tanden."

"The *tanden*? You mean the same tanden I learned about from karate?"

"Yes, it's the center of your body—four finger widths below your belly button—running right through the center of your physical body. It's where all your power is drawn from—the power coming up from the earth through your feet and legs, and the power coming down from the sky through your head, upper body, and arms. It finds its center right there." The dragon pointed one claw toward Balidova's abdomen.

The girl pressed her hand firmly against her belly, feeling for her belly button. When she found it, she placed four fingers sideways against her skin and pressed the spot directly below that.

"Oh, there it is," she said, looking down at her navel. "That's the same spot we learned about in karate, where all the punching and kicking power comes from."

"Yes, that's right. Martial arts are a tradition that has survived thousands of years. Now I will show you something that will build on what you already learned in the dojo." The dragon shook out its wings, expanded its chest, and continued. "Visualize breathing orange light in through your tanden, and with it, bring *what you want* into your physical body. In this way, you become a powerful creator—a *very* powerful creator."

"It all starts by asking yourself—"

"How do I feel now? How do I want to feel?" Balidova interrupted.

"Exactly. Because the answer to those questions will tell you what it is that you most want. <u>Everything humans do is to get a feeling</u>, whether they know it or not." The dragon paused and wiggled its golden whiskers at the girl. "Why don't you try it?"

Balidova closed her eyes, placed one hand on her tanden, and inhaled deeply. She visualized a burnt orange sunrise, with all the magic and beauty of a new day upon her. She imagined light entering her lower belly, spreading from the center of her body outward, and growing bigger with each breath, eventually reaching up to the top of her head and down to the tips of her toes. Orange light filled her up from the inside out, through all the cells of her body—so much that she even began to smell it. The scent of tangy, sweet orange zest seeped into her nostrils and eeked out her pores.

"This feels amazing," she said, dropping her hands and opening her eyes. "I just wanna hang onto this feeling forever."

Is this what being a powerful creator feels like?

What do those words mean, anyway?

The dragon laughed at Balidova's childlike delight. "Well, you *can* hold onto this feeling. Three little words will help you. Three magic words, when said aloud, will transform feeling bad into feeling good. They will help close the gap between how you feel now and how you want to feel. Three words. But you must *feel* them, Balidova. Not just say them. You must feel them fully in your body, mind, and spirit."

"What are they?" she asked excitedly. She was both stunned and skeptical at the same time. "I didn't know words could be so powerful."

The dragon paused, taking in a deep breath.

"Accept. Release. Move-on."

The dragon spoke slowly, holding up a razor-sharp talon for each word.

"That's it? But they're so simple." Balidova said, stunned.

"Life is not complicated, Balidova. Humans make it so. You can return to simplicity anytime you wish."

"Accept. Release. Move-on. Who would have thought such ordinary words could make such an extraordinary difference? What do they mean?"

"*Accept* how you feel right now. Stop pushing it away. Stop running from it. Stop denying that it exists. Just *let it be*." The dragon held the girl's gaze with its yellow eyes.

"*Release* your commitment to that emotion. You're hanging onto it with the story you tell yourself of how so-and-so did this or that to you. *Release the old story.*"

"*Move-on* to how you want to feel. Where attention goes, energy flows. There's a world of difference between pushing against what you don't want vs. moving toward what you do want. *Create a new story.*"

"I don't get it." Balidova looked puzzled.

"You will, Balidova, in time. For now, practice this motion. Place one hand on top of the other. Draw one hand up your arm as you *Accept,* turn that hand around your shoulder as you *Release,* and rub the same hand down your arm as you *Move-on,* letting it fly off your fingertips. And then do the same thing on the other arm."

The dragon ran one paw up its leg, letting its talons slide across its scales. When it reached its shoulder, it turned and slid that paw back down in one smooth motion. Balidova imitated the dragon's movement with her own hands and arms.

"Remember to arm yourself with the orange light, Balidova, while saying the words, *I am a powerful creator.* You are the author of your own story. What will that story be?"

∽

With both paws firmly on the ground, the dragon spread its rainbow-colored wings. "Speak of this meeting to no one. For they will not understand."

"Okay, I won't. I promise," the girl replied.

Right when Balidova finished speaking, the majestic beast lifted into the sky. As it flew off, it relayed a silent message to the girl through her mind:

Where two become one.
We shall meet next.

Only a small, dark bottle remained where the dragon had stood. Balidova looked dumbfounded. She repeated the words in her mind but didn't know what they meant. *Where two become one. We shall meet next.*

She bent down, picked up the bottle, and examined it closely. A label on it said, "Black Spruce Essential Oil."

The dragon must have forgotten this, or maybe left the bottle for me as a gift? Either way, there's no one else here, so I'm keeping it.

She stuffed the bottle in her pocket, feeling a strong desire to know the creature more.

Looking down at her arms, she slowly rubbed one up and down, then the other, as the dragon had shown her. She repeated the three words aloud. "Accept... Release... Move-on. **A.R.M.**"

Balidova turned and began walking down the mountain trail with Nutmeg beside her. She talked to him as they walked. "I don't see how three words can make that much difference. But I'll give it a shot. And who knows—what if it does work?" She stopped to rub his furry face with both hands and glanced back at where she'd met the dragon. Together, the girl and dog made their way back home through the forest.

Halfway down the steep slope, traveling too fast, she stumbled on a tree root that jutted above the ground. She nearly face-planted on a stick but caught her balance at the last second. Further down the mountain, she heard the distinct call of wolves howling in the distance. It was almost sunset, and the light was fading fast. Nutmeg, her loyal companion, stuck close to her side all the way back.

When they reached the house, she let out a grateful sigh, said goodnight to her dog, grabbed her backpack from beside his doghouse right where she'd left it, and went inside. She quietly dumped her jacket and runners by the side door, then tiptoed straight up to her room.

While closing her door, she heard a voice from downstairs.

"Balidova, is that you?" Her mom called out.

"Yeah," Balidova said as little as possible. She didn't want to talk to her mom, but knew that she'd dig an even deeper hole for herself if she didn't respond at all.

"Where've you been? We've been looking for you. We're having a late dinner tonight because your dad wants you girls to train first, as soon as he gets home from the hospital. Come down here soon." Balidova's Mom sounded annoyed.

"Okay." Balidova sighed, hoping she wouldn't have to explain her whereabouts. Quickly, she sat down at her desk, pulled out her journal, and proceeded to write:

Dragon Tail Breath, step 4.
Orange light. Tanden. ARM.
<u>*I am a powerful creator*</u>*. Breathe.*
Met my dragon for the first time.
Got the black spruce oil to prove it.

Looking at the words on the page, she smiled. In the solitude of her room, she thought about her enchanting evening. The beauty of the moon, meadow, and mountain lingered in her mind. She felt strangely connected to all of nature in a way she hadn't before. She also felt more connected to her thoughts and feelings. They seemed brighter—lit up—as if the balance of her inner and outer focus had shifted. As if an inner light switch had been turned on, she could now pay more attention to what *she* thought versus what everyone else thought.

Her body felt light, tingly, open, and expansive, thinking of the dragon.

Last night, when she'd argued with her dad and had loads of self-doubt about whether she did the right thing kicking Gus at school, her body felt tense, heavy, constricted, and uncomfortable.

She knew the difference now—she knew how different thoughts *felt* in her body.

Placing her hand in her pocket, she noticed something was there. She pulled out the bottle of oil the dragon had given her and opened it. A distinct woodsy aroma filled her room. She liked it, even though it was unusual to have the smell of trees in the house. Sitting in the same room where she'd felt trapped in her head, she now felt a sense of understanding, clarity, and acceptance about the world and her place in it. She felt a calm, centeredness as if a mountain of peace resided within her.

Before heading downstairs again, she looked out her bedroom window at the full moon.

The Mountain Moon.

As she allowed the moon's light to shower over her, she felt her connection to nature, her senses, and her body rhythms strengthen. No longer would she override her connection to herself with the demands of others. Unbeknownst to her, the split parts of her—loathing vs. loving herself, feeling good vs. feeling bad, wanting to learn the dragon magic vs. wanting it to go away—were slowly coming together.

Balidova felt an urgent yearning to connect with the dragon

on a deeper level, but she did not know if or when she would ever see the magnificent creature again.

All of a sudden, her eyes grew wide.

How am I supposed to call the dragon... if I don't even know its name?

CHAPTER 20
SISTERS JEALOUS

As she neared the bottom of the stairs, Balidova realized she'd forgotten to tie up Nutmeg for the night. She tiptoed out the side door as quietly as she could. Nutmeg was already in his doghouse, lying down, with his head and neck stretched out between his paws, exhausted after their arduous climb up and down the mountain.

"Good boy," she said, patting him on the head. "Thanks for coming with me. That was pretty cool, wasn't it? I bet you've never seen a dragon before."

She re-entered the house as quietly as she could through the side door, but her eldest sister, April, spotted her.

"Where were you, Balidova? Everyone's been looking for you."

"Oh, uh, I was outside."

"Really?" April looked skeptical, especially since Balidova didn't have any outdoor clothes on. Although it was spring, the weather was still chilly at night. "We looked outside and couldn't find you. Did you go down to the lagoon again? See any wolves?" Her sister smirked. Obviously, June couldn't keep a secret.

"No," Balidova replied, shaking her head. She closed her mouth and breathed in through her nose, deliberately *not* reacting to the taunt.

"Well then, where'd you go?"

Balidova sighed. *I don't wanna tell her. It's none of her business. If I tell her I met a dragon, she's just gonna make fun of me, like everyone else.*

"Why are you so reluctant to say anything? And why are you acting weird? Ever since you beat Gus in the fight at school yesterday, you've been acting very strange. You think you're a hotshot or something?"

Balidova rolled her eyes. "You don't understand. It's not like that."

"Or maybe, since we won team kata, and now that you're the champ, you think you can do anything? You don't have to tell people where you're going at night? Mom's mad at you. And so is Dad, by the way. You're not doing yourself any favors."

Balidova grabbed her jacket through gritted teeth and threw it on. "I'm going out to the barn to feed the animals. See ya later," she muttered in disgust.

"Don't take too long—it's almost dinner," April scolded her before leaving.

Balidova knew her sister's next move would be to report to Mom and Dad what she had discovered. April didn't know that Balidova had already spoken with their mom. Even though they were given a lot of freedom to roam about on the farm and surrounding area, Balidova had been away more than usual lately, attracting her parents' attention.

As she stood on the side door steps, about to close the door, her second sister, May, arrived. "Hey Dova, can I borrow that grey sweatshirt of yours? The one with a moose wearing boots on the front?"

"No, that's one of my favorites," Balidova replied.

May looked shocked that she'd been turned down. Then her tone changed. She grabbed the door before Balidova could close it and stuck her head outside, speaking in a hushed tone.

"You think you're so great just because you beat one kid in a fight at school. But remember, you lost at the tournament, and now the provincial team tryouts are coming up. There's only one person per category. That means you don't have us to rely on anymore. You gotta win by yourself."

Balidova glared at May, grabbed the doorknob, and slammed the door. May barely got her face out of the way in time. Then, Balidova heard a scream behind the door. May opened it again, crying and clutching her hand.

"You idiot, you slammed the door on my finger!! You're gonna get it for this."

Balidova walked out to the barn in stunned silence. She hadn't meant to hurt May, but realized everything May said was technically true. Provincial team tryouts were two months away, in early June. And only one person in each event would become a highly prized team member and represent the province at the national championship later in the year. Balidova wanted a spot. So did her sisters. And so did many other people from all across the province. Ironically, the sisters each knew that their most formidable competition was living in the same house. If they wanted a spot on the team, they had to beat each other out to get it.

She escaped into the barn and fed the animals their evening meal of hay and grain. While filling the horse's water buckets, she stopped to pet the barn cat, who was prowling for mice.

BACK IN THE HOUSE, Balidova headed toward the kitchen, hoping she could snag a snack before dinner.

"Glad to see you're back," her mom said sarcastically. "We

were worried about you. Next time tell us where you're going." Her mom gave her a disapproving stare.

Balidova looked at her mom and nodded. She felt sheepish about running off, but also didn't think she had a choice given the circumstances. She would have done just about anything to see the spirit elements again. She hadn't stopped to think about how her trip up Wolf Mountain would affect anyone else—she was so excited to have figured out the riddle. Yet deep in her heart, Balidova wished she could share it all with her mom. Keeping the biggest thing to happen for her a secret from everyone in her family was eating her up inside.

But I promised not to talk about the dragon.

After rummaging through the fridge and finding a leftover piece of broccoli quiche, Balidova ate alone at the table. Later, April and May walked in while she put her dishes in the sink. She noticed that they exchanged knowing glances.

They're probably glad I have to do the dishes all week to make up for leaving the dinner table early last night.

Balidova headed back to her room and saw her white karate uniform on the floor. *That's weird. I didn't put it there. It's usually hung up in my closet.* She noticed a red marking on it. Across the front of the gi, written in thick red ink, were the words 'U SUCK.'

Balidova gasped. Her head throbbed, and her ears burned. Tears welled in her eyes. She knew only a few people could have done this—her sisters.

Was it all of them? Or just one of them? May? Is this her way of getting back at me for slamming her finger in the door? She felt a stabbing pain in her chest. *But why would she write on my gi?*

Balidova looked around her room to see if anything else was amiss. If May had destroyed her karate uniform in a rage, maybe she did other damage too? But everything seemed to be in place. Balidova turned to look at the gi once more. The stark contrast of red lettering on white fabric reminded her of blood on snow. She felt a shudder run up her spine. *Wait a sec—is this why April and May were looking at each other after dinner? April's the one who said she thought I was acting like a hotshot—taking advantage of being team kata champ.*

In that moment, she realized it was not just the finger slamming that had prompted all this. It was more than that, and it was more than just May. It was her two older sisters together. They were the ones she'd be competing against at the upcoming provincial team tryouts. Being four years younger, June was in a different age category. But the older three were close enough together in age to be in the same category.

Her two older sisters knew Balidova was a threat, and they knew that she'd been gaining strength lately. They'd seen her beat up Gus at school. They'd seen her get into an argument with their dad. Where was she getting her strength from? This might be enough to push her over the edge and destroy her confidence before the next tournament—an advantage they would need since Balidova was the best one at kumite. Not only did she have longer reach, but she was fast, strong, and intuitive. She could sense things during a match that you couldn't teach. She had a sixth sense about fighting that her sisters didn't have.

May had the most to gain by undermining Balidova's confidence. At the provincial team tryouts, she would most likely lose to April in kata. And she'd lose to Balidova in kumite. Then where would she be? She wouldn't have a spot on the provincial team except for team kata.

All these thoughts went racing through Balidova's mind. She knelt on the floor and picked up her uniform. The words were written in red sharpie and wouldn't come out. As she threw the material down on the floor, she noticed something on the backside. The letters L-O-S-E-R were written in red ink along the back of the gi.

Contradictory thoughts battled in her mind.

She couldn't believe this was happening right after she'd had the most amazing experience of her life—meeting the dragon at the top of Wolf Mountain. She put her head in her hands and screamed silently.

She clenched her fists and started wailing on the inside, making little hissing noises through gritted teeth as she pounded her fists on the floor. She could feel a volcano of rage rise inside her. She was angry. Not only at her sisters but at herself—for being angry! All she wanted after meeting her guardian dragon was to remain peaceful and calm.

Just as the volcano inside her was about to explode... she caught herself and breathed deeply, remembering the dragon's words—Accept, Release, Move-on.

For a moment, her fury abated. But again, the voices inside her battled. *I can't accept this. I can't release it. And I am not moving on! Even if they acted out of jealousy, they are gonna pay for doing this. I don't know how, but they will.*

Rage rose inside her again.

Angry with herself for having such thoughts, she started whimpering and hugging her knees, rocking back and forth.

She heard muffled footsteps in the hall. She knew her sisters were spying on her. Turning around, she caught a glimpse of May and April poking their heads around the corner. Seeing them confirmed to her that both of them had done this. She slammed the door shut. She didn't want them to see her crying. She was too proud to let them know they'd gotten to her. To let them know that she was weak. She remembered her vow—to never be helpless like her mother.

Balidova felt torn between the two things she wanted more than anything else, but which seemed utterly incompatible: her mother's loving embrace and feeling powerful within herself.

∼

BALIDOVA PAUSED, took a deep breath and relaxed her shoulders. Anger had filled her up like a balloon, and now, some of that pressure was released as she breathed. She thought of the dragon's words—you are a powerful creator.

If I'm so powerful, why am I creating all this sucky stuff? I don't understand. I like how I feel when I'm with the dragon, but this doesn't make sense. Why is this happening?

She thought of her mother's supportive look at the dinner table the night before—how much it had meant to her.

Mom, I need to talk to you. I need you.

Checking to see if the door was closed, she grabbed the stone the bear had given her, the pine cone from the fish, and her favorite stuffed animal—a brown and white spotted horse that she'd named Betsy—from her desk. She crawled under her bed, something she only did in the most desperate of moments when she felt unsafe anywhere else. Lying on her chest, her chin pressed against the ground, she breathed heavily. She felt the hard, smooth surface of the rock in one hand, the jagged edges of the pine cone in another, Betsy facing her. She proceeded to have a conversation with her stuffy. Since she couldn't talk to her mom in real life, she would talk in her imagination.

"Mom, what's going on? Why is everything happening like this?" Balidova whispered, looking straight into the brown eyes of the horse.

"Balidova, it's okay. It's gonna be okay," she whispered back, moving Betsy's head up and down as if the stuffed horse was speaking.

She brought her stuffy close to her chest and felt its furry softness on her face and neck, imagining it was her mom hugging her.

"It's gonna be okay. It's gonna be okay. I'm here for you."

Even though she was nearly a teenager, she breathed in the words of comfort from the stuffed animal like a toddler clinging safely to her mother's leg in the dark. For the first time in a long time, she realized just how much she needed her mother's love.

Inhale.

Exhale.

A few moments later, she heard her dad calling all of them for a karate workout. He had just returned from the hospital.

"Girls, it's time for karate! Come on, let's go. Let's have a short workout before dinner!"

Under the bed, Balidova summoned all the wisdom and power she had learned from the Dragon.

If I can face a dragon. I can face my sisters.

Luckily, she had a spare uniform. She crawled out from underneath the bed and put it on. Having a workout was the last thing she wanted to do. But she knew she had no choice. She called up every last bit of strength inside her. Put on her spare gi and her green belt. Then she threw the marked-up gi into the corner of her closet and marched down to the basement, straight past her sisters, who watched her closely. Lining up, she started the karate workout as if nothing had happened.

At one point, halfway through their training session, Balidova felt she would lose it, and all her emotions would come tumbling out. She bit the inside of her lip hard until it bled, fighting back the tears. The taste of blood in her mouth distracted her just enough to keep her mind focused on getting through each kata. As they completed their movement forms, she avoided looking at May and April.

Sitting in seiza, meditating at the end of class, thoughts churned in Balidova's mind. Just when she'd had an incredible experience—seeing the spirit creature in its true form, dragon flesh and blood—she'd fallen to the miserable depths of her sisters cutting her down. Looking for a way out of her misery, she remembered the questions the dragon had posed.

How do I feel now?

Her eyes already closed, she scanned inside her body and noticed a tightness in her gut. *I feel mad. And sad.*

How do I wanna feel?

Immediately, an answer bubbled up. Something she wasn't expecting.

I want revenge.

Her hands already resting on her lap, she squeezed them into fists so tight, her fingernails made marks on the palms of her hands. Not a shred of light penetrated between her fingers or her thumb in that tight little ball of flesh.

She opened her eyes and for a second, had a crazy thought. *If I'm such a powerful creator, can I use that power to get back at my older sisters?*

She glanced to her right, and saw May and April sitting in seiza with their eyes closed. Something inside her told her it wasn't right, but another part of her wanted it anyways. She could feel a deep desire for revenge closing in like a dark cloak, shutting out all the light.

CHAPTER 21
TEACHER TRUST

After the karate workout ended, all four girls went upstairs for dinner. Two daughters on each side of the oval table, with Mom and Dad at either end. They all ate in silence. The food on her plate covered the image of the dragon at first, but as she consumed each bite, more and more of the dragon on her plate became visible.

There you are, just like the Dragon Tail Breath. More and more of you gets revealed with each step.

Still angry, Balidova stared into the eyes of the little red dragon looking up at her. She glanced up at her second sister—*I'm gonna ruin something of yours just like you ruined my gi—* then looked around the table. Everyone was staring down at their plate. It was a very quiet dinner table tonight. Only the slurping sound of spaghetti noodles entering hungry mouths could be heard. Suddenly, the thought dawned on her that her sisters might be feeling bad for what they did.

Good, they should feel guilty.

After dinner, Balidova ran upstairs and rummaged through her room, searching for May's favorite pen. A stack of freshly folded laundry lay on her bed. *Mom must have come in here when we were having a workout. She must have seen my gi.*

A moment later, she spotted it, buried underneath a pile of papers. Anger had a way of galvanizing her focus. She grabbed the pen with two hands, and raised it up in the air to get more leverage for a forceful snap. But her mom, who was walking purposefully toward her room, saw her.

"Balidova! What are you doing?"

She froze, hands in mid-air, and looked up at her mom.

"Isn't that your sister's pen? Are you trying to get back at her for writing on your gi?" Her mom asked sternly. "I came to talk to you about what happened. I saw your karate uniform when I came up to drop off the laundry."

Balidova didn't say a word, she just kept staring at her mom.

"**An eye for an eye makes the whole world blind**. If you break her pen, what's she going to do to you next? When will it end, Balidova? When will the fighting end?"

It won't, Balidova thought. She looked at the multicolored pen, still considering its destruction.

I know Mom's right. I'm just—arrrggghhhhh!

"Why don't you come downstairs and help me with the dishes instead. It's still your turn to do them, since you left the dinner table early the other night. Your dad's going to be very upset with you if you don't obey his note." Her mom spoke firmly but gently, looking at her daughter empathetically.

"And after we do that, I'll help you scrub the writing off your gi." She knew continued fighting between her daughters wasn't the answer. It would only make her life more difficult.

Reluctantly, Balidova threw the pen into her sister's room, which was right next to hers, and followed her mom back to the kitchen. Her anger had softened in the face of her mom's compassionate gaze and words. As Balidova entered the most frequented room in the house, she noticed that everyone else had disappeared, although they had cleared the table. A large stack of dirty dishes lay piled in the sink.

With a sigh, she decided to get started. Over the next few minutes, she settled into her task and looked out the kitchen window at the greening spring landscape, while scrubbing each plate, fork, and knife clean. As warm sudsy water enveloped her hands, and the soft sponge removed caked on debris from dish after dish, she felt something change inside her.

In the calm, loving presence of her mom, her anger at her sisters gradually subsided, and her gratitude towards her mother grew. Her mother was the only one in the family who had been there for her at the dinner table when she spoke her truth to her dad. And now her mother was here for her when she was having it out with her sisters.

Thanks for supporting me, Mom.

She no longer wanted to push away her mom and align herself with her dad, as she had wanted months ago. Instead, the opposite was happening. *I'm fed up with Dad and all his expectations—to be perfect, to win, to obey. So much pressure! I'm not doing that anymore.*

For a brief moment, she felt a twinge of sympathy for her sisters. They didn't have a dragon to guide them in the face of such pressure, like she did. She wondered if they had been affected by the dark cloak like she had. Still, it was not an excuse for what they did. But the idea that it wasn't all them—that other forces had influenced their behavior—lessened her desire for revenge.

As her frustration abated, she felt more and more drawn toward her mother's love. *Even though I haven't spoken to Mom for months, she's still there for me. She still makes lunch for me every day. She still waves goodbye before I go on the bus. She still kisses me good night. She even offered to help clean my uniform. I guess everything isn't so black and white,* she thought to herself as she cleaned spaghetti sauce off the bottom of the pot. *Mom's not all that bad.*

As she scrubbed the metal basin caked with food debris, the old grudge toward her mother got scrubbed off too. For the first time since she'd made her vow of silence toward her mother back in January, she spoke to the woman, not out of necessity, but out of desire.

"Mom."

"Yes, Balidova?"

"You know when I got in trouble at the principal's office for kicking Gus?"

"Yes…"

"Well, the principal winked at me and said I wouldn't be punished. She seemed glad that I had taken care of things myself."

Her mom smiled. "I'm glad you put that boy in his place too."

After finishing the dishes, Balidova and her mom walked together into the laundry room to wash the writing off her gi. Unfortunately, it wouldn't come out because it was written in permanent marker. For a brief moment, upset flared in Balidova once again, but her mom reassured the girl that she'd buy her a new uniform.

Later that evening, her mom helped Balidova confront her older sisters about the marked-up uniform. After speaking to her mom and seeing May's bandaged finger, Balidova decided revenge wasn't necessarily the best option. She chose to A.R.M. herself and just let it all go.

Accept.

Release.

Move-on.

That night, she lay in bed, pondering all that had happened. So many new ideas challenged what she previously thought. The world was not as it seemed—contrasting events were popping up everywhere. From avoiding to appreciating her mom. From revering to rejecting her dad. From wanting revenge on her older sisters to forgiving them. From miraculous encounters with dragons to dangerous brushes with bullies.

It seemed like every time she learned another piece of the Dragon Tail Breath, every time more of the magic was revealed, the more volatile her home and school life became. She didn't know how to bridge the gap between the mystical world and the real world. She didn't know how to make sense of all the contradictions. All the violent swinging back and forth made her dizzy, creating a growing chasm inside her.

THE NEXT MORNING, Balidova woke up remembering she had a science lab that day. She quickly pulled on blue jeans and a black, long sleeve shirt. Her clothes reflected how she felt—she had not done her homework.

Maybe Mr. Winston will take pity on me? He does seem to like me—he always wants to talk about dragon stuff.

I wonder if he knows what it means to be a powerful creator?

What did the dragon mean when it said that?

Why am I so confused?

Is there a scientific explanation he can give me to help make sense of all this?

When science class came around, Balidova took her place at the lab table. She sat near the back of the large room, with shelves full of equipment and textbooks behind her. Mr. Winston's glasses slid down his nose as he started to sweat and he pushed them back onto his bulbous nose with his middle finger. Balidova smirked, noticing that the teacher had just given her class the finger. She wondered if anyone else had noticed.

He was giving the preamble. "Listen up, class. You need to understand three points in order to do the lab today. Number one.

Everything is made of energy. Everything from the hardest rock, to the fluid ocean, to invisible rays of light. E v e r y t h i n g, including you, is energy."

One student put up their hand. "Mr. Winston? What about thoughts? Are those energy too?"

"Yes, but let's save that for later. We'll get to it. Good question."

Mr. Winston paced around the classroom, enjoying his soliloquy. "Think about you for a second. Are you really solid? Actually, you're made of 60 trillion cells. And inside each of those cells are electrons, neutrons and protons—vibrating rapidly. So actually, you're not really solid. Plus, you're mostly water. You're not solid at all. You're just being held together by a thin membrane called your skin, and by a bony calcified structure called your skeleton. Think about that."

A murmur went through the class, then someone coughed. "If we're not solid, then why does Tony feel it when I shove him?" Someone in the back of the class laughed as he pushed the boy in front of him.

"Quit horsing around," Mr. Winston said sternly.

Balidova squirmed in her seat.

Hmm, is that why the tree spirit could appear like flowing branches at first and then morph into the bear?

The fish appeared out of water?

The sunflower out of fire?

And the dragon came out of a swirl of sticks and dirt?

Mr. Winston continued. "Number two. Once you get that everything is made of energy, then you need to understand that energy moves in waves. There's a movement to energy. It doesn't just travel in a straight line. There's a frequency and vibration to those wave movements. All energy is in constant wave motion. Look at nature. It doesn't stop. The ocean tide is relentless, whether big or little, it never ends. The seasons also, they just keep going. The earth's orbit around the sun, the moon's orbit around the earth, the planets keep going too, without stopping. Every natural thing we know, operates in a universal dynamic flow. Including you. Your breath doesn't stop. Not for long, anyway, unless you have a death wish. Your heartbeat, same thing. It doesn't stop. And it moves in waves."

Wow, that's so cool. Balidova was stunned by the connection between the human body and nature.

"Number three. States of Matter. The same thing can be in different states," Mr. Winston went on.

"You mean different locations in the US?" someone asked.

"No, not those kind of states—not countries. States of being—that's what I'm talking about. For example, water. At different temperatures, it can be solid, liquid or gas. Under zero degrees Celsius, it becomes solid. The water molecules crystalize and become as hard as ice. Above zero degrees, it's a liquid. It flows and can be poured, dripped, shaken, or stirred. Heated to about 100 degrees Celsius, water becomes a gas—steam. Almost invisible. The same thing changes form, as the space between the particles expands and the water molecules grow further apart. The human body is no different. You have solid parts like your bones, liquid parts like your blood and gaseous parts too."

Balidova looked out the window, thinking about the events of the past several months.

If water can appear in different states, then other things can too.
The wind spirit and the owl were the same thing, in different forms.
The tree spirit and the bear,
the water spirit and the fish,
the fire spirit and the sunflower,
all the elements and the dragon,
They were all the same thing.

Mr. Winston kept talking, "The last thing you need to understand, is that we are made of the same things that the stars are made of."

A hush came over the whole room.

"What's that?" someone asked.

"Mostly hydrogen, carbon, and oxygen," Mr. Winston answered.

The class was listening closely now, instantly enraptured by their own similarity to the galaxy.

Balidova too, was stunned. *Really? We're made of the same stuff as stars? But planet earth is a star. That means we're made of the same things the planet is made of—the four elements.*

Fire, water, air, and soil.

Right on cue, Mr. Winston confirmed Balidova's own thoughts. "Literally the same elements that make up the stars and the earth, make up us. We are creatures designed to live on the earth,"

Mr. Winston was really in his groove now. "The energy that's all around us, flows within us and connects us too. All energy moves in waves—cell phone waves, light waves, gamma waves, radio waves. Our body also has energy within it. What do you think keeps our heart beating and our lungs pumping? We are electromagnetic beings."

He extended his arms and splayed out his fingers as if mimicking an explosion. "The energy within us moves in waves too. There's a rhythm to it. You can feel it in your heartbeat. Today's experiment is to play with that energy through the states of matter."

All of a sudden, he stopped talking. "Okay, enough from me. Get out your materials and get started." He pointed to the lab procedure written on the smart board. "Follow the process. You know what to do."

Students mobilized around the class, pulling equipment onto their lab tables, chatting in excited yet hushed tones with their lab partners. Balidova got out a blow torch to heat water, and liquid nitrogen to freeze it. She put on her goggles and gloves and prepared a flask of water. She was excited about what she had just heard. It helped her make sense of all the strange occurrences she had witnessed over the past several months since she turned twelve. Her teacher's words helped solve a puzzle in her mind.

Meanwhile, Mr. Winston was patrolling the room, helping some students and reprimanding others as he saw fit. He sauntered over to Balidova's table and stood nearby, watching her. She decided to ask him something that was on her mind, something she figured he might know about since he knew so much about invisible energy.

"Uh, Mr. Winston—what does it mean to be a 'powerful creator?'"

"Where'd you hear that phrase?" he asked, surprised.

"Well, I have a crazy story to tell you…"

Mr. Winston quickly looked around and cut her off before she could continue, "Stay after class Balidova. We'll talk then."

Almost an hour later—after ice, water and steam had filled the classroom—all the students cleaned up their 'states of matter' experiment and left the lab as the bell rang.

Only Balidova stayed behind.

After making sure her table was clear and her notebook was safely back in her pack, she walked over to Mr. Winston's desk.

"Where'd you hear about being a powerful creator?" he asked.

"You're not gonna believe me," Balidova shuffled her feet, nervously.

"Try me," he said, looking straight at her.

"You know all those Dragon Tail Breath lessons I was telling you about?"

"Yes, you were up to Step Two, was it?"

"Well, now I'm on Step Four, actually. You won't believe this, but do you know who taught me Step Four?"

"No," he said expectantly, leaning forward.

She looked around to see if anyone else was in the room. She'd already been ridiculed enough. "An actual dragon." she whispered.

Mr. Winston gasped. "Really?"

"Yes," Balidova said, matter-of-factly. "I couldn't believe it either."

Mr. Winston's eyes grew wide. "That's amazing. I didn't know that was possible." He rubbed his finger on his chin, as if he were remembering something, although she didn't know what. Then he shook his head and got back to the conversation in front of him. "What did the dragon teach you, exactly?"

She proceeded to tell him about breathing in the orange light. She told him about being a powerful creator and the three magic words—Accept, Release, Move-on.

"Wow. That's a lot to take in," he said. "The dragon sure packed it in, didn't he?"

"How do you know it's a he?" Balidova asked him, tilting her head sideways.

"How do I know?" Mr. Winston seemed taken aback. "What do you mean? I just know. Such a powerful creature must be."

Despite her growing confidence in him, Balidova didn't like his assumption, but she kept her opinion to herself.

"Mr. Winston, I have a question for you. You talked about everything being energy. Energy moving in waves and being in constant motion. And we're made of the same stuff as everything around us. So, is being a powerful creator when we line up our energy waves with the energy that's out there? Is that how we're able to make things happen?"

"Yeah. I guess that's a good way of looking at it. I never really thought about it like that." he adjusted his bow tie as he spoke.

"There's something else," she said, "you said we're electromagnetic beings. So, do we attract certain things with our energy? Like a magnet?"

"Yes." Mr. Winston seemed surer of himself now. This question was more familiar to him. "Whatever energy you put out is what you attract back. If you send out a low vibration, you get a low vibration back. If you send out a high vibration, you get a high vibration back."

"I don't know what that means," Balidova said, confused.

"Well, you asked how we create stuff. Attracting energy waves at different vibrations is part of it."

"Is that why, when I feel bad, everything seems to go wrong? And when I feel good, everything seems to go right?" She pulled at the rough edges of her fingernails.

"You could say that."

Balidova looked down at her watch. She only had a couple minutes to get to her next class, so she started towards the door.

"Balidova, before you go, I have an unusual request. Could I have one of your, um, fingernails?"

"What? What for?" she asked, shocked.

All of a sudden, Mr. Winston recognized what he'd asked. "No, no, not the whole thing," he laughed. "Just the clipping off the top."

What in the world do you need that for? She creased her face quizzically.

As if reading her mind, he said, "I need it for… an experiment. I need a calcified body part, but not my own."

"You mean—bone?" she asked, even more puzzled.

"No, a fingernail clipping will do."

"That sounds really strange Mr. Winston. But what the heck, you answered my weird questions, so, here you go. This piece was coming off anyway." She ripped a small bit of nail off her thumb and handed it to him.

"Thanks," he said with a smile, surprised that she had obliged him.

As she turned to go, she noticed him take out a small, black box from his desk drawer and place her fingernail in it, very carefully.

Whatever, she thought, shaking her head while walking out the door.

A FEW STEPS into the hallway, she passed Angel. Her friend's bright pink hair scrunchie contrasted sharply with her orange and yellow tie die shirt.

That shirt's the same color as the dragon's eye.

"Hey Balidova, what's up?" Angel said.

"Hey Angel, how are you?" Balidova was genuinely happy to see her friend, even if she was surprised Angel was speaking to her.

"I just wanted to say, it's pretty cool what you did with Gus the other day. He did have to be stopped. I'm glad you kicked him even if you didn't do anything when he came after me." She smirked. "You're kind of a hero, you know."

Balidova shook her head. "Well, thanks, but my dad sure didn't think so. He got mad at me for using my karate at school."

"Well, everyone at school thinks you're pretty cool, including me." Angel smiled.

She seems to have forgiven me for what happened months ago. I guess you can only hold onto a grudge for so long? Balidova reasoned.

"See you around?" Angel waved a two fingered peace sign at her friend. "Oh wait, there's one more thing—you wanna do the science fair project together?"

"Yeah, that'd be awesome." Balidova grinned, glad to be on talking terms with her best friend again, and even happier that Angel asked to work with her. "See you around." She swung her book bag happily in sync with her long stride, her black ponytail bobbing from side to side.

Funny how everything comes full circle. Maybe all these energy waves, including the colors of light, are connected. I can use them to change my state of being too.

Struck by curiosity, Balidova pulled out her phone and looked up the meaning of the word "light." She wanted to know the exact definition. She was surprised by the answer—"the natural agent that stimulates sight and makes things visible."

That's what the dragon's doing—helping me see things in a different way. She felt a pang of hope. *Maybe there isn't such a big gap between the dragon world and my world after all.*

CHAPTER 22
BULLY BREWING

Just after Balidova left the science lab—Gus entered it. Gus had Mr. Winston for science too, right after Balidova, but they had never crossed paths because Gus was usually late, rushing in at the last moment after hanging out with his friends at the east side doors, near the other end of the school.

He walked in just as the bell rang, his grey t-shirt hanging out of his baggy, ripped jeans, shaggy blonde hair falling across his chiseled face. Mr. Winston called him over while everyone else was taking their seats. "Gus, come over here, I'd like to speak to you for a minute."

While Gus sauntered over to the far side of the room, Mr. Winston addressed the rest of the students. "Class, pull out your lab books, we'll be doing an experiment on the States of Matter today. We're gonna be using liquid nitrogen and bunsen burners."

A small cheer went up. They would be repeating the same experiment the previous class just completed—turning water into ice and steam.

"Yeah, what's up?" Gus said, a big wad of chewing gum in his mouth.

"I need to talk to you after class, something urgent has come up," Mr. Winston said, adjusting his bow tie.

"What is it? Same thing as before?" Gus asked coolly.

Mr. Winston's eyes darted around to see if anyone was listening, but all the other students were preparing for the lab, paying no attention to them. He lowered his voice, "Balidova Forester..."

"Again? I can't stand her." Gus sneered. "She thinks she's so good."

"Yes, I know. I want you to do something for me. Come and see me after class."

Mr. Winston gave the same lecture about everything being energy—about energy moving in waves, and about people being made of the same stuff stars are made of—hydrogen, carbon and oxygen. Plus, he added a component he didn't mention to the last class. A part he'd only discovered after talking with Balidova—*when we align our energy with universal energy, we can command the elements.*

After he spoke, a big hush fell over the class and Mr. Winston wondered whether he should've shared that at all. *Maybe this stuff is just too potent for 8th graders. Maybe it's too much information?*

Dark stains marked the armpits of his shirt. Something was making him nervous.

Oh well, these kids won't know what to do with it. Balidova's the only one learning that.

Exactly fifty-five minutes later, the bell rang and the classroom emptied out. Gus stopped by Mr. Winston's desk again, casually twirling a pencil in his fingers.

"What do you want me to do to Balidova? I already shoved her into her locker, trying to get the lock of hair you wanted."

"Which you failed at, I'll remind you." Mr. Winston replied sharply. "Weren't the scissors I gave you good enough?"

"No. She was just, uh, tougher than I thought." Gus didn't like being dressed down. He stopped twirling the pencil and held it in his hand. He felt he had to make it up to Mr. Winston. "What do you want me to do now?"

"I want you to stop her," Mr. Winston said simply.

"Stop her? From doing what? I'm not sure I can stop her from doing anything. She just kicked my butt. Literally," Gus frowned. He looked down at the butterfly tattoo on the inside of his left wrist, tapping his pencil on it.

"Well, it might take some planning to pull it off, but here's the situation." Mr. Winston leaned in closer to the boy and lowered his voice. "She's been learning a secret energy technique called the Dragon Tail Breath."

"What's that?" Gus pulled back, raising his eyebrows. His pencil dropped out of his hand.

"A special way of breathing the seven colors of light through the seven energy centers of the body," Mr. Winston continued.

Gus shrugged. "So what? Sounds simple enough."

Mr. Winston shook his head. "You don't get it. It's simple, yes. AND it's incredibly powerful. Not just anyone can do it."

"Oh, okay." Gus replied, still not fully understanding. He stooped down to pick up the pencil he dropped.

"You know the lecture I just gave about energy today? Well, this breathing technique boosts and elevates your energy to a whole new level. It makes you a hundred times more powerful than you've ever been. Maybe even a thousand times. It's what allows you to align your energy with universal forces and command the elements of fire, water, air and earth. She's already learned four steps out of seven. She must not get to number seven!" By now, Mr. Winston was speaking as emphatically as he could while still keeping his voice at a whisper.

"So, what do you want me to do?" Gus asked. "I already threatened her friends because you said she knew something about my dad illegally hunting the ghost bear? Look where that got us—nowhere. Angel and Balidova are back together again. I saw them talking in the hallway." He pointed his pencil toward the door.

Mr. Winston glared at the boy. He did not appreciate Gus belittling the situation, or doubting him. "Do you know how important this is? Do you know *why* she must not get to Step Seven?"

"No, I just don't like her. That's why I'm willing to do it." Gus said, defending himself.

"Well, you'll be greatly rewarded if you stop her, and not by me. By forces far more powerful than you can imagine," Mr. Winston winked.

"I don't really get what you're talking about Mr. Winston. I mean, why should I put myself at risk? She's already embarrassed me at school, in front of all my friends." Gus remembered lying on the ground after she side kicked him. Unconvinced, he balanced his pencil on one finger, as if he were weighing his options.

"Gus, this isn't about you." Mr. Winston dropped his voice to a low whisper. "There are forces battling in the universe. Balidova holds the key. She has the ability to tip the balance of power. The Dragons of Light are teaching her a secret breathing technique. The dark dragons—the Drakoban—must not let her complete it or the Dragons of Light will win. The Cloak of Fear will never have a chance to seal over the earth, and the Drakoban will lose their control over human souls—forever."

Gus's eyes went wide. He had no idea this whole situation went beyond his tiny little world. For once, he was speechless.

He gripped the pencil with his fist and held it tight. "The Cloak of Fear?" he whispered.

"Yes. The Drakoban have installed a dark cloak around the planet, which amplifies and combines human fears into a thick energy layer. It's becoming stronger, trapping more and more humans in fear. It must seal completely before she comes fully into her powers, or the Cloak of Fear will shatter and be useless."

"Whoa, I had no idea."

"Is that what you want to happen? The Drakoban lose control and power, forever?" Mr. Winston exclaimed.

"No!" Gus shouted back.

SNAP!

Without realizing his own strength, Gus had busted the pencil in two. The broken pieces fell to the floor.

Mr. Winston watched them roll on the grey linoleum.

"Fear—that's how we maintain control, isn't it?" Mr. Winston was getting worked up now, speaking louder and becoming more animated, even though he was careful to keep his voice low. Even if the boy didn't know about the high stakes, he knew how to use fear to do his bidding. That's why Mr. Winston had sought him out in the first place. It was something they could bond over. That, plus the fact that Mr. Winston had dirt on Gus' dad—Balidova had told him months ago that Gus's dad had illegally hunted the spirit bear.

"Yeah, you bet. Keep 'em scared of you," Gus agreed. He looked down at the shattered pieces of lead on the floor and smiled.

"When people are afraid, they remain small and powerless. We must plant the seed of fear within Balidova so she no longer pursues the Dragon Tail Breath."

"I can probably cook something up. Let me talk to my buddies," Gus grinned mischievously, stepping on the pencil pieces to see if he could smash them into even smaller bits.

"No. Don't tell anyone about this. You must do it alone."

"But I don't do anything alone," Gus balked. "I'm always with my friends. We're a gang. We do everything together."

Mr. Winston looked around, noticed some students still cleaning up from the lab experiment, and lowered his voice to be sure the two of them wouldn't be heard. Realizing there was no one else he could trust with this task, he said, "Okay, but only one friend at the most. Make sure it works—or else."

"Yes sir." Gus realized he was on notice. Mr. Winston had a very serious look on his face.

"If you do this, you're gonna pass science with flying colors." Mr. Winston winked. "If you don't, you're gonna flunk," he finished, locking eyes sternly with the boy. A moment later, Mr. Winston turned away without so much as a goodbye.

"Oh, and pick up your garbage."

Gus stooped down, retrieved the pencil fragments and chucked them in the waste bin as he left the classroom, but not before Angel, who was tidying up at the back, noticed the long conversation they had. She had put her books away slowly, prolonging her departure. She couldn't hear what they were saying, but she noticed that Gus didn't look like he was getting in trouble. He and Mr. Winston seemed to be planning something together.

"That's weird," she thought as she left the classroom, entering the masses of kids in the hallway. "I didn't know they even talked to each other."

A FEW WEEKS WENT BY. All the excitement about the fight between Balidova and Gus at school died down. Angel and Balidova were back on talking terms and hanging out together. Balidova even told Angel about the Dragon Tail Breath and the four steps she'd learned already. She couldn't keep the secret from her friend, any longer.

One day after school, Balidova was at home in her room, finishing her homework. Her shoulder started twitching in rapid spasms, reminding her that there was more going on below the surface than meets the eye. Some nerve in her body had gotten crossed somewhere, and it was causing her right shoulder to twitch uncontrollably. Was her body literally showing her that she was an electromagnetic being, just as Mr. Winston had described?

How do I make it stop?

Maybe I need to drink more water?

She was just about to grab her water bottle and take a swig when she heard a loud *crash*! A rock came hurtling through her bedroom window—a large stone, the size of a fist. A note was attached.

Quickly running to the window, looking down from the second floor to see who was there, she spotted the backsides of two people running into the forest—and a flash of dirty blonde hair.

Turning back toward her desk, she picked up the rock and read the note. In scribbled black ink, it said:

> *Stop learning the Dragon Tail Breath*
> *or we'll turn the whole school against you*
> *for good.*

Who would do that? she wondered. She noticed that her shoulder had stopped twitching.

Her eyes narrowed. There was only one person who came to mind—Gus Polter.

But how does he even know about the Dragon Tail Breath?

I haven't told anyone except Mr. Winston and Angel.

Why does Gus care?

Why does he want me to stop learning it?

It doesn't make sense.

Right then, there was a knock on the front door. Balidova ran downstairs to get it.

It was Angel.

They had planned to work on their science projects together.

"Hey Balidova," Angel said cheerily, as the double door swung open. She stepped inside the Forester home in her striped skirt, flower patterned blouse and hot pink ear phones.

"Hey Angel." Balidova ushered her in, her eyes darting around. "Quick, shut the door."

"What's going on? What happened?" Angel whispered, removing the headphones from her neck, not sure why Balidova was acting all skittish.

Angel took off her shoes before both girls headed up to Balidova's room.

"Look what just happened. Someone threw a rock into my window. There's a note attached." Balidova handed her friend the crumpled paper.

Angel looked startled as she read the note. "Oh—this reminds me—there's something I forgot to tell you. I saw Gus and Mr. Winston talking after class a few weeks back. It was kinda unusual. They were talking for a long time. I couldn't really tell for sure, but it didn't look like Gus was getting in trouble. It seemed like they were planning something together? I wonder if this rock is related to the conversation they had..."

"Why didn't you tell me earlier?" Balidova asked.

"I dunno, I just forgot," Angel shrugged. "I didn't think it was that big a deal." She smoothed her hands over her skirt.

Balidova studied her friend to see if she was telling the truth. Although they were longtime buds, their breakup earlier in the year had made Balidova wary. But she did not detect that her friend was lying to her.

"Why would Gus care so much about the Dragon Tail Breath? It must be more than the fact that I know his secret." Balidova put her hands on her hips.

"What's that?" Angel asked curiously.

"He's actually a softie inside."

"Oh, he'd die if anyone knew that," Angel confirmed. "He puts so much effort into keeping up his 'tough guy' image."

"The Dragon Tail Breath must be more powerful than I thought." Balidova scratched her head. "I wonder what he was talking to Mr. W about?"

As she paused to think, Balidova spotted pieces of glass scattered across her bed. The reality of the situation suddenly hit her. *What if I was lying on my bed when it happened? Glass coulda gone in my face and taken my eye out! He musta thrown it super hard to get it through my window on the second floor.*

All at once, she remembered. "Gus is good with a slingshot—almost as good as me. A long time ago, we used to play together and try to hit squirrels. I nailed one once, but felt so bad for killing it, I swore I'd never hit a living creature again. Gus didn't have good enough aim back then, but I guess he's gotten better."

"Yeah," Angel piped up. Gus really has it in for you. What did you do to him?"

"Nothing." Balidova let out a big sigh, suddenly feeling vulnerable. "Maybe I shouldn't learn any more steps of the Dragon Tail Breath. They've raised the stakes. They're not playing around. Shoving you in the hall, pushing Jojo down the stairs, and slamming me into my locker at school is one thing. But this is on a whole different level. Now they're coming after me at home—in my room. I'm lucky to be in one piece."

She looked at Angel with fear in her eyes. "Maybe I *should* stop. Maybe it's just not worth it?" Balidova's shoulders sagged and she hunched forward, her head drooping. "Maybe my sisters are right. I am a loser. I do suck." Suddenly deflated, she flopped down on the edge of her bed.

Angel stared at her for a second. She wondered what Balidova was talking about. She had kicked Gus's butt. Yet she could understand her friend's fear. People had gotten hurt, including her. Gus was a formidable enemy.

Angel looked around the room. She saw the karate uniform with the words "U SUCK" written across the front. It was balled up in the corner of Balidova's closet, but the words were still visible. She put Balidova's comment together and realized her sisters must have done it. She gasped, knowing how much of a tightly knit unit the Forester sisters were. That would have cut Balidova deeply. But she also saw the karate medals and trophies stacked on the shelf. Angel saw the poster on her friend's wall that read 'Run Like A Girl', and the outline of a hole punched in by the door. All signs of a different Balidova than the one before her now.

"Seriously? You're gonna let Gus stop you? If you do that, he'll think he won. You're the one who kicked his butt at school. Remember?"

Balidova looked up from staring at the floor, and caught her friend's eye. A smile crept across her face as she saw the belief in Angel's eyes. "Well, I don't always feel invincible, you know. Especially when my sisters turn against me. You saw what they wrote on my karate uniform, didn't you?"

"Yeah, that was mean. What're you gonna do about it?"

"I dunno. My mom said not to do anything. I can't fight with everyone—at least not at the same time," she laughed. "And I do have the provincial tryouts coming up soon. I don't have time for this dragon magic stuff!" Balidova threw up her arms in frustration.

"Wait a sec." Angel was the level-headed one now. That's why she and Balidova were such good friends. She always brought reason to Balidova's un-reason. "You don't have time to learn magic from a dragon? Are you kidding me? I wish I could. I wish I was the one. Maybe I can go instead." She put a hand on Balidova's shoulder.

Immediately, like a toddler with toys, someone else wanting what was hers made Balidova want it more.

That's MY dragon. Those are MY lessons.

She snapped back to her senses.

"No. It has to be me. It can only be me."

Balidova gritted her teeth and steeled her jaw as her mind turned around. Instead of the rock through the window deterring her, it made her even more determined to continue on the path of the Dragon Tail Breath. To prove to her sisters and to herself, that she was *not* a loser.

She shook Angel's hand off her shoulder, turned back to her desk, and searched for her journal. When she found it, she flipped through the pages. Although it had only been a few weeks since she'd met the dragon, so much had happened—it felt like a lifetime ago.

Less than a minute later, she found it.

"Here," she said under her breath, "the place where I meet the dragon next." She traced the words with her finger—*where two become one.*

"Now if I could just figure out what that meant."

She looked up, about to ask Angel—who had already shifted her attention to their science fair project—then decided against it. She had not told Mr. Winston this riddle either. She got up from her chair to go downstairs. She would need her mom's help to clean up the broken glass and cover up the hole in the window before bedtime, so the chilly spring night air didn't blow in.

Should I ask Mom about the riddle? she wondered, silently.

No, she decided, *this is for me.*

Me alone.

CHAPTER 23
NOT ENOUGH

A few days later, on the night of the May full moon, Balidova rode the bus home after school. When she arrived at the farm, she went through her usual routine—dropping her backpack and grabbing a snack from the fridge. This time, she found a big hunk of leftover chocolate cake. She wrapped it in a piece of white paper towel and slipped out the side door. She had reason to celebrate. Not only was she heading out to find the dragon, but it was Friday, the end of the school week.

She stuffed a few big bites in her mouth as she ran out behind the house to the edge of the forest. Her jeans soon had brown streaks on them as she wiped her chocolaty fingers on her legs. She knew if she ate the whole piece of cake, she'd feel sick, so she decided to save the rest for later. Wrapping it up in the paper towel, she left it wedged in a tree branch, a few feet off the ground, at the edge of the property.

A smile spread across her face as she reveled in the free time she had at her disposal. As her mind drifted, she thought of the little blue bird that had guided her to the meadow in the past. But the bird was nowhere to be found, so she stepped into the forest on her own. She simply couldn't wait.

"It's okay. I can do this myself," she whispered.

Balidova's self-confidence had grown. She had begun to trust herself.

She paid attention to where she was going, keeping an eye out for broken twigs, old footsteps in the mud, and any recognizable marker she could find. After a while, when the meadow was nowhere in sight, a subtle yet gnawing feeling gradually began eating away at her core—doubt crept into her mind.

She bit her fingernails as she walked. *Should I have waited for the bird to guide me? Am I going in the right direction?* She was about to give up and turn around when a dragonfly buzzed overhead.

She paused and looked up, turning in a full 360-degree circle. The dragonfly flew off, but a beautiful blue sky remained—a vast expanse framed by evergreen trees towering above her like tall sentinels.

She closed her eyes and breathed.

She could hear the hum of the forest, and smell the distinct aroma of cedar and pine. She placed her hand on a tree and felt its rough yet familiar bark on her skin.

"It's okay Balidova, you're okay. Just calm down and relax."

She breathed in the fresh air a few more times, allowing the taste of the forest to tickle her throat. All five of her senses—taste, touch, sight, smell, sound—were heightened and alive, in tune with the woods.

WHEN SHE OPENED her eyes again, she saw with different vision. Her doubt had vanished. In its place, she felt joy.

Joy, standing in the middle of the trees.

Joy, moving toward the place where she had met the dragon

before.

Joy, deciding to continue with the dragon magic lessons.

Joy, trusting herself enough to find her own way through.

She had crossed that invisible, thin line inside herself from fear and doubt, and stepped into excitement and joy. With a smile, she grabbed the end of her ponytail and twirled it in her fingers.

Thank you, trees.

Picking up the pace, she jogged through the woods, trusting the subtle, almost imperceptible feelings inside, giving herself just enough time to sense yet not enough time to overthink. She became aware of the sound of birds chirping and insects singing. She listened to the forest as it guided her toward the meadow.

When she spotted an opening in the trees, a huge grin erupted across her face. She clenched her fists and pumped her arms in a quiet victory gesture. But as she came up to the edge of the forest, she was surprised to find she wasn't in the meadow at all. She must have made a wrong turn somewhere? She had reached a cliff overlooking the ocean!

Kitimat lay at the tip of the Douglas Channel, a 90km long seawater fiord leading to the Pacific Ocean.

Horrified that she'd come to the wrong place, Balidova ran to the edge of the cliff and looked down. Dark blue seawater marked by greenish brown pockets of kelp, greeted her. She thought of the hundreds of sea creatures who made their home in the sea forest. *Too bad one of them's not a dragon. This is not where I want to be! I'm never going to find the dragon now...*

Not knowing what to do next, she watched waves crash onto the rocky shore. As she stared below, her breathing slowed and began to match the rhythm of the water. Breathing in as waves rolled in. Breathing out as waves rolled out.

Soon enough, her heartbeat slowed to match the rhythm of her breath. Her mind slowed to match the rhythm of her heart.

Calm again, Balidova looked up and turned her gaze away from the seascape, toward the land behind her. It was the middle of spring, and plants sprouted up quickly during the short growing season. Tall grass and yellow flowers swirled around her, purple fireweed swayed in the breeze. Her green sweatshirt blended in with the new growth.

When she listened closely, she could hear the sound of mice scurrying through the grass. *If I can hear those little creatures, the dragon must be able to hear me,* she reasoned. *Maybe it can hear me even if I'm not in the meadow, but by the sea?*

She decided to give it a shot. But instead of calling the dragon with her voice, she used the power of her mind. She closed her eyes and saw the dragon in her mind. Long sleek body and tail, powerful feet, wide chest, and wild mane framing a face marked by fierce, yellowy orange eyes. She could see the beautiful shades of green of the dragon's scales, and the array of colors in its rainbow-colored wings. The dragon was so real in her mind's eye, Balidova could almost touch it.

The vision evoked a strong feeling and she allowed it to flow through her—a feeling of safety, strength, and pure unconditional love. As if she were being hugged by an angel and held in an embrace of white light.

Balidova steeped herself in this vision until she felt a breeze on her cheek and heard a rustling of leaves. She opened her eyes, and turned to look at the edge of the trees. She couldn't see anything, so she walked closer. A squirrel stopped in its tracks and stared up at her. "Are you kidding me?" she frowned. I thought you were—something else."

Balidova stuffed her hands in her jean pockets and felt a stone there—the stone the spirit bear had given her. She had a habit of keeping it in her pants pocket. It reminded her of the dragon magic even when she didn't feel magic around her. But now it wasn't working.

There was no dragon.

In a moment of frustration, she pulled out the stone and threw it as hard as she could. She watched the grey rock fly through the air.

Suddenly, she realized what she'd done. She raced after it, searching the ground for any sign of grey. Luckily, the snow had melted, otherwise the rock would have blended into the landscape and disappeared forever.

A moment later, she spotted it, wedged between some tree roots. As she retrieved it, she noticed how odd those roots were.

Just a fleeting thought...

But instead of dismissing it, she examined closer.

Roots cascaded everywhere. Her eyes followed the roots along the ground, back to the trunk, and up the ridged bark of the tree. All at once, she noticed two trees emerging from the root system.

Clutching her prize, she stared at the tree, not sure what to do next. Once again, she turned to her breath.

Breathing in...

Breathing out...

Slowly and steadily, again and again.

Accepting that she might not see the dragon this time, even though she desperately wanted to, she reluctantly turned toward home. But a buzzing sound caught her attention.

It was Bumby. The bee landed on her arm, bent antenna and all. She wondered how the little bee had found her in its condition.

She kept walking, then quickly spun around again.

"Wait, that's it! The double-tree.

Where two become one.

Two trees become one at the base! The riddle—this is where I meet the dragon next!"

A surge of excitement swelled in her chest, and thrill bumps erupted down her arm. She couldn't believe she'd figured it out!

She couldn't believe she had been so close, yet almost turned back. She closed her eyes and placed her hands together in a moment of quiet thanks. When she opened them again, there stood the dragon.

Balidova was speechless.

She walked over to the creature, reached up and placed her hand on its leg. The dragon's legs were thick and strong, with wide, round paws at the base. Three sharp talons extended from each foot, jutting out in different directions. On the muddy ground, its footprint looked like a cross between a bear and an eagle.

"Wow, you're actually here." Balidova said in awe.

"Your curiosity has rewarded you," the dragon smiled. "You called me?"

"Uh, well, kinda," Balidova responded, still amazed that she'd unlocked the riddle and found the meeting spot. "Not with my words. This time I called you with my mind."

The dragon chuckled. "Come out here into the open where I can see you better. We dragons can't see so well in the dim light, you know, although our sense of smell is phenomenal."

"Really? I didn't know that. I thought you could do anything."

"We do have our limitations. Much fewer than humans—but yes, they do exist," the dragon shook its mane as if brushing off an insignificant fact. Its golden hair swished from side to side, reminding Balidova of Melody's mane, except that the dragon's was ten times longer, thicker, and more coarse.

"What's going on in your world Balidova?"

Balidova looked at the beast. The question snapped her back into the present moment. She wanted to tell it about the rock smashing through her window, her sisters writing on her karate uniform, and her conversation on energy with Mr. Winston. All these things had happened in the month since the last full moon, when they'd met on the mountain. But there was something she wanted to talk about even more than all that stuff. Something that bothered her deeply.

"Why do some people want to stop me from learning the Dragon Tail Breath?" she asked, thinking of the note attached to the rock. She twisted the black hair tie on her wrist.

The dragon shifted its stance, pausing for a moment before responding.

"There are dark forces on the planet, Balidova. And they come in many different forms—some human, some dragon, some other like the Cloak of Fear. You need not know all right now. But know that they exist. Fear always tries to win. But you have strength within you—strength to overcome that fear."

Balidova looked solemn. "Two moons ago, the sunflower told me about the Cloak of Fear. Please teach me more. I can't let fear win. Not mine or anyone else's."

The dragon blew out a gust of air, shaking the thick branches of the double tree. Balidova clung onto its trunk to avoid getting blown over.

"Just as the Dragon Tail Breath is about breathing the seven colors of light through the seven energy centers of the body, the Cloak of Fear is about weaving the many forms of fear through the human heart."

"What are the many **forms of fear**?" Balidova asked, curiously.

"Anger, worry, hatred, helplessness, shame, jealousy, revenge, sadness, and doubt." The dragon replied matter-of-factly.

"What happens when the many forms of fear weave through the human heart?"

"The Cloak of Fear will be complete. It will seal over the earth and snuff out hope, forever. Chaos will exist in homes, schools, companies, and governments. Freedom will be lost." The dragon lifted its paw, clenching its talons together in a tight ball, so that the only thing visible was a series of sharp, black, calcified points.

"Oh wow. But a lot of those things have happened already!" Balidova sounded alarmed. She thought about her own family. She herself had experienced anger—lots of it. Hatred too, as well as shame and jealousy, sadness, doubt, and definitely worry.

She had seen tremendous anger between her parents, when her dad cut the dishwasher cord. She had experienced hatred toward herself. She had seen jealousy between sisters when they wrote on her karate uniform, and revenge when she wanted to get back at them. She had felt helplessness between friends, when Angel had cut off their bond.

She furrowed her brow in contemplation. "If I've already experienced so many of these fears in my own family, others must have too."

"That's right Balidova. The Cloak of Fear is spreading quickly. It's a contagion that passes from person to person, and family to family. You must complete the Dragon Tail Breath before it infects everyone and forms an impenetrable seal over the earth."

Balidova was silent. She sighed at the gravity of the situation, and the weight of her role in it. Her task seemed impossible.

"First... I have a question. A very important question."

"Yes?" the dragon said, bringing its head down and shifting its ears forward. "What is it?"

Balidova paused. "What is your name?"

The dragon trembled. Its whole body and tail shimmered in the sunlight. Its scales appeared to glow.

"My name is Luminora."

"What does that mean?" Balidova asked, mesmerized by the sound of the word.

"Luminora means 'gift of light.' I am a being of light, as are you."

"Okay, if you say so," Balidova replied tentatively. "Can you teach me how to do that, too? How to have more light?" Balidova looked discouraged. "I just feel like I don't have much of anything inside me right now, or ever. I mean, except for when I'm with you," she looked up and smiled briefly.

"Life just feels heavy sometimes, you know? I'm weighed down by all the things I have to do, all the things I'm supposed to do—all the fighting and arguing and just... stuff. It seems like there's a lot of have tos and should dos. They kinda squeeze out all the wanna dos. What about what *I* want? Isn't there any space for that?"

The dragon paused. "Hmm, yes. The life of a human, it's not easy, not easy at all. But it does come with benefits."

"What do you mean?" Balidova took the hair tie off her wrist and started playing with it in her hands.

"Well, you get to be here now, in this body, at this time. With all the diversity of planet earth at your fingertips. You can create great darkness or beautiful light. The choice is yours."

"It sure doesn't feel like that," Balidova said. "It just feels like something's not right. Like it's never enough. Like whatever I do is never enough. Like I'm never enough."

"Never enough what?" the dragon said.

"I don't know. I can't really put my finger on it. The other day a rock came flying through my bedroom window with a note attached—threatening me to stop learning the Dragon Tail Breath. I was scared! Am I supposed to learn it or not? It feels like it's never okay to be completely me. Everyone's trying to get me to do one thing or another. I don't even know who I am sometimes." She threw her arms up in frustration.

"Mom, dad, sisters, bullies, teachers, friends—it's like... practice karate, practice piano, get good grades at school, do your chores, win the tournament, be a good friend, be strong but not *too* strong," Balidova huffed. "Where am *I* in this whole mix? I feel kinda lost. Like there's no space for *me*." She snapped the hair tie like an elastic band and it went flying off into the tall grass.

She wouldn't be able to find it now.

CHAPTER 24
INDIGO LIGHT VISION

Balidova sat dejectedly at the edge of the cliff. She watched the seagrass flow back and forth onto the shore below, and breathed with the ocean waves, imagining herself swimming through tall underwater forests. *Combined with the land forests, these plants produce all the oxygen on the planet. Half from sea. Half from land. So I can breathe. So the whole world can breathe. One breath. One world. One world breath...*

After a while, she looked up at the beast. "I only seem to feel totally amazing and good when you're around. I'm starting to feel that again, just being near you."

"Yes, that's because I'm holding space for you." The dragon wiggled its snout, making its long, golden whiskers move in a wavelike motion.

"Holding space? What does that mean?" Balidova asked.

As the dragon brought its head closer to the girl, she noticed that the dragon's eyes contained the same brilliant yellow hue as the dandelions around them.

"I'm holding a container, filled with a high vibration of unconditional love, that you can step into and accept *all* that you are." The dragon gazed deeply into the girl's eyes as it spoke, as if peering into her soul. It could see both darkness and light in the girl, both fear and love. Which force would win the battle going on inside her? That would depend on which one she fed—with her thoughts, emotions, actions, and words.

"Oh, vibrations..." Balidova said. "We learned about that in science class. Is that related to wavelength, frequency, and energy?" She felt slightly uncomfortable under the beast's intense gaze.

"Yes. Can you feel the high vibration in your body?" Luminora said, backing off slightly, noticing the girl's discomfort.

"Yeah, it feels tingly and light. My body feels happy." Balidova replied, glad to have a little more space.

"So, you're ready to learn Step Five of the Dragon Tail Breath then?"

"Yes!" Balidova said jumping up with excitement.

"Well then, explain to me the first four steps." The dragon sat back on its haunches, its front legs off the ground, curling its tail around its body for stability.

"Okay," Balidova took in a big inhale, then began, "Step One is breathing the emerald green light in and out through my heart, like a stream passing through me. *All is well.*" She placed both hands on her chest, right where her own heart was located.

"Good."

"Step Two is when I breathe in the golden light through my solar plexus. *Here now.* I come into the present moment as golden light enters my chest and spreads across my body." She pressed one hand to the top of her belly, just below her rib cage.

"Mm-hmm," the dragon confirmed.

"In Step Three, I breathe blue light in through my throat. Light that's as blue as the sky, feeling that expanse enter my body. *What do I want?*" She moved both hands to her neck, rubbing both the front and backside with her palms.

"Yes, yes," the dragon said, clapping the end of its tail on the ground in approval.

"And Step Four is breathing in the orange light, through my lower belly, my *tanden*. The center of my physical body. Knowing that *I am a powerful creator*. I get to decide how I feel using these two questions: *How do I feel now? How do I want to feel?* I can move between these two feeling places with three simple words: *Accept. Release. Move-on.* If I truly take in their meaning, that is." Balidova placed one hand on her lower abdomen, four finger widths below her belly button.

"Very good!" the dragon said in a booming voice. "You *have* been paying attention!" The dragon's voice reverberated across the entire cliff. Its satisfaction with Balidova resounded loudly and all the animals stopped what they were doing to look. The chirping of birds, the singing of insects, the sound of mice scurrying through the leaves, all grew quiet for a moment. As if Mother Nature herself paused for a split second and nodded her head towards Balidova. As if all the animals gathered round and silently clapped for her. For a brief moment, all was still. Then the sounds of nature's orchestra continued their hum once again.

She noticed this moment, and a smile broke out on her face.

"You see," the dragon said in a whisper, "All of life loves and supports you."

Balidova laughed. She did a little J-O-Y turn with her arms outstretched above her head. The dragon spread its wings in synchronicity with Balidova's outspread arms, enjoying the playfulness of the girl.

Then, with a snort, it said, "Okay, let's get down to business."

Across the water, the sun was setting and the moon was rising. There wasn't much time left before it would be dark. The beast placed all four feet back on the ground and gave each one a stomp, as if counting the four steps Balidova had just outlined.

"Step Five of the Dragon Tail Breath is breathing indigo light in through the third eye."

"What's indigo?"

"Indigo is a deep, rich, cobalt blue, like royalty. Use this color to bring in the royalty that you are through the richness of your inner sight."

"Inner sight? What's that?" Balidova asked. "And what's the third eye? I thought I only had two?"

"You have two physical eyes, and something more." The dragon elaborated, pointing a single talon to a spot on its forehead. "Right between your eyes, is your third eye, the home of your inner sight. That's what you used to call me earlier."

"I don't know what you mean," Balidova shrugged her shoulders and turned up her palms.

The dragon looked at her with a sideways glance and deliberately took its time. Balidova huffed, stared, and waited. She wanted to understand Step Five immediately, especially since daylight was running out.

A few moments later, wiggling its long, golden whiskers at her, the dragon asked quietly, "Are you ready now?"

"Yes," Balidova replied, sitting still, listening with every ounce of her being, like she'd learned to do in her karate practice when she meditated. She realized the dragon would not be rushed, but would go at its own pace, no matter what she did.

"You have three levels of senses," the dragon continued. "The first is the physical level: sight, sound, smell, taste, touch. Right?"

"Yeah," Balidova replied, pointing to her eyes, ears, nose, mouth and fingers, going through five senses in her own mind.

"You see with your eyes, hear with your ears, smell with your nose, taste with your mouth, and touch with your skin, particularly your fingers," the dragon said.

"Yeah, we learned that in elementary school. The five senses," she confirmed.

The dragon ignored her comment and continued.

"Right. Did you know that humans are more than five sense creatures? Did you learn the next five and the next five?"

"What are you talking about?" Balidova retorted. "There are only five senses. That's it."

"Well actually," the dragon said, "there are more—a lot more. Those are your five *physical* senses. Then you have your five *intuitive* senses and your five *knowing* senses. You have three levels of senses, and at each level, they become more subtle, yet more powerful at the same time. If you can pay attention to them, hear them, and follow them, that is."

"Whoa," Balidova exclaimed, her eyes widening in amazement. "Nobody ever told me that."

"That's because most humans are limited to their physical senses. They have not yet grown to fully trust their intuitive and knowing senses. Don't get me wrong, there are some people who have the ability to go beyond their five physical senses. But they are few and far between." The dragon waved one wing in the air.

Balidova was confused. "I get the physical senses. But what are these other levels? Tell me more about them. What's the difference between the intuitive level and the knowing level?"

"Well," the dragon smiled, glad the girl was asking questions. "What's the difference between *believing* something and *knowing* something?"

"Hmm," Balidova looked up at the treetops as if they were talking to her. She paused for a moment, placing her index finger on her lips. "Knowing is more solid than believing."

"Exactly." The dragon blew its nose, spraying snot in all directions.

"Ew, gross! Did ya have to do that?!" Balidova shouted, wiping slimy goop off her arms.

The dragon chuckled. "When you *know* you like or don't like something, what does it feel like inside you?"

Balidova stood up and secured her feet firmly on the ground in a martial arts stance. "Knowing something feels like the deep roots of a tree."

"Like an unshakeable truth?" the dragon smiled.

"Yeah, sorta. Like no one can move me off of it," Balidova stood tall as she spoke, her voice sounding firm and confident. "It feels really certain and strong." She clenched her fists. "Like when I *know* I don't want you blowing snot all over me!" Her whole body shook as she giggled.

"Yes, exactly. That's the *knowing* level of senses," the dragon continued. "It is really certain, and strong, when you can hear it."

"And what about the intuitive level?" Balidova asked.

"Intuition involves believing. What does believing something feel like to you?" the dragon asked back.

"It feels like I need to have faith. It feels like it might be true and it might not be true. I'm not really sure, but I'm hoping that it is? It feels like there are roots.... maybe like the roots of a sapling, instead of a tree? They don't really go as deep, but there's still something connecting me to the ground." She tilted her head from side to side. "Like when I believed I could find my way through the forest to the meadow again? I wasn't 100% sure. But I was more than 50% sure I could do it. I didn't find the meadow, but I found the meeting spot."

"That's right. The intuitive level is between the physical sensing and the knowing sensing. It's more than what the physical environment tells you. It's something you sense. Some people call this our sixth sense. You can process millions of bits of information in a split second through this sense—much more than your physical capacity and much more than you can do with your logical, rational mind, which is limited."

The dragon paused to scratch the side of its body with its hind leg. Long talons sprung from its back paw and delicately rubbed a spot on its underbelly. Balidova watched in awe, noting that the dragon was so big and powerful, it could squash her in a second.

Yet the girl, dwarfed by this colossal creature, did not feel an ounce of fear.

"And yet, you may or may not trust your intuition yet," the dragon continued. "So, intuition is between what you sense physically, and what you know to be an unshakeable truth within you."

"That makes sense," Balidova thought. "Logic tells me I should be afraid of you, but my intuition tells me not to be."

Just in that moment, the dragon opened its wings to their full expanse. The sudden movement startled Balidova, and she jumped back, her heart racing.

I guess I'm not 100% sure about you yet, she chuckled inside her own head. *I know you won't hurt me on purpose, but you might by accident!*

Balidova's whole body shuddered as she came back to the conversation, sitting down on a tree root by the dragon again.

"So, when Gus pushed me into my locker awhile back, I felt the cold, hard metal pressing on my face and it hurt. I felt the shove. I heard the footsteps. And I might have even smelled the guy. I looked, and I saw him smirking."

"I know."

"Wait, how do you know about that when I didn't tell you."

"I know many things about you Balidova. I can read them in your energy field. All your emotions and experiences are stored there, like a sort of energy signature."

"Will I be able to learn how to do that?" Balidova looked hopefully at the dragon.

"Yes, in time."

Satisfied, Balidova got back to the conversation about the fight at school. "So, if feeling the cold metal on my face was the physical sensation, what's the intuitive level?"

"Well, what did you do next?" The dragon asked, peering at her with fiery eyes.

"When I saw him smirking, I knew it wasn't an accident. And I sensed there were no adults around. I had to do something, I couldn't just let this pass, but I wasn't really sure."

"Okay, go on."

"I also sensed that other people were looking at me and wondering what I was gonna do. There was more at stake here than just me, because he'd bullied other people in the past. If I didn't do something, he would keep up his bullying nonsense."

"Yes," the dragon said, opening its eyes wider.

"All this passed through my mind in a split second—not in words. It's kinda hard for me to even explain it to you now."

"That's your intuitive sensing," the dragon said, blinking a few times.

"Oh." Unconsciously, Balidova mimicked the dragon's eye movement and blinked also.

"And what about your *knowing* senses? What did you do next?" the dragon asked.

"Then I knew." Balidova's voiced lowered and gained a steely tone as her eyes narrowed. Something hardened inside of me and I made a decision. All in that split second. I took one step and I just kicked. I didn't really even think about it. I just did it. I knew I was strong enough. I knew my training would back me up. I knew it was in me."

A wide smile broke out across the dragon's snout as Balidova continued.

"As Gus sat on the floor, gasping for air, I saw this flicker in his eye, and I knew he was thinking about getting revenge right then and there. So, I didn't look away, on purpose. I didn't back down. Because if I did, he would have come after me. I kept up the energy. I knew I had to continue being strong and let him know that his actions weren't okay. It was kinda like a tipping point right then, where he could either counter-attack, or retreat. I just *knew* it."

She paused for a moment, pressing the fingers of her hands together in front of her chest.

"I couldn't have explained this to anyone at the time. It all happened within me, in a split second. There was no doubt. There was no hesitation. There was no questioning. There were no thoughts going through my mind. I just *knew*. And I did it."

Feeling the energy swirl of that incident within her as she spoke the words, she let out a deep sigh, breathing through the fingers of both hands, which were pressed against her lips now, in a prayer position. As the tension released from her body, she dropped her arms by her side. Girl and dragon sat together in silence for a moment.

"You used each level of sensing." The dragon broke the silence. "Physical sensing. Intuitive sensing. Knowing sensing." The beast extended its talons one at a time. "How did that feel?"

"It felt amazing," Balidova said, lighting up. "Absolutely amazing. It felt like my whole being was there. Not just my body—but also my mind and spirit—all connected and lined up like a laser beam in a massive focus of energy. It felt really good. I felt strong, and complete. There was no doubt. I totally trusted myself."

"And how did it feel after?" The dragon asked, stretching out its long, elegant neck.

"After it was done, I collected up my books and was walking to class, and it felt like I had broken through to a new level within me, a level where I can trust myself. I felt somehow like I knew myself more." Balidova stretched out her own neck and shifted her feet on the ground. "But later, the energy faded. It didn't last forever."

She looked around. Spotting some tall grass swaying in the breeze, she sat up a little straighter, while at the same time wiggling her body to imitate the flexible, flowing movement of the grass.

"You know, it's kinda strange. The part of me that *knew* what to do has always been there. I just couldn't really put my finger on it. I didn't know it had a name. I didn't know there were words to describe it."

"Yes, all of us have three levels of senses within us." The dragon smiled, retracting its three talons, one at a time. "You didn't have a language for these three levels of senses, or permission to use them. But you do now. You *know* what the difference is. You've *felt* the difference. And you have words for them. This will help you distinguish between the choices *you* want vs. the choices you think someone *else* wants you to make."

"Is that why it felt so bad when my dad criticized me for getting into a fight at school? Because I knew it was right and he thought it was wrong?"

"Yes. When you allow others' choices to override your own, it doesn't feel good inside you."

"I get it now. It's like a battle going on inside you. That's what it felt like."

"Exactly," the dragon nodded its head. "Only *you* know what is right for you and what is not."

"Only I know. Only Balidova knows." She started saying the words, then singing them, gradually louder and louder, imagining a deep blue light entering into her body between her eyes.

"I know, I know, I KNOW." She stood up as the stream of light grew stronger and brighter. She was laughing now, gaining speed and momentum, soaking in the delicious feeling of giving herself permission to trust herself, once again.

"Only I know!"

Oh my goodness, I love that!

The stream of indigo light felt as expansive as a mountain range now. As wide as the deep blue sea. Streaming down from her forehead and filling her whole body with light, including her brain cavity.

The dragon smiled. "Until next time, Balidova. Remember—you have to be the one to carry the energy you want. You are the one you've been looking for."

With a sudden swoosh and a flash of light, the dragon extended its long tail, lifted its wings and disappeared into the evening sky.

Balidova stopped for a moment and blew a kiss into the air, in the dragon's direction. She felt beyond happy—grounded, strong and true. Skipping home through the forest, gripping the stone in the palm of her hand, she sang, "Balidova Knows... Balidova KNOWS... BALIDOVA KNOWS!"

By now the sun was setting. She had to get back home before dinner time. She looked up at the sky and saw a round, white sphere in the fading evening light. *Hmm, what should I call you?* She stopped skipping for a moment, thinking of the double tree by the sea—the magical place where she'd met the dragon for a second time. She smiled in silent thanks for her friend in the sky.

The Tree Moon.

Out of the forest and back onto the farm property, Balidova spotted something white in a tree, about chest high—her chocolate cake. She had left it there when she first entered the woods. By now, a long line of red, fire ants had found it. They wound around the tree, swarming the mountain of sweetness.

Balidova watched the tiny creatures for a while. Slowly, the corners of her eyes lifted and her brow smoothed as a smile spread across her face. She could feel herself sparkling. She decided to leave the dessert for the ants. She admired their work ethic. Each one laboring tirelessly as a member of a group, banding together for the good of the whole. With a flash of insight, she knew both land and sea forests, and all their inhabitants, were doing the same thing for her. She suddenly realized she was part of something much larger than herself.

Thank you to the forests, and to all creatures... big AND small.

CHAPTER 25
THE KNOWING

That weekend, Balidova was so excited about what she had learned she could barely contain herself. Even so, she didn't dare tell her sisters.

They'll just ridicule me, like they did before. I don't wanna go there again. Besides, we're gonna be competing against each other very soon. I don't wanna give my superpower away. Sharing with them that I'm learning a special breathing technique from a dragon is not gonna do me any good. No. Even though I want to—I don't dare tell them.

On Saturday evening, she was in the barn, brushing Melody after a ride, getting ready to feed the horses their evening meal. The barn was Balidova's safe place, where she felt totally at home. But it didn't belong to just her. It was her mom's favorite place also—to hang out with her own horse, Gypsy.

Balidova knew she owed one of the best parts of her life to her mom—the freedom and joy she had in the barn with her horse, Melody. Ever since her mom helped her navigate the karate gi debacle, Balidova felt a longing to reconnect with her mother even more deeply. She missed her.

Balidova heard footsteps outside the barn door. Shortly after, the sound of the big wooden door sliding open, filled the room.

A stout figure in a black and red checkered jacket, and olive gumboots entered her sanctuary. Wisps of shoulder length, silver hair were visible under the light of the bare bulb hanging in the hall ceiling. Surprised by the unexpected visitor, Balidova quickly turned around.

"Oh, hi Mom." Balidova smiled. She paused from picking dirt out of Melody's hooves.

Her mom was startled to hear Balidova address her. She knew her daughter might be in the barn—where she'd escaped to so often during winter and spring—but assumed she would be silent, as she had been for so many of the past several months. She didn't know exactly what was going on inside her daughter's head, but she knew enough to give the girl space to figure it out.

Pleased to hear Balidova talking to her, she walked toward Melody's stall and opened the door. She had come out to the barn to check on the horses and do the evening feed.

"Hey Balidova, what are you doing?"

"Melody and I went for a ride. Now I'm just brushing her down. We're just having a little time together." Balidova said, giving her horse a pat on the neck.

"Hmm, that's nice," her mom said wistfully, as if remembering a time as a young girl when she did the same with her own horse, Gypsy.

"Hey Mom..." Balidova continued hesitantly.

"Yeah?"

"Can I tell you something?" Balidova cocked her head to the side.

"Sure." Her mom replied, taking care not to sound too interested—even if she was happy to have Balidova opening up to her again.

"I know we haven't talked a whole lot in the last while. But, there's something I wanna tell you." Balidova said slowly.

"Ok, what is it?" her mom said, stepping closer.

"Well, I've been learning the steps of the dragon tail breath on the full moon for the last several months. And yesterday I learned another one—step number five." Balidova blurted out her story before she could think too much about how it sounded.

"Is that why you've been slipping off a lot lately—rushing outside right after school and not telling us where you're going?" Although Balidova's mom had not said much, she was not too happy with her daughter's behavior over the past months, and now it showed in her scolding voice.

Balidova's jaw dropped open. She looked like she'd been slapped in the face—crestfallen at her mom's negative reaction to something so meaningful and magical to her. "Uh, I guess so," was all the response Balidova could muster.

Realizing she had inadvertently crushed her daughter's excitement, Balidova's mom changed her tone.

"Wow. That sounds really amazing. I didn't even know there was such a thing." She wanted to support her daughter after all.

Balidova paused, not sure which reaction to believe—the scolding or the support. Cautiously, her excitement returned. "Yeah, so much has happened, Mom. There's so much I wanna tell you."

Balidova stepped closer. She knew her Mom's mood could change quickly, yet she wanted to confide in her. They both stood next to Melody's head. The little brown mare nudged each of them with her muzzle, looking for treats.

"The Dragon Tail Breath lessons have been amazing. They've taught me how to breathe the colors of light through the different energy centers of my body."

"Like a rainbow?" Her mom asked.

"Yes, exactly!" Balidova said, happy that her mom seemed

interested, and was letting go of any previously held annoyance. "The last lesson I learned, just yesterday, was breathing indigo light in through my third eye. It was all about trusting myself." She touched her index finger to a spot right between her eyes as if to emphasize the point.

"That's something I'm still learning, and I'm in my forties," her mom said, as she stroked Melody's face. "It's amazing that you're learning something so important at this age, Balidova. You're really lucky. How did all this happen?"

"Oh geez, Mom, I don't even know where to begin." Balidova flopped her arms down and leaned against the mare. She proceeded to tell her mom about the wolves and the wind spirit in the lagoon, about the tree spirit and the white bear in the meadow, about the water spirit turning into a fish at the river, and about the fire spirit forming magically into a sunflower. Her mom listened, transfixed.

Balidova searched her mom's eyes for any signs of disbelief, but found none. So, she continued. "And then, best of all, I met the spirit creature in its true form on top of Wolf Mountain."

"What form was that?" Her mom asked, leaning in toward her daughter with growing curiosity, and a hint of concern.

"A dragon!" Balidova said with a flourish.

Her mom gasped, shaking her head. "Wow, I can't even imagine. What did it look like?"

As Balidova described the dragon, her mom watched her daughter's body language, eyes and facial expressions closely. She knew her well, and could tell that Balidova was completely enraptured by this creature and all the new experiences it had brought into her life. However unusual the story was, she became convinced that Balidova was not making it up.

"Do you believe me?" Balidova asked, looking hopefully at her mom.

"Yes," her mom replied, smiling quietly and nodding her head. "Yes, I believe you."

They hugged each other tightly, and Balidova just cried. All the tears that had been held back for so long, because of her pride, all poured out now. She cracked open and allowed herself to be vulnerable in the presence of her mom.

"Thank you for telling me," her mom whispered in her ear. "I love you, Balidova."

"Thank you for listening. I love you too, Mom." Balidova whispered back.

They hugged tightly some more. Then her mom pulled away and said in a matter-of-fact tone, "Okay, now finish up with Melody, feed the rest of the horses and come in for dinner. It's time to get going. We don't have all night."

Balidova nodded, familiar with this very down-to-earth side of her mom, yet grateful for the magical moment they had just shared. She hummed happily to herself as she finished her barn chores, closed the big red doors for the night and headed back to the house.

Before she reached the side door of the house, Balidova looked up and spotted a hawk in the sky. The majestic bird flew in circles, watching her from above. In that moment, with her heart full of love and trust, she too could see things from a higher perspective.

On Monday, when Balidova spotted Angel's pink backpack in the hallway at school, she couldn't help but tell her too. Although they were friends, they looked like complete opposites. Balidova's grey sweater and blue jeans were so boyish, whereas Angel wore a frilly shirt with flowers on it—something Balidova wouldn't be caught dead in.

"Did you know there's something called the knowing senses?" Balidova said, after the two girls greeted each other.

"What? What're you talking about?" Angel replied, walking with Balidova toward their classrooms, which were near each other.

"Yunno when you just *know* something?" Balidova continued. "Even though you can't explain it?"

"Yeah, so?" Angel shrugged.

"Well, it's a thing. It's real. It's called *the knowing*." Balidova lowered her voice, grabbed Angel's wrist, and pulled her to the side of the hallway—moving them both out of the way of the masses of kids who were heading to class.

"Okay, so what?" Angel said, a little alarmed by Balidova's sudden secrecy.

"It's a part of you. Everyone has it," she whispered, eyeing the kids walking by. "But we don't really think of it as something important, and we don't trust it."

"I've never really thought about it," Angel replied nonchalantly.

Balidova removed her hand from her friend's wrist and adjusted the straps of her backpack. She leaned in and whispered in her friend's ear, "I learned lesson five of the Dragon Tail Breath. Breathing indigo light through my third eye. It's all about *the knowing*. About listening to what's inside of you. The dragon showed me how to do it."

"What? You did the next lesson? Despite the note?" Angel said incredulously, pulling away from Balidova and looking her friend in the eyes.

"Well, yeah, the full moon was last Friday." Balidova replied, as if it were obvious.

"Oh yeah, right." Angel paused. "Good for you, Balidova. Good. For. You." She nodded her head with approval and respect. "I knew you wouldn't let Gus's threat stop you. You're way too stubborn for that."

"Thanks Angel," Balidova said with a tilted grin. "Thanks for encouraging me."

"No worries. What're friends for?" Angel smiled and shrugged her shoulders at the same time. "So, what's this *knowing* stuff all about? How do you do it?"

Balidova paused for a moment, not sure how to put what the Dragon had taught her, into words. "Yunno how sometimes you wish for something, and then later, it happens?"

"Yeah, so?" Angel shrugged her shoulders.

"Well, that ride, from wishing to knowing, is what I'm talking about."

"What do you mean?" Angel squeezed her face, confused.

"If you really want the thing you wish for to happen, you can't just wish it and hope for the best. You have to do more than that." Balidova raised both arms, gesturing with her hands.

"What else *can* you do?" Angel looked puzzled.

Balidova looked her straight in the eyes and grinned. "Believe."

Angel paused, then frowned. "How're you supposed to believe if it hasn't happened?"

"That's exactly what belief is. It's an energy. A feeling. A vibe. You gotta carry some of that in you." Balidova extended both hands out wide, palms facing each other, as if holding an invisible ball of energy around her.

"Until it happens?" Angel was curious now.

"Until you *know*." Balidova pressed her lips together. She had a twinkle in her eye as she looked at her friend.

"And then the thing you wished for happens?" Angel was looking totally fascinated now.

"Yup." Balidova nodded her head. "The energy inside you

changes from wishing to believing to knowing. That's how it works."

"Cool." Angel nodded her head in agreement.

The two friends gave each other a high five, a low five, a tap on the shoulder, and slid their hands down each other's arms, snapping their fingers at the end when they flew off into the air—their signature hand shake. Then both girls went their separate way to class.

It's been months since we did that. Things are on the up and up. Balidova chuckled as she walked down the hall with a skip in her step.

A WEEK WENT BY, and Balidova didn't think much about the dragon, distracted by all the other activities on the farm, in the dojo and at her study desk. Until one day, she was walking in the school hallway and noticed a group of students had gathered. A big commotion ensued, as a bunch of kids laughed and pointed at something on the wall near Balidova's locker.

What is it?

Balidova strained to catch a glimpse of what they were making fun of, but couldn't see through the mass of bodies. Gradually, she inched closer to the front of the crowd, which seemed to part as she came near. She gasped when she saw what everyone was staring at—a poster of a dragon with a big X through it.

It said, "Bali-don't-va. Weirdo. Know-it-all."

She could hear chatter amongst the crowd:

"Yeah, she's so weird."

"What's her obsession with dragons all about? She thinks they're real."

"What's up with that?"

"She's living in make believe land. Come back down to earth."

As she slunk her way out of the crowd, Balidova saw Gus standing with his gang of friends and overheard what he was saying too.

"Earth to Balidova. Earth to Balidova! Dragons aren't real. You're such a dumb butt—don't you know that?"

How quickly things have changed. What happened to the admiration for the girl who stood up to the bully?

Immediately, she realized what Gus was doing. If he couldn't beat her by force or threat of force, he would beat her with humiliation and embarrassment. Oh, how quickly the other students followed suit—teenagers could be so fickle sometimes.

Balidova walked quickly to her locker. She felt an overwhelming urge to punch his lights out, again. But she took a couple deep breaths, calmed down, and knew it wasn't the right thing to do.

Just then, Angel walked up to her from the other direction. "Hey Balidova, what's up?

"Did you see that poster?" Balidova huffed.

Angel glanced over her shoulder and caught a glimpse of the image and the words. "Oh my gosh, I can't believe it."

"What? You know something about this?"

"I'm really sorry Balidova," Angel looked sheepishly at the ground. "Last week Gus asked me if you'd learned the next lesson. He threatened that if I didn't tell him, he'd shove me down the stairs too. I didn't wanna break my arm or my leg! So, I told him that you learned lesson five and it was all about 'the knowing'."

No wonder they wrote 'know-it-all' on the poster.

Balidova practically shouted in shock. "You what? You told him? That's between you and me! That was a secret! How could you do that?" Now it was Balidova's turn to be mad at Angel.

"I'm really sorry Balidova. I didn't mean to. It's just that he scared me and I kinda let it spill."Angel pleaded.

"Okay, whatever," Balidova said, turning toward her locker,

stuffing her books in her bag. She slammed the metal door shut and walked off. "See ya," she glowered at Angel.

BACK AT HOME, Balidova desperately needed to talk to her mom. She had no one else to confide in. She found her mom in the kitchen, cooking dinner—coconut chicken curry. The smell of spicy curry powder, fragrant jasmine rice, coconut milk, garlic and onion, filled the air. As her mom chopped raw chicken into bite-sized cubes on the wooden chopping board atop the dishwasher, Balidova told her what had happened at school.

"You must've been really upset," her mom said as she continued chopping.

"Yeah, I was," Balidova replied.

"But did he threaten you physically, Balidova?" Her mom interjected.

"Well, no."

Her mom looked at Balidova squarely in the eye. "Then you have to take the high road. Words can only hurt you if you believe them—if you let them in. Don't lower your vibe, Balidova, not for him, not for anyone. Trust me, I know what happens when you do that. It's not good. You become someone you don't like." After she finished speaking, she threw some chicken cubes in the hot oil of the pan and a loud sizzling sound erupted.

Balidova felt the sides of herself sizzling too. Frustration and anger boiled inside her. Yet she knew her mom was right. She would have to take the high road, again. *Just like I did with the karate uniform my sisters wrote on. But at least I got a new uniform out of it.*

"This sucks," she said aloud.

"Life isn't necessarily fair, Balidova. But you do have choices."

Yeah, I get to choose who I trust. I'm so glad to be talking to you, mom. But what if things between us change again? I was glad to be back with Angel, but now we're off and on. There's lots of people in my life, but at the end of the day, the person I really need to trust, who can always be there for me... is ME.

The dragon was right—*I've been looking in the wrong places.*

I'M the one I've been looking for.

She clenched her fists and took a deep breath, staring into the pot of food gently boiling on the stove. For a brief moment, she caught a glimpse of her own reflection on the silvery surface of the wok. She smacked her lips as the sweet and spicy aroma of coconut curry wafted into her nostrils.

With a renewed sense of self-trust, she thought, *that's gonna be so good when it's done.*

CHAPTER 26
ELIMINATION ROUNDS

Several weeks later, Balidova entered the regional karate competition in the neighboring town of Prince Rupert, a two-hour drive from Kitimat. Like Kitimat, Prince Rupert was a coastal port city nestled in the mountains. The entire region was in the heart of the Great Bear Rainforest, where grizzlies, black bears, wolves, eagles, and the rare white bear roamed freely. Not only were land animals plentiful, but sea creatures were too —orcas, humpback whales, and salmon lived here. So abundant was deep-sea fishing that Prince Rupert was known as the halibut capital of the world.

The tournament was held at the Northwest Community College, next to the famous *Eternal Torch,* a gas-lit flame that burned year-round, representing the Northern Lights—a spectacular, multi-colored display of light that erupted across the night sky and became visible during the fall and winter months.

Balidova wore her new karate gi and newfound confidence. The re-connection with her mom had given her strength. Wearing the new uniform her mom got for her, she felt her mom's support.

Balidova also liked that her mom didn't care about whether she won or lost, but cared more about her daughter's well-being.

Balidova felt a certain acceptance from her mom. Their touching conversation in the barn, her mom's calming advice about her sisters, her help replacing the karate gi, and the woman's quiet but steady support during the dinner blowout with her dad all added up to a changing feeling towards her mom.

The newfound trust Balidova felt toward her mom—and herself— came out in her karate fights. She blew through the single-elimination kumite rounds that day. She was less hesitant and more sure of herself. Her punches and kicks had a commitment and force she had not felt before. She was more focused and less fearful—as if fear itself were transformed into power.

Balidova knew which techniques she was good at and capitalized on them repeatedly in many different matches. Whereas a split second of hesitation used to cost her the point, a split second of confidence now gave her the point. This slight, invisible shift made all the difference in the kumite ring. The internal switch changed everything, turning the tide from losing to winning.

By her last match of the day, she felt calm and confident as she entered the ring. She stepped onto the blue and red tatami mats, feeling focused, yet relaxed at the same time. As the referee said, "Hajime," and motioned for the fight to begin, she moved lightly on her feet, dancing effortlessly around the ring. When she executed an attack, her techniques were explosive and powerful. After a series of attacks, she'd return to her free-flowing footwork, staying out of her opponent's way.

Her mind, too, was free-flowing, absent of thought. She had none of the usual mental chatter and self-doubt, wondering whether she should attack or not. All her techniques, honed by years of training, flowed out effortlessly. Her body knew what to do—she didn't even have to think about it.

When she finished the match, she couldn't remember what

techniques she'd done. Her mind had merged with her body and her spirit. Everything flowed easily. She loved every minute of it and felt like she had fought her absolute best.

She beamed and bowed after receiving the win. For the first time in a long time, fighting felt fun. She was filled with a sense of love for the sport, the match, and even herself.

So this is what it feels like to be in the zone—everything flows so easily, effortlessly, and enjoyably.

As the day went on, Balidova noticed that she wasn't the only one in her family who was on a winning streak. Her second sister, May, had also won all three of her matches that day. They were on opposite sides of the draw, which meant they would face each other the next day—in the final.

BALIDOVA PACKED up her gear and headed to the dorm. Because the regional championship was an out-of-town tournament, the Kitimat Karate team was staying in the community college dormitory, next to the gymnasium where the tournament was being held. It was an exciting adventure to have left Kitimat! The only unfortunate thing was that her sister May was her roommate.

In their room, Balidova and May unpacked their overnight bags in silence. Even though they shared the same sleeping quarters, they both knew what the next day would bring—facing each other in the ring. They ate dinner in the cafeteria with their teammates, sitting at different tables, avoiding each other as much as possible. Then they went back to their room, brushed their teeth, and changed into their pajamas.

A few minutes later, when they were both getting into bed, there was a knock on the door. Balidova opened it. It was their dad. He stepped inside.

"Well done today—both of you. Congratulations on making it

to the finals tomorrow. An excellent showing for the Forester family."

"Thanks, Dad," May said from the other side of the room.

Balidova didn't say anything. She wasn't mad at her dad anymore—for making her do dishes for a week, or for not believing her when she said kicking Gus was the right thing to do. She was feeling way too good after winning three fights for all that. It was nice of him to congratulate them both.

"Dad..." she paused for a while.

"Yeah? What is it, Balidova?"

There were a lot of things she wanted to say. A lot of thoughts and emotions swirling inside her. She felt like a pendulum, moving towards her dad, then away from him. And now, she felt neutral. She still wanted to win the championship tomorrow, but not for him—for herself.

The only word that came out of her mouth was a simple, "Thanks."

"Okay, good night, girls," he said as he walked out and shut the door.

Both girls turned their lights off and lay on their beds across the room from each other.

"Dova, can I talk to you for a second?" May said.

"Yeah, sure. What is it?" Balidova turned on her side when she heard her sister speak.

"I'm a little scared."

"What?" Balidova wasn't expecting that. May was normally the tough one amongst the four. "What're you scared about?"

"Well, you might not know this, but you know that boy you kicked in school?" May continued.

"Yeah, Gus. Gus Polter. What about him?" Balidova was curious now.

May paused before responding. "Well, he's been coming after me."

"Really? Why would he be coming after you?"

"He's been threatening me—turning my friends against me by spreading rumors that I'm dragon crazy just like you. He wants to bring me down." May added indignantly. "And you know what?"

"What?" Balidova paused, a sense of dread filling her stomach.

"It's working," she said solemnly. "Some of my friends have been ignoring me."

Balidova was confused. She could sense an accusatory tone in her sister's voice. Was May blaming her?

"It's kinda your fault," May continued. "If you hadn't got on his bad side, none of this would be happening."

Balidova rolled her eyes in the dark. Then turned on her light. She saw that her sister's eyes were welling up with tears.

"Are you crying?" she asked in surprise. She couldn't remember the last time she'd seen May cry.

"Yeah, it's awful, Dova. I'm being pushed out of my friend group. I used to be the one who decided things, and now nobody listens to me. I don't know what to do," May whimpered.

"Geez," Balidova sighed. She threw off her covers and walked over to her sister's bed, sitting next to her. "Well, you don't need to cry about it. It'll all work itself out." She leaned down to hug her.

"What if it doesn't?" May moaned. "I'll be a reject forever, all because of you."

Balidova sat on the edge of the bed for a moment. She didn't know what to say. It was true, even if it wasn't entirely her fault. She hadn't started the feud with Gus, but she'd been part of it.

"Hey, I can't help it. I don't control what he does."

"You need to make it better," May said, her tears turning into a stream now.

Balidova interlaced her fingers in her lap and hung her head down, looking toward her belly button. She'd never seen May this vulnerable before—it took her by surprise. She felt terrible that her sister was suffering because of her.

"Okay, I'll see what I can do," she consented.

"Thanks, Dova. I knew I could count on you," May smiled.

"Yeah," Balidova murmured. She went back to her bed and turned the light off. Turning onto her side, her back facing May, Balidova was alone with her thoughts in the quiet, dark.

What? My fault? Thoughts swirled in her head. *Now I feel sorry for May. A minute ago, I was ready to beat her. What should I do tomorrow—try to win or go easy on her? How does the stuff she just told me have anything to do with our fight tomorrow?*

Balidova tossed and turned in her bed, tempted to say something to May. *If I go easy on her, what does that say about me? I wanna win. I want a spot on the provincial team. I've worked hard for it, and I know I'm good.*

She bit the inside of her lip to prevent herself from saying anything. She knew nothing good would come of it, this late at night, with both of them about to sleep. She sat up in bed and looked over at her sister's curled figure across the room.

But if I'm too fierce, is that gonna hurt her even more? She is my sister, after all. We live in the same house. And we've gone through so many things together—we train together, we've won team kata together, we've endured our parents' endless arguments together. Am I supposed to look out for her?

Balidova felt confused. Quietly, she got up, and put her shoes and blue track jacket on.

"Where are you going?" May asked drowsily.

"To the bathroom," Balidova replied.

"With your jacket?" May sounded suspicious.

"I just need to get some fresh air."

Balidova stepped out of the room quickly, before her sister could ask anything else. She closed the door quietly and tiptoed down the hallway, slipping out of the dorm.

Only one creature knows what to do when I don't.

Balidova looked up into the sky. The white light of the full moon illuminated the building and grounds in an eerie silver glow.

I have to find Luminora.

CHAPTER 27
ALL TIED UP

Balidova stepped out into the night, closing the building door behind her. By this time of year, nearing summer, daylight hours had reached their peak. The sun rose at 5:00 a.m. and set at 10:00 p.m., delivering seventeen hours of light each day. It was now after 10:00 p.m., and Balidova was not normally outside this late. The white orb of the moon shone magnificently, lighting up everything around her.

It's way brighter than I thought it would be.

She pulled her jacket around her. It was still chilly, even in June.

She took a few steps forward in the dark, silvery silence. She was wearing black sneakers with no socks, and every time she stepped, she could feel the squishiness of the shoe soles on her skin. No one else was around—all the other karate competitors were asleep in the dorms. The fierce competition of the day had died down into the quiet stillness of night.

She looked around, but didn't know where to find the dragon. All she knew was that she wanted, more than anything, to see Luminora again—tonight. It was the full moon, when all her dragon lessons had occurred, yet she worried the dragon would not show. Her pulse quickened as anxious thoughts entered her mind.

Soon enough, she realized what she was doing—working herself into a frenzy.

"Stop it, Balidova! Stop it right now."

Suddenly, she remembered what the fish had taught her—S.D.R.W. Stop. Detach. Remove your commitment to that emotion. Wrap it with love and let it go.

She said the words out loud so she could hear them, not just in her head but also in her ears. After taking a deep breath, she pivoted on her heels and began to focus.

Okay, I know how I DON'T want to feel—worried and stressed.

But how DO I want to feel?

I want to feel calm.

I want to feel like I know what I'm doing.

She was in a full-blown conversation with herself now. Luckily there was no one nearby to hear her.

Tap into the knowing, a voice inside her said.

Tap into the knowing, Balidova.

All the answers you seek are already within you.

Breathing in the words, Balidova spread her arms out wide, letting the moon's white light soak into her face, hands, and body, all the way down to her feet. She stood facing the moon, allowing its silvery glow to hit the front of her body. After a while, she turned around, allowing its luminescence to hit her back as well.

As the moon's glow swept over her entire body, it scrubbed all her fears, worries, and doubts away. And as she relaxed, she knew what to do. *Go to a large open area. The dragon is too big to land in between these buildings. Go to the fairgrounds, Balidova.*

She looked to see which way that would be, but honestly had no idea. There were buildings in all directions, separated by cement sidewalks, lampposts, and small grassy areas with shrubs and flowers. Since she couldn't tell which way to go, she decided to turn to her intuition to guide her. She rotated in a circle slowly, sensing the energy within her. As soon as she felt a surge of energy, she stopped.

This way.

Balidova started walking in the direction she was facing. But as she rounded the building, she saw two figures walking toward her—one large and one slightly smaller. From the way they walked, they both looked foreboding.

Her body bristled.

What are they doing here late at night?

As they came closer, under the street lamp, she could make out the features of the two men. She was both relieved and alarmed to recognize both of them. The taller one was wearing a sports jacket, dress slacks, and leather loafers. The shorter one was wearing a hoodie, jeans, and sneakers. The taller one was holding something in his hand.

"Mr. Winston? Gus? What're you doing here?" She knew it was her science teacher from the patch on his throat, which was visible now, since he wasn't wearing a bow tie.

She breathed a sigh of relief when she saw him.

"Oh, we're just out for a walk, enjoying the moonlight," Mr. Winston said, glancing at Gus. "There's a teacher's conference in Prince Rupert this weekend. You know—continuing education."

"Why's Gus here?" Balidova asked, confused.

"I brought him with me." Mr. Winston reassured her.

"Why?"

Mr. Winston didn't answer her question this time. He just stepped closer to her.

She could sense that something wasn't quite right. Why was Gus visiting the same town she was in during the provincial tryouts? She spotted the thing Mr. Winston was carrying in his hand. It looked like a piece of rope.

"What's in your hand?" she pointed. She was already wary of Gus but had no reason to be mindful of her science teacher, who had only shown her support and understanding over the past several months as she'd learned more and more about the dragon. Both men were close to her now—only a few feet away.

Before Mr. Winston could answer, Gus stepped to the side to make her think he was moving away—so she would drop her guard—then lunged toward her, grabbing both her arms, so they were trapped beside her body. He might not have been an expert fighter, but he was still a big, strong guy.

Balidova reacted immediately, trying to get free, but her arms were locked at her sides. She leaned her head back, then smashed it forward to hit him with her skull, but nothing was there. He knew that trick—the head bash. She moved on to her next option. But just when she was about to stomp on his foot with her heel, Mr. Winston sprang into action also.

"Quick, get her hands behind her back!" he said. "Get her down on the ground." It took both of them to wrestle her down to the pavement. Mr. Winston tied her feet with rope before she could kick him, while Gus held her upper body.

"Mr. Winston, what are you doing? Why are you helping him?" she asked in shock.

Mr. Winston didn't say anything right away, but a crooked grin slid across his face. "I'm not helping him, Balidova. He's helping me."

BALIDOVA FELT like she'd been punched in the gut. She was so stunned that she didn't strike out when they pushed her onto the lamppost and tied her arms around it, behind her back. She couldn't muster up any words that reflected the extreme level of disgust she felt for him. She just spat on him.

He looked down at the globule of saliva on his chest and said something she wasn't expecting. "Thank you. I was wondering how to get that from you. You don't know what you've just done."

He reached down, collected it onto a small piece of paper, and tucked it into his pocket.

Balidova's mind reeled. Suddenly everything was off-kilter.

"Don't you dare," were her last words before Gus stuffed a bandana in her mouth and tied it behind her head to prevent her from screaming.

Gus pulled out a pair of scissors. "Remember these? I was holding them when you kicked me at school. Now I'm gonna use them on you, just like I was trying to do then." She squirmed violently and tried to yell, but the bandana muffled the sound.

Her eyes grew wide as Gus leaned in close with the scissors, waving the shiny metal near her face. He opened them up, the sharp edge next to her skin, and lifted the blades toward her eyes.

She turned her head away, too terrified to see what he would do next. She was completely defenseless and weaponless.

For a few agonizing seconds, she waited. Then she heard a clipping sound and felt a tug on her head.

"Got it," he said, holding a small lock of her hair.

"Good. Let's go." Mr. Winston replied. "We've got what we need. She's not going anywhere. And she's certainly not learning the next step of the Dragon Tail Breath," he smirked, looking up at the full moon.

"Balidova's muffled sounds permeated the night.

"Don't worry, Balidova. Somebody will find you—in the morning." Mr. Winston smiled smugly. Both he and Gus laughed.

"Nighty night!" said Gus.

But before turning to leave, Gus went right up close to her face and said, "I've wanted to do this ever since you knocked me down at school." He took one step back, still facing her, and landed a kick right in her gut.

She doubled over, sucking wind. For a moment, she couldn't

breathe at all. He had kicked her in the solar plexus, the most vulnerable spot. As her muscles contracted violently, she felt a searing pain course through her body. It started in her core, then radiated throughout her back and into her lungs and heart. She couldn't breathe through her mouth with the bandana stuffed there and panicked.

But eventually, her breath returned through her nose.

SOME TIME WENT by as Balidova sat there simply breathing—she didn't know how long. Just when she started sinking into a panic again, she heard footsteps coming from the opposite direction. She turned to look, recognizing the red and black checkered pants. It was May. Balidova stomped her feet on the ground so her sister could hear her.

"Balidova, is that you?" May called. "What're you doing out here?" She saw that Balidova's hands were tied behind her back around the pole.

"Oh my gosh, are you okay?" She rushed over and saw ropes binding Balidova's feet and hands, and a bandana around her mouth.

As quickly as she could, May untied the bandana gagging her sister.

"Mr. Winston and Gus," Balidova said through deep lungfuls of air, "they tied me to the pole and took a piece of my hair. Then, Gus kicked me in the stomach."

"You mean Mr. Winston, the science teacher?" May untied her sister's hands, and Balidova placed them on her stomach, still in pain from the kick.

"Yeah, can you believe it?" Balidova said, still reeling from the experience.

"You didn't come back, so I came looking for you. I was worried." May said.

"Thanks, sis," Balidova replied, reaching out to hug her sister. "Thank goodness you came to get me. I could have been out here in the dark all night."

They embraced each other tightly. Then May pulled back, her hands still on Balidova's shoulders.

"Are you okay?" May looked concerned.

"Yeah. Gus kicked me pretty hard, but I can breathe again now. It's not the first time I've been kicked—I'll get over it." Balidova leaned her head back on the pole and let out a long sigh of relief. "I'm really glad you came."

"Yeah, me too." May dropped her arms by her side. For a moment, they both looked at each other in silent solidarity.

"It's the full moon." Balidova pointed up toward the sky. "Tonight's the night I learn the next step of the Dragon Tail Breath. I have to find the dragon."

"The what?" May looked startled and clasped her hands together. "You're not making any sense."

"The dragon," Balidova said, matter-of-factly, looking into her sister's eyes.

"I dunno what you're talking about, Dova, but it's too dangerous. You can't stay out. They might come back for you. You've gotta come back inside the dorm." May's eyebrows were raised as she spoke.

"No. I have to." Balidova thought about Mr. Winston's betrayal. That's what hurt the most— even more than the kick. She had trusted him, and he had betrayed her—it made her question her own judgment. Yet something in her knew.

"There's no way I'm going back to the dorm yet."

May recognized the steely tone of Balidova's voice. Even though she didn't understand why Balidova had to stay out, she knew there would not be any changing her sister's mind. The only thing to do now was help her.

"Okay, then I'll go back to the dorm and cover for you." May sighed. "The night monitor's gonna be checking to see that everyone's in their rooms. I'll put some pillows on your bed and cover them with a blanket to make it look like you're sleeping."

"Thanks," Balidova replied.

"I still don't think you should be out here alone." May tried one last time to persuade Balidova to come inside with her. But when her sister stood staring at her, May capitulated. "Oh, whatever, we don't have time to argue. Just go."

Balidova turned to go, her whole body prickling on high alert as if sharp spruce needles pressed against her skin. She began walking in the same direction she was headed when she first ran into Gus and Mr. Winston—the direction her intuition had told her to go.

And the direction they had left in.

CHAPTER 28
RED LIGHT ROOT

Balidova picked up the pace and ran out to the fairgrounds beyond the community college. Once there, she paused and looked around. Just as she was about to shout Luminora's name, she stopped. She didn't want to let Mr. Winston and Gus know she was untied.

Standing tall at the edge of the field, she closed her eyes and pictured Luminora's kind eyes, flowing mane, muscular body, and brilliant wings. She imagined the dragon's long tail winding around her body with each breath.

She breathed in and out, and heard a voice speaking to her.

*When your inner fire subsides,
go to where the firelight resides.*

Her eyes popped open. She looked around but saw only darkness.

Then it struck her.

The community torch next to the totem pole.

She ran to the gate, passed through, and stood squarely in

front of the lone torch lighting the entrance to the community fairgrounds. Next to it was a totem pole with a bear, fish, and eagle carved into the wood—or was it a dragon?

Looking into the flickering flame, she spoke aloud, all the affirmations she had learned, as she breathed in and out.

All is well. Deep breath.

Here now. Deep breath.

What do I want? Deep breath.

I am a powerful creator. Deep breath.

Balidova knows. Deep breath.

With each word and each breath, she felt more and more centered in the dragon's energy—a feeling of deep calm. She closed her eyes and let the sensation flood through her, basking in its glow.

～

When she opened her eyes again, the dragon was there. She ran and hugged the leg of the beast, which was as large as a tree trunk.

"Thank you for coming," she sobbed. Now that she felt safe, the roller coaster of emotions she'd just been through overwhelmed her—a river of tears poured out.

"There, there, dear one," the dragon said, bending its head down to meet her. "Come under the light. It's hard for me to see you in the dark, although I can smell you miles away."

The dragon's calm, still presence soothed Balidova. After a while, she collected herself again, stepping into the torchlight. "Am I ever glad to see you," she sighed. "So glad to see you—you have no idea."

"Why, what happened?" the dragon asked, raising its eyebrows. "You were so happy when we last met. What could have happened in such a short time?" Luminora chuckled, knowing the range of possibilities—both positive and negative—that could occur in Balidova's life.

"Mr. Winston and Gus," Balidova said breathlessly, "They attacked me, tied me to a pole, and took a piece of my hair. Why would they do that? I thought I could trust Mr. Winston. I feel terrible now. Like I can't trust anyone—including myself," she groaned.

"Hmm," the dragon replied, lowering its head to her level. Nostrils poked out from the smooth surface of the dragon's snout, rising like mountain caves above the ground. "It's time to tell you, Balidova. Mr. Winston is not who he seems."

"Yeah, I figured that out, but why? Why attack me? I never did anything to him."

"He is one of the leaders of the Drakoban," Luminora said, matter-of-factly.

"The what?" Balidova's eyes widened.

"The Drakoban." The dragon thumped its tail on the ground emphatically.

"What's that?" Balidova sounded confused.

"A secret order of Dark Dragons." Luminora raised its head again.

"Dark dragons? I didn't know there were different types of dragons. Then what are you?"

"I am one of the Dragons of Light." Luminora looked at the girl, saw that she was baffled, and decided it was time to explain more to her. "Two groups of dragons are battling with each other—over human souls. The dark dragons seek to control humans with fear. The light dragons wish to free people with love."

"Who's winning?" Balidova asked, as if it was the next obvious question.

"The Drakoban are gaining power. They have placed a Cloak

of Fear around the earth, and soon it will seal completely, trapping human souls in fear forever. Once it seals, humans will only know the different versions of fear—anger, rage, frustration, hatred, helplessness, shame, jealousy, revenge, sadness, and doubt. Unless a human—the one—learns the Dragon Tail Breath and shatters the Cloak of Fear, tipping the scales of justice toward the light."

Balidova stopped talking for a moment.

Instantly, it all made sense.

"The Cloak of Fear is what I've felt when I'm at my worst. In my bedroom, when I hated myself and felt trapped in my head. In the dojo, when I believed what I was feeling was wrong and just went along with what my sisters wanted. At school, when I felt like an outcast after Gus put up that poster. When I punched a hole in the wall of my room after shouting at my dad."

She was picking up steam now.

"When I wanted revenge against my sisters for writing on my gi. When I was mad at Angel for telling Gus about Step Five of the Dragon Tail Breath. When I panicked and didn't believe in myself."

All the times that Balidova had felt terrible over the last seven months came flooding back to her. By focusing on one of those negative thoughts, she opened a gateway to all of them, and they came surging in.

"Yes, the Cloak of Fear magnifies your fears with the fears of others. We are surrounded by energy, Balidova, and everyone's energy can affect everyone else. We are all connected." The dragon wrapped its tail around its body, enveloping Balidova as well.

"I didn't realize how *everywhere* it is." She felt shaken, as though she couldn't trust anything or anyone anymore. Then she placed one hand on the dragon's scales, which felt silky smooth yet impenetrably firm at the same time.

"Fear is a learned behavior that all humans acquire—some

more than others." The dragon responded. The creature's neutral tone calmed Balidova momentarily, even amid such a foreboding topic.

"It affects others too. Not just me?" Balidova had learned this from the sunflower but somehow wanted it confirmed by the dragon. She wanted to know more about this invisible dark cloak that seemed to significantly impact her life without her ever seeing it.

"Yes, the Cloak of Fear affects *everyone*," Luminora confirmed.

"My dad, mom, sisters, Gus, Mr. Winston, Angel, Jojo, and Mrs. Marsh?" Balidova persisted with her line of questioning. Although she sensed it was true, she did not want to accept just how invasive the Cloak of Fear was.

"Yes, all of them. It turns mild emotions like doubt and worry into even heavier emotions, like anger and depression." Luminora repeated. "Emotion, after all, is simply *energy in motion. E-motion.*" Luminora's golden whiskers wiggled up and down in a wave motion to emphasize this point.

Hey, that's what I learned in karate too.

Balidova was comforted that her karate world and her dragon world overlapped.

"Energy draws similar energy to itself. Fear draws more fear. Love draws more love."

The dragon blew a plume of smoke from its mouth, allowing the smoke to form a circle in front of them. It covered Balidova's face, and for a moment, she couldn't see clearly. "The Cloak of Fear, wrapping around the earth like a cloud of darkness, makes it more difficult for humans to see the truth of love, and much easier for them to fall back on their fears."

"Is that why the world is full of war, chaos, fighting, and deadly diseases?" Balidova had watched the news with her dad and noticed how horrible most of the stories were. Countries were going to war with each other, and neighbors were turning on one another for stupid reasons like the color of their skin, the way they talked, or the kind of clothes they wore. Terrible things were going on all over the globe as more and more people chose fear over love.

"Yes. The Drakoban are very powerful. Their Cloak of Fear is building, Balidova. It's having a stronger effect on more humans. If you feel something often enough, it becomes ingrained in you, laying deeper and deeper tracks in your mind. The Cloak of Fear is not something humans can see with their eyes—only something they can feel with their heart."

"Does it affect you?" Balidova looked hopefully at the dragon. There had to be some way to stop this sinister dark cloak from spreading. It seemed to be everywhere, and it was growing—like a virus.

The dragon smiled at the girl's logic.

She had a mind like a steel trap—logical, analytical, critical. The creature knew this was both a blessing and a curse. Every human had the possibility of darkness within them, including Balidova. She could use any of her powers—including her reasoning mind—for good or bad. The girl had already displayed anger, rage, frustration, jealousy, doubt, self-hatred, helplessness, shame, sadness, and a desire for revenge, and yet, she was "the one."

"No. The Cloak of Fear does not affect me. I am not human. I am dragon." The creature spoke with a calm, commanding tone that signaled an end to this part of the conversation.

But why do the dark dragons want humans to live in fear?

Balidova restrained herself from asking this last question, respecting the dragon's tone. She paused while taking everything in, then lifted her head, remembering something else Luminora had said earlier.

"What's 'the one'?" she said cautiously, as if she knew the answer but was afraid to ask.

"Not what, but *who*," Luminora stared at the girl through yellowy-orange eyes.

"So, who is it?" the girl asked again, slowly, returning the dragon's gaze.

The mighty creature lowered its head to look even closer into the girl's eyes.

"It is *you*, Balidova."

BALIDOVA STEPPED BACK. Her left eye—the one with the green tinge—twitched. She paused, curling her fingers into a fist, listening to the sharp, cracking sounds her knuckles made.

"Me? Is that why I've been learning the steps of the Dragon Tail Breath, because I have a task to do? Nobody told me. You didn't even tell me." She was feeling wary of Luminora, too, now.

"You were not yet ready, Balidova. Everything has its time," Luminora spoke steadily, reassuring the girl, knowing she was still reeling from the betrayal by her science teacher.

"Really? When were you going to tell me that in addition to fighting my sister in the finals tomorrow, fending off attacks from someone I thought I could trust, and defending myself and my friends against the school bully, I would have to save the world!"

The dragon looked at her with knowing eyes, as if the creature were wrapping her with love.

Balidova threw her arms up in the air. "This is great. This is just great. Right when I don't know if I can even trust myself, the one creature I *do* trust says the well-being of the whole world is riding on me! That's just what I need now. Thanks." Balidova turned around, covered her face with her hands, and started to sob.

Again, the dragon did not speak. The beast just looked at Balidova, supporting the girl, not with wings but with a certain energy—holding the girl in a field of pure unconditional love.

Slowly, Balidova felt it. She could feel the love within.

Shortly after, she stopped crying.

As she calmed down, she returned to her senses and turned toward the dragon.

"That's it, Balidova. Good."

The dragon sensed the shift in the girl immediately. "Come back into your *knowing* senses. Come back into the wisdom of your body." The dragon trembled its skin, making its scales shimmer in the moonlight.

Balidova sighed deeply, then spoke quietly.

"So, what am I supposed to do?"

"Learn all seven steps of the Dragon Tail Breath before the seventh moon passes."

"The seventh moon?"

"Yes. The seventh moon after your twelfth birthday. That is the legend passed down for generations—*before seven moons pass in the twelfth year*. The world began with the dragons of water, earth, fire, and air. It must be completed with dragon magic, but this time, channeled through a human."

"But that's coming up soon—only one full moon away," Balidova said breathlessly. "I turned twelve on December 31st. The first moon was in January when I met the spirit bear in the forest. The second moon was in February when I met the fish at the river." Her eyes drifted up to the left as she pulled the images from her memory.

"The third moon was in March when I met the sunflower in the meadow. In April, the fourth moon was when I met you, the dragon, on top of the mountain. The fifth moon was in May at the double tree." Her gaze returned to look at the dragon.

"And the sixth moon is now, in June, here in the fairgrounds.

I've learned one step of the Dragon Tail Breath on each of the full moons."

"Yes, and you will learn the final lesson on the next full moon. You must not let anyone stop you. Especially a seventh-level demon like Mr. Winston," Luminora looked intently at the girl.

"A seventh-level demon?" Balidova looked puzzled.

"Yes, the most advanced kind. They not only harbor darkness but give the illusion of light."

"What do you mean?"

"Their skill lies in getting you to trust them."

"Oh, so that's how he fooled me. He seemed so understanding and nice, but deep down, he wasn't." Balidova paused as if forgiving herself, just a little, for not seeing this before.

"They also have the power to shapeshift." The dragon continued.

"You mean they take on other forms? Like an animal or something?"

The dragon remained silent.

Wanting to know more, Balidova continued with her questions. She remembered what she'd seen at the hospital months earlier.

"What's up with that patch on his throat?"

"Ah, that's one of the telltale signs of a seventh-level demon. They have inexplicable ailments that don't seem to make sense, most commonly in the throat area, because their physical bodies absorb the negative energy from all the lies they speak and break down."

"That must be why he wears bow ties all the time—to cover up the patch," Balidova reasoned.

"Perhaps. Such a low vibration creates disease in the body. Demons try to cover it up in many different ways," the dragon continued.

Balidova cocked her head sideways, "Okay, but why did he need a piece of my hair?"

"They're making a potion, Balidova—a potion to stop you and make you forget everything you've learned. It consists of different parts of you representing each of the four elements—your blood, hair, fingernail, and saliva."

"Oh my gosh," she gasped. "He's got three of those parts of me!" She remembered how he had touched her bloody hand at the hospital, asked for a piece of her fingernail in class, and now Gus had just cut a lock of her hair.

But the fourth part—how would they get the saliva?

Then she remembered how she had spit at Mr. Winston when he tied her feet with the rope. He had laughed at the glob of saliva that landed on his jacket.

"Oh no, he's got all the ingredients," she moaned. "That's what he meant when he said, 'you don't know what you've done,' after looking at my spit." Balidova covered her face with her hands and whimpered softly.

"Now, what do I do?"

The dragon watched her quietly the whole time. The creature saw something in the girl that she did not yet see in herself.

"The only thing you can do, Balidova, is use your growing powers. Continue studying the steps of the Dragon Tail Breath and use what you learn to defeat the Drakoban. As you breathe in the colors of light, wrap yourself with love. That is the only antidote to the Cloak of Fear."

"Really?" Balidova asked skeptically. "Wrap myself with love?" She did not yet believe in her own powers. "Is that all you can give me?"

"Remember the essential oil I gave you when we first met? Keep it close, for it will come in handy at the right time," the dragon said, winking at her.

Balidova let her hands fall by her side and looked down at the ground, overwhelmed by the task ahead. *How am I supposed to defeat a seventh-level demon and the order of dark dragons?*

Sensing her confusion, Luminora explained more. "Dragons are incredibly creative creatures. They have the power that creates worlds flowing through them. The world began with the dragons of earth, water, air, and fire, but if they don't harness their incredible power, it starts to go dormant. Even though they are enormous beasts, they have this one weakness—if they retrace their physical steps with the same mental intention, their power is cut in half."

Balidova looked up at the fantastic creature, buoyed by a glimmer of hope. It seemed to believe in her more than she believed in herself. But then, the reality of her situation came rushing in, and she cast her eyes down again. Her chances seemed so slim and her responsibility so great. There was no way she could do this alone.

Both girl and dragon stepped back from each other, letting the space between them grow. A ray of moonlight shone down and seemed to make a line in the grass, illuminating the distance between them—between the physical and magical worlds.

"One who is connected to the light is more powerful than millions who are not," the dragon continued.

"Although the dark dragons need some light to survive, as do all living things, too much of it will destroy them. The Drakoban disintegrate in bright light."

Balidova inhaled deeply, taking in the dragon's words. They seemed familiar to her, even though she had not heard them before. She felt as though she were not learning them for the first time, but remembering them from long ago.

She closed her eyes and breathed, just as the dragon had taught her...

Breathe in four seconds.

Breathe out four seconds.

Repeat four times.

Noticeably calmer, she looked around, shook out her hands, and shifted her feet, taking everything in.

"Would you like to learn Step Six of the Dragon Tail Breath?" the dragon asked. "You've demonstrated confidence—in the Dragon Tail Breath and yourself—coming to find me in the night, even after being attacked. So, I know you are ready."

AFTER CONTEMPLATING FOR A MOMENT, Balidova looked up. "Are you sure I'm ready? It sounds like I haven't been doing such a great job."

"On the contrary," the dragon said. "You've been doing a wonderful job. This isn't about getting everything perfect."

"It isn't?" Balidova asked. "I thought that's what everything was about." Puzzled, she took another deep breath. "Then what *is* this about?"

"Being *present*." Luminora paused. "Coming in and out of the energy. Being curious. Being willing to grow and learn. The greatest warriors are not the ones who never fall. They are the ones who simply get up faster than the others after they fall. You are doing this perfectly already, my dear."

After soaking the idea in, she said, "I assume you want to know the first five steps before showing me the sixth?"

"You're a quick study," the dragon nodded, returning its wing to its normal position.

"Okay, here goes. Step One, breathe emerald green light into my whole body. *All is well.*" Balidova opened her arms wide and then brought her hands to her heart, placing one palm on top of the other.

"Yes," the dragon affirmed.

"Step Two, breathe in golden light through my solar plexus.

Here now." Balidova shifted her feet, firmly rooting them on the ground.

"Good," the dragon said encouragingly.

"Step Three, breathe blue light into my throat. *What do I want?* Speak my truth and understand the power of words," Balidova said. She stood up tall, pulling her shoulder blades back.

"Nice."

"Step Four, breathe orange light into my tanden, the physical center of my body, knowing *I am a powerful creator.* Accept, Release, and Move-on from what I DON'T want, to what I DO want." Balidova tucked her hips in, lending even more support to her powerful, tall stance.

"Okay," the dragon smiled.

"Step Five, breathe indigo blue light in through my third eye, seeing and using the different levels of my senses—physical, intuitive, and *knowing.* I know, I know, *I KNOW!*" she said loudly. She dropped her chin down and straightened her body even more. Now she stood tall and strong, like a warrior—feet planted, hips tucked in, shoulders back, chin down, hands at her heart.

"Well done!" the dragon said. "That's a lot of information—you've accumulated a lifetime of learning in such a short time." In one magnificent motion, the dragon sent a ripple down its whole body, from head to tail, displaying the full brightness and beauty of its rainbow-colored scales under the torchlight.

Balidova watched in awe, grinning with delight. She rubbed her hands together in anticipation, "Okay, so what's Step Six?"

Balidova had shaken off the feeling that she wasn't ready. Going through the first five steps—breathing, speaking, and moving her body—had transformed the feeling inside. She accepted her destiny now. She wanted to learn more.

Luminora leaned in close to the girl.

"Step Six is breathing in red light through the root of your body."

"The root of my body? What's that? I thought only plants had roots."

"Right between your legs. There's an energy center at the base of your torso, like the roots of a tree, from which everything grows."

Balidova looked down at her groin, then started laughing. "Are you joking?"

"No. We're talking about energy, Balidova. These are the *energy centers* of your body."

"Uh, okay. So, breathe red light into there?" She pointed between her legs.

"Yes. Breathe red light in and let it rise through your torso, all the way up to your head and neck, down your arms and legs. Breathe red light in until it fills up your entire body."

"Okay, whatever you say," she said skeptically.

Balidova resumed her strong, tall stance.

She took a deep breath.

Then another, and another.

After about thirty seconds of breathing, she said, "Whoa, I feel like a fireball!" she shouted.

"That is the fire at the core of your being. As you breathe the light in, repeat these words—*I love and accept myself.*"

"Hmph."

The dragon waited. "Well?"

"I love and accept myself," Balidova mumbled.

She mulled the words over in her mind, wondering, *what does that even mean?*

"What was that?" Luminora asked, bending an ear toward the girl. "I can't hear you."

"I love and accept myself," she repeated quietly.

"I still can't hear you."

The dragon's ear was so close to Balidova that she could reach out and touch it.

"I love and accept myself!" Balidova shouted at the top of her lungs.

All of a sudden, she felt it. A pang of energy shot up from the root of her body, through her tanden, solar plexus, heart, throat, and between her eyes. A vertical line of energy extending from the ground, through her body, right out through the top of her head.

She stood increasingly straighter as she felt the physical, emotional, and mental centers of her body connecting, lining up together in one invisible pillar of energy—

third eye (mental center),
heart (emotional center),
tanden (physical center).

She stood tall, as if someone was pulling her up from the hair on the top of her head—her pelvis tucked in, shoulders back, chin in. A martial arts stance—straight, strong, and true.

"Oooh, that feels good!" she said.

"I love and accept myself."

The feeling reverberated inside her being with each word, as if every cell were drinking it up. Red light expanded and grew, lighting and sparking the root of her body up through her entire torso and into her energy field—an explosion of fireworks erupting from the inside out.

"Wow, that is so cool." A big smile snuck across her face.

The dragon watched her, noticing what was happening. "Yes, indeed. You're waking up, Balidova. Waking up to the dragon magic." The dragon smiled wide, opening its jaw and revealing a long row of dragon teeth, each as big and sharp as a knife.

Balidova saw those teeth, then lifted her gaze to the dragon's golden eyes. She drank in the CALM, STRONG, VIBRANT feeling that engulfed her body. Even though she was much smaller, less colorful, and in a different shape, she somehow felt powerful, like a dragon. She felt the truth of the dragon's words—*you're waking up to the dragon magic.*

The dragon opened its wings, getting ready to fly away.

"No, don't leave. Not yet." Balidova pleaded. "I feel so good. Please stay a few minutes longer."

"It's almost time to complete the last stage of the Dragon Tail Breath. You will be able to use it in all parts of your life. And you will need it to defeat the Drakoban," Luminora announced. "But that is enough for today. Until next time."

"No, don't go, don't go!" Balidova scrambled over and wrapped her arms around the dragon's leg. "I feel so good."

"Take this feeling back into your life, Balidova," the dragon said. "Do not let others crush it down. Know that you can come back to this feeling simply by taking a deep breath. Breathe in the red light and focus on lining up your body, mind, and spirit while saying *I love and accept myself*."

Balidova pressed her face against the dragon's scales.

Then slowly released her grip and retreated.

She knew she would have to go back to the dorm, to the competition ring to fight her sister tomorrow. She would have to face the Drakoban—who knew when?

She wasn't sure if she could do any of it.

She was scared yet hopeful at the same time.

Running her fingertips over the callouses on her knuckles, she felt the skin of her own hands, toughened from hundreds of punches on the brown leather heavy bag in their home dojo. She looked up at Luminora and asked a simple yet troubling question.

"How will I know I'm the one?"

The dragon looked down at the girl and spoke in a soft, low voice. **"When you realize you're good enough just as you are."**

THE DRAGON UNDERSTOOD the girl's hesitation yet nudged her toward a new possibility that it could already see for her. "Believe in yourself, and *any*thing is possible. Without that, nothing is possible."

Perplexed, Balidova scrunched her face. "How am I supposed to believe I can beat my sister or the Drakoban if I haven't done it before?"

"Belief comes from the inside, Balidova. Don't think. Feel..."

The dragon's words trailed off into the wind. The majestic beast looked at her one last time, and for a moment, Balidova thought she saw her reflection in the dragon's eye.

All at once, with a flash of indigo light and a gust of wind that almost extinguished the fairground torch, Luminora was gone.

Balidova was left standing in the dark, alone. She looked at the moon, illuminated by the spectacular Aurora Borealis dancing in the sky, lighting up the night. As she walked back to the dorm, her bare toes squished together in her shoes once again. She brought her gaze back to eye level, cast it upon the totem pole, and watched the flickering fire of the fairground torch where Luminora had appeared. Gently, she whispered into the flame.

Thank you, Fire Moon.

CHAPTER 29
THE FINALS

After thanking and naming the moon, Balidova scanned the fairgrounds and the forest beyond once more. She hoped to see Luminora but knew the dragon had disappeared. She saw the *Eternal Flame* burning bright in the night and, for a moment, thought she saw red flames reaching up like a dragon's tail. The sky was dark and motionless, except for the glow of the Fire Moon and a lone bird soaring high above the trees, past the edge of town. Walking back toward the community college, she realized she didn't want to get caught out in the dark—or get caught by Mr. Winston and Gus—again, so she broke into a jog, then a full-out run across the open field.

Back in the dorm, she tiptoed into the room she shared with her sister, removed her sneakers and jacket, and crawled into bed. She moved the pillows May had placed under her blanket to make it look like she was sleeping there. Conflicting emotions tugged at her heart. Tucked under her blanket, she repeated the words she had learned as part of Step Six of the Dragon Tail Breath—*I love and accept myself.*

She looked over at her sister and saw a wisp of dark brown

hair peek out from the top of the blanket. *How am I supposed to unleash myself on her when she saved me? I wouldn't even be here right now if it wasn't for her. I'd still be tied to that lamppost out in the dark—alone, cold, and scared.* She felt a wave of gratitude towards her sister, sleeping peacefully.

Balidova rolled over onto her other side, facing away from her sister, and pulled the blanket up to her chin. *But if I don't fight my best, what's that doing for me? The dragon said to 'love and accept myself.' I've put in so many hours of hard work for this. I can't just give that up. 'Always be true to you.' But which one is true—being powerful and going for the win, or being loving and letting May win? Even after seeing Luminora, I still don't know what to do.*

That night, she tossed and turned in her bed, trying to get some sleep before the sun came up.

WHEN SUNDAY MORNING CAME, the two girls rose and got ready without saying much. They ate breakfast in silence in the cafeteria, packed their bags, and headed out the door to the competition arena. Once there, they went to different corners of the warmup area. Each one intuitively knew she needed her own space before facing the other in the ring.

While May was walking to her corner, she glanced at Balidova. "Remember what I told you about Gus," she said. "He's after me and will be even more now, especially if he finds out that I saved your butt last night."

Great. Balidova wanted to throw up her hands in reaction, but restrained herself to only a slight head shake. She didn't want May to know what was happening inside her right before they stepped on the mat to compete against each other. It would give her sister an unfair advantage.

What am I supposed to do with that?

Balidova turned away and distracted herself by digging through her karate bag and putting on her kumite gloves. She shook out her whole body vigorously—the way a dog shakes water off its fur—shaking off a feeling of guilt and gratitude mixed with pity.

Just get ready for the fight.

She slipped on her mouthguard, preparing for the finals of the open weight category. The winner of this match would automatically earn a spot on the provincial karate team and attend the British Columbia Winter Games next year.

Balidova was taller than her sister, so they were not the same weight category. But this was the open weight division—any girl of any size could enter. You'd think that bigger people would win, but that was not always the case. Often, being larger meant being slower and more cumbersome. Smaller fighters who were quick and agile could outmatch a heavier fighter as long as they could get in and out quickly, without the bigger competitor landing a blow on them.

Balidova looked at her sister across the ring. They were evenly matched. Balidova was taller and had longer reach with her punches and kicks, but May knew Balidova's weak points, was a year older, and had more experience.

The two girls bowed and entered the ring, stopping precisely on their starting lines, just two meters of empty space between them. Both wore an all-white karate uniform that extended to their wrists and ankles. Balidova tied her gi with a red belt and wore matching red gloves. May wore blue gloves with a matching blue belt. The colors distinguished the competitors and matched the red and blue flags carried by the referees sitting on the corners of the ring. Even black belts had to remove their regular belt and wear these colors during competitions. The girls stood on their lines, feet shoulder-width apart, hands in fists by their sides, staring into each other's eyes.

"Hajime!" the referee shouted, initiating the start of the match.

As the fight began, both girls stepped toward each other, moving cautiously while sizing each other up. May smiled at Balidova for a brief second, and Balidova smiled back–something she didn't normally do in the middle of a kumite match, but it was her sister, after all.

Without warning, May attacked with a flurry of punches.

Balidova was caught off guard, but with her quick reflexes, she managed to block and move out of the way just in time.

Okay, game on.

Not seeing Balidova's block, the referee awarded a point to her sister, who smiled again. A different smile this time.

Both girls stared at each other.

When the match re-started, May kept the pressure on. She came forward, closing the space between them. Balidova's nagging thought that she owed her sister—both for the trouble she'd caused with Gus and untying Balidova from the lamppost—made her hesitate ever so briefly before she launched each kick-punch combination. This allowed her sister just enough time to block or get out of the way, so Balidova's attacks didn't score.

Balidova couldn't help feeling like she'd given up some power to her sister, and now it was too late to get it back.

May capitalized on Balidova's momentary hesitation, winning the next two points.

Balidova's confidence was starting to waver. *It's 3-0. This is ridiculous. I worked hard for this, and I'm letting my sister beat me.*

As she stood on the line and watched another point being awarded to her sister, Balidova had a sinking feeling in her stomach. She felt awful inside, yet May was smiling. Balidova steeled herself and clenched her fists.

I'm getting the next point.

This time, when the referee said 'go,' she decided *she* would control the space between them. Something had changed in her mind. She wasn't letting her sister's smile get to her anymore.

Balidova lunged in with a double punch followed by a roundhouse kick to the head, scoring two points at once.

Yeah, that's more like it.

Her sister looked surprised, as if she wasn't expecting Balidova to wake up.

The two-minute match was almost over, and Balidova was still down 2-3. She came blasting off the line with one of her favorite techniques—a front kick to the chest, followed by a face punch over the top.

"Kiaaaaiiiii!"

All four red flags shot out, unequivocally indicating the point for Balidova.

Just then, the bell rang. Time had run out.

"Hikewake," the referee announced. *Draw.* The referee held both hands palm side up, one toward each girl, indicating a tie.

"Now we go into sudden death over time. First point scores," he commanded. He stepped one foot back, stretched his arms out, and pointed one hand toward each competitor, preparing to relaunch the fight.

With heightened awareness, both girls stood at the ready, their bare feet gripping the tatami mat. *So, this is what the dragon meant when it said, 'Always be true to you.' Lowering my level for anybody, for any reason, at any time—including my sister—is not being true to me. Hmph, that's the same thing Mom said—'don't lower your vibe for anyone.'*

Balidova shifted her weight from one foot to the other, feeling the floor beneath her feet.

What do I want?

I want to win this match.

I'm going to win this match.

A new resolve came over her as she narrowed her gaze, staring at her sister with tiger-like intensity. In an instant, she realized the truth about the situation. Two fights were going on here, one in the ring with her sister and one in her heart with herself. She was determined not to lose either one.

May was no pushover. She looked right back at Balidova, knowing what was happening. Consciously or unconsciously, her softening tactic was wearing off. She knew she'd better be ready because Balidova would come at her full force. May could read it in her sister's eyes.

The moment the referee called 'Hajime,' the two girls sprang at each other. Unlike the earlier part of the fight, there was no time to make up a lost point. The two sisters knew each other's strengths and weaknesses better than anyone else. They lived and trained together. They grew up together. Although they both desperately wanted to win, both were wary of the other person's ability.

For a few moments, tension built as they sized each other up, testing the distance between them to see if they could draw the other person out. It was one of the oldest tricks in the book—fake an attack, so your opponent launches their attack right at that moment. Then you know what's coming and have the best chance of a counter-attack. Both girls attempted this trick on the other, but neither was successful. They both knew what to look for.

Then May went for it—for real. Her signature move—sidestep roundhouse kick to the lower belly followed by a backfist to the head. But when she moved in, something unexpected happened. Balidova did not move back or block. She did something completely counterintuitive.

She went forward.

As May's body came hurtling toward her, Balidova did not flinch, blink or back up; she attacked with *her* signature move—a simple, precisely on target, timing punch. Her reaction speed was so lightning fast that the moment May initiated her kick, Balidova exploded forward without hesitation.

The result? Balidova's punch landed on her sister's gut before May's kick was complete.

The referee stopped the match immediately. Two of the corner referees raised blue flags. Two raised red flags. Depending on where the judges were sitting, they saw the clash of techniques from different angles.

Two judges thought Balidova's punch was first.

Two judges thought May's kick was first.

The head referee would break the tie.

He paused for a second—which to Balidova seemed like an eternity—then pointed toward her and awarded the point.

Balidova had won.

Now it was Balidova's turn to grin. She felt elated. She wanted to celebrate her victory over her sister and, even more importantly, over her internal battle. But with great self-restraint, she held back from pumping her hands in the air. Because staring back at her was a seething mad and hurt older sister, who she knew she had to return home and live with. Instead, she breathed in and out, enjoying the feeling of euphoria flowing through her body.

The two girls bowed to each other, then stepped forward and shook hands curtly, part of the etiquette of a kumite match. Then they turned their backs on each other and returned to their respective sides of the ring.

As Balidova walked off the tatami mat, she spotted her father, who nodded briefly at her. Although she was happy to be recognized by her dad, she had won not for him but for herself. Despite her mixed emotions before, during, and after the fight, she was extremely pleased to have fought her best and held true to what she wanted. She felt a deep sense of satisfaction within.

Maybe love and power aren't so separate after all.

CHAPTER 30
POTIONS

After the karate tournament ended on Sunday afternoon, the Forester family drove home to Kitimat. It was a quiet car ride, with their dad driving and all the girls retreating to their phones rather than talking to each other and risking confrontation. A lot of mixed emotions from both winning and losing swirled in the car. In addition to Balidova winning open weight kumite and May placing second—losing to her sister—April had won the individual kata event. June had placed second in the younger kumite division. Balidova's father would not take sides with one daughter over the other, so he remained neutral. Balidova's mother, sitting in the passenger seat staring out the window, was simply happy that none of her daughters had gotten injured.

The next day, walking through the large front doors of the school, Balidova felt confused. She was disturbed yet happy at the same time, a jumble of emotions coursing through her body. She'd had the best experience—beating her sister in the finals of the Regional Championship—and the worst, most terrifying experience—being attacked by Gus, betrayed by Mr. Winston, and tied to a lamppost, left out in the cold dark night alone—all in the last forty-eight hours.

She cast her eyes down on the linoleum floor as she walked, not wanting to make eye contact with anyone, fearing they would see her confusion and start asking questions she wasn't prepared to answer.

She wanted to tell her classmates about the dragon and the Dragon Tail Breath. The swings back and forth between her two worlds were making her dizzy.

Do I need to keep it all secret anymore? The circle of people who know about the dragon is growing bigger and bigger. Mr. Winston knows, Gus knows, my mom knows, Angel knows, and now May knows.

She paused her train of thought as she focused on the white lines zigzagging across the grey floor.

But I can't possibly tell anyone else. No one will believe me.

She looked realistically at the facts of her situation as she passed by the spot in the hallway where Gus had put up a poster of a dragon's face with a big X through it, mocking her.

I'm already an outcast. Everyone thinks I'm a weirdo. My friendship with Angel is on the rocks again, and I can't trust Mr. Winston. I just beat May, so she's not talking to me, and my other sisters don't usually say much either.

By the time she reached her locker, a feeling of isolation had engulfed her.

I need support from someone.

Removing one set of notebooks from her backpack and grabbing a granola bar that she had stashed in her locker, Balidova noticed how quickly the euphoria she'd felt after beating her sister had faded. As she placed her textbooks in her bag and slung their weight onto her back, she felt burdened by worry. She was aware that she had powers she didn't fully understand. But she also felt a growing doubt about everything she'd learned thus far from Luminora. All the steps of the Dragon Tail Breath... all that

Luminora had taught her... and her relationship with the dragon itself... were cast into question by the fact that she had a task to do—which Luminora hadn't told her about.

Is that the only reason the dragon's teaching me? Because it wants me to do something? Does it even care about me?

Balidova tore open the wrapper of her granola bar and took a bite. *There has to be somebody I can talk to about all this.* She slammed her locker shut and headed off to class.

When she neared her science class, she stopped just before crossing the threshold and setting foot in the room. She knew she'd have to pretend as if nothing had happened, but she also knew the confrontation with her teacher was far from over.

If she went to the police or the principal and said her teacher had attacked her and tied her to a pole, the authorities would ask for evidence, of which she had very little. Her sister had seen her tied up to the pole, but not who'd done it. Besides, she didn't want to drag May into this mess, especially after she'd just beaten her at the tournament.

That meant a showdown between a student's word vs. a teacher's word. She would be drawn into a quagmire of publicity, and everyone would know everything. She'd have to talk about the Dragon Tail Breath and divulge her relationship with Luminora. That was the last thing she wanted.

Balidova crossed her arms, walked into the classroom, and took a seat, eyeing Mr. Winston cautiously. She went about her own business, laying low, not rocking the boat—yet.

What she didn't know is that he was also wary of her—unsure of who she would tell and what she would do next. He had heard through his informants that Balidova had escaped with her sister's help and learned Step Six of the Dragon Tail Breath, despite his efforts to stop her. As a high-level Drakoban, he had eyes in places Balidova did not know about.

Only two weeks of school remained before summer break. Mr.

Winston knew he had one last chance to stop Balidova from learning the final lesson of the Dragon Tail Breath. His only hope rested with a principle of energy that formed the backbone of all scientific teaching:

Energy cannot be created or destroyed. Yet it can be transformed.

He needed to transform Balidova's knowledge of the Dragon Tail Breath before it was too late. Her rising powers could still be converted into dark energy for the Drakoban.

One last way remained.

Luminora had already explained the danger to Balidova. Mr. Winston was embedded with the Drakoban. He was a master of illusion—a seventh-level demon—who gave the impression of light where there was none. This kind of demon was the most treacherous because it was expert at tricking you into thinking it was good. With your defenses down, you would trust it, revealing your secrets, just as Balidova did when she told Mr. Winston more about the dragon lessons than anyone else.

Gus, on the other hand, was merely Mr. Winston's sidekick—a conveniently placed kid who could execute specific tasks that the Drakoban leader needed to be completed. The school bully, yes, but one who didn't think for himself enough to wonder what Mr. Winston was really up to.

And so, Mr. Winston operated unchecked at the school—plotting his last and greatest deception yet. Something he'd been planning for months, ever since he'd met Balidova at the hospital and first learned about her encounter with the wind spirit—an unexpected gift he received when he asked about the rip in her red jacket.

He had slowly but surely been collecting components of a brew—an elixir that would make her forget everything she had learned of the Dragon Tail Breath. She'd be left with only her martial arts training. All the power she had gained from Luminora would be transferred—to him.

The pieces of her that he'd collected were four-fold: a drop of her blood, a piece of her fingernail, a lock of her hair, and a globule of her saliva. He had carefully saved and collected these bits of her in a special metal box, kept in a locked drawer in his desk.

Knowing he could transfer her powers into his was why he'd encouraged her to continue learning in the first place. This was his last chance to exercise his ability before she learned the final step of the Dragon Tail Breath, and it was too late.

AFTER THE BELL rang and all the students left the classroom, Mr. Winston unlocked his desk drawer and pulled out the box. He was holding it in his hands when Gus walked in.

"Mr. Winston, you called me?" Gus said, his long hair swishing from side to side as he strode into the room.

"Yes, Gus. I have a special job for you," Mr. Winston looked up from the metal box, straight into the boy's eyes, as if testing to see whether or not he would be up for the task.

"Another one?" Gus responded, chewing a wad of pink bubble gum.

"Yes, one last task before the school year ends," Mr. Winston smiled slyly, caressing the box with his hands.

Gus paused for a moment. "Okay, I'm up for it. Who does it involve this time?"

"Let's just say, our dearest friend."

"Oh, her again." Gus blew a bubble with his gum, and when it got huge, let it burst with a loud pop. "Aren't we done with her? We gave her a pretty good scare last time. I don't think she's gonna bother us anymore."

"You underestimate her." Mr. Winston carried the box over to one of the lab tables and placed it on the smooth, black countertop, where it landed with a clink.

"Maybe," Gus shrugged, thinking of the solid kick in the gut he'd given her. "My dad doesn't like her either." Gus followed him. "She saw him hunting the spirit bear, illegally, a few months back. Big fine if you get caught, and he doesn't have the money. He'd rather she forget all that, if you know what I mean."

"Well, isn't that perfect then." Mr. Winston pulled a blow torch, beaker, and glass vial from the cupboard under the table. "Because what I'm about to make is a *Forget Potion*. When you place all these ingredients—which I collected from her person—in a flask, and join them together with water raised to the boiling point, and add a little dark magic," he chuckled, "they create a potion that will make her forget everything about the Dragon Tail Breath. Everything she's learned from the Dragons of Light will come to me instead."

"Whoa, that's epic!" Gus looked surprised at Mr. Winston's ingenuity. "Is that why we needed to cut a piece of her hair the other night?"

"Yes," Mr. Winston replied, turning on the blowtorch and placing it next to the beaker. He filled the beaker with a bit of water, then dropped all the ingredients from the box into it. Finally, he added a drop of his own blood. As the water heated up, the red blood cells broke down and created a ribbon-like thread of color through the liquid. The saliva dissolved, and little bits of hair and fingernail swished around the bubbling mixture. It boiled for a while, then Mr. Winston turned off the flame, said some unintelligible words, poured the contents of the beaker into a small vial, and placed a stopper on it. He held it up toward Gus, letting it cool as he showed the boy.

"Your job is to make sure she drinks it."

"And what do I get out of it?" Gus said, never one to miss seizing an opportunity to advance himself.

"You get not to be reported for assaulting a fellow student," Mr. Winston growled, his face quickly turning to a frown as he stared through the boy's cold blue eyes. He did not like Gus questioning his authority.

Gus paused, reconsidering his position in the face of Mr. Winston's threat. "Yeah, I think I can come up with a way to get that done." He nodded slowly, a wry smile sliding across his lips.

"Well then, here you go." Mr. Winston carefully handed him the vial. "All you have to do is get her to drink this. How you do it is your business. Whether you do it is my business. Do. Not. Fail." He spoke the last words slowly, emphasizing each one, as he stared at Gus with a menacing look in his eyes.

Gus was momentarily taken aback by Mr. Winston's intensity. Then the boy shuffled his feet, stood tall, and collected himself. He, too, was a master of manipulation. He looked the teacher straight back in the eyes. "Okay, Mr. Winston. I got it." He would do Mr. Winston's bidding but work the situation for his purposes as well. He had his own reasons to dress Balidova down—so she couldn't tell on his dad, and he could establish *himself* as the toughest kid in the school, permanently, with no one to oppose him.

Right then, Angel walked toward the classroom. She had science with Mr. Winston immediately after Balidova. She saw Gus holding a small vial and putting it carefully in his backpack. He held it as if it was hot. As she peeked in the room, she saw Mr. Winston put some equipment away and take a metal box from the lab table, placing it back in his desk drawer.

"That's weird," she whispered to herself. "Looks like they just made something. I wonder what it is?" She looked closer, trying to figure it out, but couldn't. "Oh well, maybe later." She stepped inside the science lab and put it out of her mind.

A COUPLE WEEKS LATER, on the last day of school before summer break, Balidova was joking around with the kitchen staff in the cafeteria as they doled out her food. Since nearly all the students had ostracized her, she'd made friends with the adults who fed her.

"Can you believe this is my last lunch in this place for the whole school year?" she said, grabbing a green juice to go with her burger.

"Isn't that great?" one staff member replied. "No more rock-hard pizza slices or rubbery chicken!"

"Hmph," Balidova smirked. "No more chips or licorice from the vending machine either."

Angel walked into the cafeteria and spotted Balidova sitting alone, her green juice open on the table.

CRASH!!

At the other end of the cafeteria, someone in the food line dropped their tray and everything on it. Two kids in the line started shouting and swinging at each other while other students ran over to watch the fight. Balidova moved toward the ruckus as well, thinking she might be able to break it up.

Amidst all the commotion, when Balidova was far enough from her drink, Gus snuck up and poured something into it. Balidova didn't see him because she was facing the opposite direction, paying attention to the fight going on at the other end of the cafeteria.

But Angel saw it from across the room.

A few moments later, Balidova—realizing it was just a member of Gus's gang who was creating all that trouble—returned to her seat, grabbed her juice, and put it to her lips, ready to take a sip.

Gus watched her from about forty feet away.

"Balidova, stop!" Angel yelled. She ran over to her friend, grabbed her arm, and yanked the juice bottle from her mouth.

"Angel, what's going on? Take it easy. I'm just drinking my juice! I know we're not on the best of terms, but don't you think that's a little aggressive?"

Angel pulled up a chair and sat down next to Balidova, lowering her voice to a whisper. "No. I don't. I saw Gus drop something in there."

Suddenly Angel remembered what she saw outside the science classroom a couple weeks earlier, and it clicked. "The vial—that's what Gus was gonna do with the vial."

"What vial?" Balidova looked puzzled.

"I saw Gus leave Mr. Winston's class with it a few weeks ago," Angel explained. "When I peeked into the science room, I saw Mr. Winston cleaning up some equipment, like he'd just made something. Then he carried a metal box back to his desk and put it in his drawer."

Balidova wrinkled her brow as if she remembered something too. She also spoke in hushed tones. "A metal box...." She paused for a moment, then lit up as the memory came back to her. "That's the box he put my fingernail in!"

"What fingernail?" Angel asked as quietly as she could, although she had to raise her voice. The cafeteria had erupted into total chaos with students throwing food at each other.

"He asked me for a piece of my fingernail months ago. Weird, huh? And that piece of glass—the broken prism—had a drop of my blood on it." It was all flooding into Balidova's mind now. "Luminora told me about a potion that requires four parts of me. That's why they cut a piece of my hair when they tied me to the lamppost."

Balidova's eyes went wide.

"What is it?" Angel asked, worried for her friend.

"That's why he laughed when I spit on him. He said, 'you don't know what you've just given me—a gift.' They needed a drop of my saliva! And I just gave it to him—the last part of the potion." Balidova smacked her forehead with her palm. "Thanks, Angel." She turned to face her friend, placing both hands on Angel's shoulders. Their eyes locked as their heads drew near. "You saved me from the potion. I woulda lost everything I've learned so far about the Dragon Tail Breath. You have no idea how important this is. Luminora explained the potion to me." Balidova spoke with sincere gratitude in her voice.

"Glad to be of service," Angel smiled, tossing her strawberry blonde hair behind her shoulders. "But wait, if Luminora explained the potion to you, then the dragon already knew this would happen?"

"I don't know." Balidova dropped her hands from Angel's shoulders. "Maybe—but it doesn't make sense. Why wouldn't the dragon stop Mr. Winston from making the potion in the first place?"

"Hmph," they said simultaneously. Neither of them had an answer. Somehow, their combined puzzlement only drew the two friends closer together. They looked at each other, shrugged, then grinned.

Gus was standing nearby, watching them.

What Balidova didn't know is that Gus would soon face Mr. Winston's wrath for failing to deliver the *Forget Potion*. Mr. Winston knew what the boy cherished most, and he would take that away. Not his science grade. Not his ability to get away with assaulting Balidova. Not even his relationship with his father. But his reputation as the meanest, toughest guy at school—the leader of the east side door boy's gang. Mr. Winston would take away from Gus the only bit of self-respect and confidence the boy had, by exposing his weakness to the student body.

As a member of the Drakoban, Mr. Winston had certain powers—the ability to read a person's energy field and know what had happened in their past, was one of them. He knew about the butterflies in Gus's youth. He knew about the friendship between Gus and Balidova. And he would tell everyone. And after punishing and humiliating Gus, the Drakoban leader would take on the task he'd given the boy himself, and find another way to transform Balidova's growing power.

BALIDOVA AND ANGEL got up from the table and walked out of the lunch room together, one last time before summer break. Upon reaching their lockers, they stopped by the side of the hallway in a huddle, and Balidova turned to face her friend.

"You know, Angel. Even though you told Gus about the dragon when you weren't supposed to, you saved me just now."

Angel grinned and nodded her head. "Yeah, even though you didn't stand up for me when Gus first pushed me, you kicked his butt later."

"I guess we've both let each other down, haven't we?" Balidova looked down sheepishly.

"And we've both propped each other up," Angel replied cheerily.

"Yeah," they both smiled.

"It feels better to be there for each other than not, doesn't it?" Balidova said, examining her friend in the eyes.

Angel replied by holding out her pinky finger. "Let's make a promise to always be there for each other. No more bickering and no more secrets, okay?"

"You got it." Balidova held up her baby finger. They interlocked pinkies and did their signature handshake.

Turning to leave, Balidova said, "You know Angel, there's something I wanna tell you." Balidova felt like she could trust Angel now, and she desperately needed to trust someone at school. She couldn't keep all this info to herself. Nor did she want to keep secrets from her best friend anymore.

"You know Mr. Winston?"

"Yeah."

"He's part of the Drakoban," Balidova said, dropping her voice.

"The what?" Angel looked startled. She didn't know what it meant, but the way Balidova said it, the word sounded ominous.

"Remember what I was telling you about Luminora and the Dragons of Light? Well, there's the opposite also. The Order of Dark Dragons—the Drakoban. They're trying to cover the earth in a Cloak of Fear so all human souls will be trapped in fear forever." Balidova blurted out the whole thing in one breath, then sucked in a lungful of air, bracing herself for the flurry of questions she knew would come.

"Whoa, that's heavy," Angel took a step back, lacing her fingers around the shoulder straps of her backpack as if to steady herself from the weight of the idea. She adjusted her feet on the floor and breathed in slowly. Then let out a long, slow exhale. Unexpectedly, her eyes lit up. "I wonder if the Cloak of Fear affected *me* when I was so mad at you. I mean, why else would I turn against my best friend?!"

"Good question. I don't know, but Luminora did say that the Cloak of Fear affects everyone by bringing out their worst." Balidova pursed her lips. "That's partly why Gus and Mr. Winston attacked me. It affected them too."

"That's pretty sick," Angel continued. "I mean, people would really get messed up if there was no hope of feeling good anymore. What would stop everyone from turning into jerks and monsters?"

"Yeah, no kidding." Balidova leaned in close. "You already know that I've been learning the Dragon Tail Breath. It's the only thing that can stop them. But I have to learn all seven steps before the seventh moon of this year passes. Otherwise, it'll be too late."

Angel stood speechless in the hallway, staring at Balidova,

deciding whether to believe this new twist in the story. "Now there's a deadline to saving the world?"

Eventually, Angel took a deep breath. As she exhaled, she released all the doubt that had built up about Balidova before. Every time she'd doubted her friend, Balidova had come back stronger. "Okay, yeah," she said, encouragingly. "I have a million more questions, but okay, go on."

Buoyed by her friend's faith—or was it just curiosity?—Balidova continued with her story. "Mr. Winston and Gus came after me during the tournament in Prince Rupert because they didn't want me learning the next step of the Dragon Tail Breath."

Angel paused, dumbfounded. "Why? Why's it such a big deal?"

Now it was Balidova's turn to pause. "Because I'm 'the one'."

"The one what?"

"The one who has to defeat the Drakoban by shattering the Cloak of Fear."

"Whoa. Are you serious? How the heck are you gonna do that? Angel whispered. "Isn't the Drakoban—the order of dark dragons—super powerful? That sounds intense."

"I dunno. But here's the thing," Balidova said, leaning in toward her friend. "Luminora didn't tell me any of this until a few weeks ago. I feel like I've been led on." She stepped back to get a good look at Angel so she could examine her friend's body language before asking the next question. "Am I being played? Is Luminora just using me to save the planet, or does the dragon actually care about me?"

Angel didn't respond right away. She was taking it all in—processing the fact that her friend, Balidova Forester, was the one who had to take on this impossible task. She began walking down the hall toward class. Balidova followed her.

"It makes me wonder if everything I've been learning is true?" Balidova continued, speaking quietly. "If Luminora does believe in me. If the dragon does think I'm capable. If I really am 'the one.' It just makes me question everything and wonder if I can do it." Balidova held her books tight to her chest as they passed other students in the hallway, creating a shield between herself and all the expectations of the outside world.

Angel stopped and turned to face her friend. "Well, can you? I mean, *I* believe in you, Balidova. Come on—you're Balidova Forester!" As Angel spoke, it all became clear. "You're my best friend. What's not to believe in?" She smiled and pushed Balidova gently on the shoulder." If you can beat Gus and your sister, you can learn the Dragon Tail Breath and destroy the Cloak of Fear. After all we've been through, are you seriously going to let yourself be taken down by your fears and doubts?"

Balidova noticed Angel's use of the word 'we.' It gave her strength. She couldn't do this alone, even though she knew she had to.

"I guess that's what's happening, isn't it?" Balidova said as they continued walking, glad to have her friend act as a mirror for her so that she could see her thoughts.

"Come on, Balidova, you can do it. When did you say the last lesson is? On the full moon?" By now, they had reached the outer door of the school, and both girls stepped outside. Angel looked up into the sky, where the faint outline of a crescent moon was visible.

Balidova followed her friend's gaze above the treetops. All of a sudden, she spotted a bald eagle looking straight at her. Its stare was so piercing that it unnerved her. She let out a rush of air from her lungs as if she'd been holding her breath for a long time.

"Okay. I'll do it."

Balidova clenched her fingers into a fist so tight that her fingernails dug into her palms. "I can do this," she muttered, taking one last deep breath. "But I don't have much time to learn the last step."

More than telling Angel, she was convincing herself with the sound of her voice.

"What was that?" Angel asked.

"I can do this," Balidova repeated, louder.

"Yes, you can," Angel smiled at her.

"Yes, I can." Balidova repeated the words slowly, letting each one roll off her tongue. "Yes. I. Can."

At that moment, seeing the sunlight along with the moon, she remembered that today wasn't just the last day of school. It was special for another reason. Today was a marker between seasons, and from one half of the year to the next—a transition point. It felt odd to talk of dark dragons on the Summer Solstice, the longest day of the year—the one with the most light.

Suddenly, Balidova realized that true friends are like bright lights, guiding you to do the things you might not otherwise have the courage to do.

Angel's right.

She smiled, straightening her back and holding her head up high. She thought of the six steps of the Dragon Tail Breath she'd learned already.

I can do this.

I do have the dragon magic in me.

CHAPTER 31
PURPLE LIGHT CROWN

The full moon arrived soon enough—on the first weekend of July. Balidova got up and put on a pair of grey sweatpants and a purple long-sleeve t-shirt. Today was a rare day when there was no karate, no school, and fewer barn chores for her. School was on break for the summer, karate was on the back burner for the long weekend, and today was her eldest sister's turn to do the morning feed. Her only job was to muck the horses' stalls. But she could do that later.

As she changed out of her pajamas, Balidova felt goosebumps appear down her arms, even on the soft inner fleshy side—not because she was cold, but because she was excited.

For some strange reason, she grabbed her slingshot and the rock the spirit bear gave her and stuffed them both in her back pocket. Maybe she'd find more rocks along the way and do some target practice. She tiptoed downstairs before anyone in her family woke up. Stealthily, she made her way down the hallway and out the side door without even brushing her teeth. She had to get to the meadow as soon as possible to tell Luminora about her newfound confidence. She *could* learn the final step of the Dragon

Tail Breath and shatter the Cloak of Fear. She *believed* in herself. She *knew* she had the dragon magic in her.

As soon as she was outside, she took a deep breath of fresh morning air. Nutmeg came bounding up, ready to accompany her on the adventure, but she commanded him to stay put.

"I don't want you scaring Luminora away," she said to him.

A moment later, she realized how ridiculous that sounded. She laughed, rubbing Nutmeg's ears, tempted to change her mind.

"Naw, I still don't need you coming with me." She tied him up as he looked at her curiously, sensing something different about her. She patted him on the head, looked him straight in the eyes, and said, "Nutmeg, you stay here and guard the house, okay? I'll be back soon."

In a split second, Balidova spun around and took off at a full sprint across the backyard, past the horse paddocks, and down to the edge of the wood. She paused briefly to find the trail, saw it, then took off again as fast as she could run through the forest. She was 80% sure she was going the right way, and didn't bother giving herself time to worry about the 20% of doubt that crept in.

'*Don't think, feel...*' the dragon said.

"Feel your way through Balidova. Feel your way through," she said to herself out loud, confirming the idea with her voice.

She used all her senses to guide her. The sight of familiar trees, logs, and stones, the smell of the cedar and pine groves, the movement of her body along the path, and the rhythm of the turns. She also used her intuitive and knowing senses. When she wasn't sure which way to go, she tuned into the subtle feeling within her pulling her this way or that, without giving her rational mind time to override it.

Before long, she saw rays of morning sun rising above the horizon and peeking through the trees, illuminating the clearing beyond. She picked up her pace and burst into the meadow at full speed.

She couldn't contain her happiness and just kept running, doing laps around the meadow—arms spread out wide as she ran, touching the tall summer grass. She made long, graceful strides through the wildflowers as birds, insects, and leaves rose up to meet her, sharing her joy.

Balidova loved this place.

She kept running at full gallop, unleashing her exuberance into the open space. Sunlight streamed through the trees, flickering in her face. The wind ran its fingers through her hair.

Freedom.

When she started to tire, she slowed to a jog, then a walk, and finally stopped, bent over with her hands on her knees—panting for air.

About a minute later, after catching her breath, she stood up straight, stretched her arms wide, and faced the sun full on. Soft, golden rays stared her directly in the face and washed over her. She stood still, letting mother nature's love in.

Then she tilted her head back and called the dragon.

"Luminoraaaaa!" she sang, without a hint of desperation in her voice. Pure, unleashed joy spilled from her mouth. She held the final vowel until she ran out of breath. Then brought both hands to her heart and bowed her head in a moment of gratitude.

Out of the corner of her eye, she saw a speck in the sky. As she turned to look, it became bigger and bigger until she could see the color and shape of a flying object.

Is that what I think it is?

But as it came closer, she realized it wasn't a dragon. It was a hawk. She ducked at the last second as it flew over her. When she stood up, she saw a piece of paper on the ground. The bird had dropped a message for her. She unfolded the paper and read the words. Once again, she wished she had her golden frames:

*Meet me where
the light does not reach
save for the rocks
that glow from within.*

Balidova looked up to the sky for more signs, but the hawk had disappeared. The message was clearly from Luminora. But what did it mean? It didn't make sense to her. Another riddle?

Sobered by her uncertainty, the girl clutched the paper in hand and looked around the meadow. Seeing no clues, she headed toward home, thinking about the words the whole way.

For the rest of the day, pulling weeds in the vegetable garden, then helping her dad fix the tractor, the note was all Balidova could think of. By late afternoon, after trying one answer after another in her mind, she had a flash of insight while mucking the horse's stalls.

She noticed how nuggets of fresh horse manure produced heat from within. She thought of other things that lit up from the inside. *Compost and poop both produce heat from fermenting organic matter. Is there something that produces light from a natural process? Luminora's name means 'gift of light.'*

She mulled the name around in her head.

Luminora... Luminous... Luminescence! Isn't that when something lights up from the inside? From a chemical reaction or something? Like fireflies! Wait, no, that can't be it. The riddle says, "Rocks that glow," not "Bugs that glow."

"Oh, I know where it is!" she barked suddenly.

Melody lifted her head from munching on hay to look at Balidova, then returned to her meal.

'Where light does not reach,' that must be underground—a cave or

a tunnel. 'Save for the rocks that glow from within.' I've heard about a crystal cave where luminescent rocks glow—never been in there myself because I was always too scared. Is that what Luminora's talking about?

She threw down her pitchfork and ran to the door of Melody's stall. Then paused for a moment, turned back, grabbed her pitchfork, and stood it up in the hallway. *I don't want Melody stepping on it and getting lame.*

Careful to make sure all the stall doors were shut, Balidova exited the barn and took off at a sprint. She grabbed her bike from the garage and jumped on when she stopped, ran to the house, and flung open the side door.

"Mom, I'm going for a bike ride," she yelled.

"Okay, but did you finish the stalls?" her mom yelled back.

"Yes. I'll be back before dinner!" Balidova slammed the door and tore out the driveway before her mom could change her mind. *The stalls are mostly done. Not perfect, but good enough,* she smiled mischievously.

SHE PEDALED down the street as fast as she could. The crystal cave entrance was on the outskirts of Cablecar, just far enough for her to be breathing heavily by the time she got there.

When she arrived at the entrance to the cave, she jumped off her bike and threw it down, staring into the big black hole. *No wonder I've never been in here. It's so dark and spooky.*

As air filtered back into her lungs, courage slowly gathered in her heart. She looked up into the sky and saw the familiar white circle of the moon, faintly outlined in the late afternoon light. Taking a deep breath, she walked toward the cave and entered the underground world.

A swarm of bats flew out of the cave, startling her, but she squelched down her fears and continued on.

"Sorry to disturb your home, but that makes more space for Luminora and me," she said to the odd-looking creatures.

Her eyes adjusting to the darkness, Balidova called Luminora, at first with her voice, then again, silently, deliberately talking to the dragon with her mind. As she tuned in, a part of her sensed that Luminora was already there watching her. With each step the girl took, she sensed that Luminora was very close, waiting for her to realize the dragon had been there all along.

Balidova walked further into the cave and came upon a large, glowing rock amidst a sea of glittering stones. At that point, the cave opened up to a large cavern. Crystals lined all sides of the enormous space, including the ceiling. Balidova's jaw dropped as she looked up and around, in awe of the sea of luminescent stones. She stood still for a moment, enraptured by the twinkling light.

Just then, she sensed the presence of something large, even though she couldn't see it. Spinning around, she saw the dragon's silhouette against the cave wall.

Balidova gasped. "I knew it! You're here!"

Luminora stepped toward her. "Greetings Balidova. I see that you solved the riddle."

Balidova stepped toward the dragon. "Yes, I did." She paused. "And I sensed that you were here."

"Good, good." Luminora chuckled. "Your *knowing* sense is getting stronger."

"I have something to share with you."

"What is it?"

The girl looked down at her feet and said, "I know I'm the one." She paused, releasing a deep sigh. "But I'm not sure I can do it."

"Do what?" The dragon seemed unperturbed.

"Shatter the Cloak of Fear. How's one person supposed to destroy something that's taking over the whole planet?

"Focus on overcoming your own fears, Balidova. Like you did when you ventured into this cave."

"How's that gonna change anything?"

"It changes more than you know," Luminora chuckled. "Everything is connected, remember? When you overcome your fears, it inspires others to overcome theirs. Soon enough, the whole system of fear topples."

The dragon paused a moment to adjust its grip on the rocks with its long talons. "Shall we continue then?"

"With what?"

"The Dragon Tail Breath."

"Oh yeah, of course," Balidova laughed.

"The final step—seven," Luminora announced solemnly.

Balidova released a whoosh of air as if she were releasing any remaining hesitation she had.

"Okay, let's go."

The girl knew there was very little time between her and the monumental task she'd been assigned to complete. Tonight was the seventh full moon after her twelfth birthday.

"A little more enthusiasm, perhaps?" Luminora suggested. "You're about to learn a secret passed down for thousands of years to only a select few. A secret that carries the ability to harness infinite power within."

BALIDOVA RELEASED another stream of air from her mouth. "It's almost too much to take in."

"Well then, we'd better get started. Show me that you know the first six steps."

Balidova raised her arms above her head, reaching as high as they would go and making her body as big as possible. Then she brought her arms down by her sides, tracing a circle around her until she stood tall and strong. She wanted to DO the breathing as she recounted the steps to the dragon. This wasn't just a mental exercise but a whole-body experience. She needed to convince herself, more than anyone, that she could do it.

"Okay, here goes—Step One. Breathe in emerald green light through my heart. *All is well.*" Balidova inhaled deeply and exhaled with a whoosh. Her whole body filled with light, and she stood taller and straighter.

"Step Two. Breathe in golden light through my solar plexus. *Here now.*" She inhaled deeply again. And as she exhaled, she closed her eyes to absorb the calm feeling that began to drift through her.

"Step Three. Breathe in blue light through my throat. *What do I want?*" She smiled, just thinking of the possibility that she could have what she wanted. Merely asking the question made her feel more powerful.

"Step Four. Breathe orange light in through the tanden. *I am a powerful creator.*" She felt it now. Orange light washed over her entire body, starting from her belly and spreading everywhere—up to her head and down to her toes, forming a belt of energy around her hips.

This feels like a belt of power—kinda like my karate belt. Not a scary power, but a loving power.

Balidova's karate lessons and dragon lessons were merging within her now. She breathed out, basking and settling into the vibe of that loving power.

It anchored her.

She felt stable and steady in the orange light, and all the colors she had breathed into her body so far. She took a few more deep breaths, wanting to stay in this moment.

The dragon nudged her with its snout, and Balidova was shaken out of her reverie. She glanced at the orangy-yellow eyes and green scales of the dragon.

Those are the colors I just breathed in.

"Step Five. Breathe indigo light through the third eye, and see with my inner vision. *I Know.*" A rich, cobalt blue light spread over her body like a deep ocean of peace, covering her with brilliant blue. She took several more deep breaths, basking in the knowing vibe.

"Step Six. Breathe red light in through the root of me, letting it shoot up my whole torso like an explosion of fireworks. *I love and accept myself.*" She felt a beam of light go through her entire being, like a pillar of light forming the center of her core, shining out in all directions.

She opened her eyes. "Those are the six steps so far."

"Yes, yes." Luminora nodded with a chuckle. "And to finish it off, Step Seven will take the whole thing to another level, connecting you firmly with everything around you and the heavens, anchoring you completely in the dragon magic." With its talon, the dragon tapped on a large icicle-shaped stalactite that hung down from the cave's ceiling. It made a deep, musical bell sound that resonated throughout the underground cavern.

Balidova could feel a powerful energy swirling within her. She desperately wanted something to anchor, solidify, and secure it to her for good. She listened to the ethereal bell tone for a long while.

When the sound finally faded, Balidova asked quietly, "What is Step Seven?"

Luminora looked at her. This young girl was the one.

She had demonstrated a consciousness—of herself, the world around, and the magic—coming this far. She had traveled a great distance inside herself since their first encounter, yet she still had a long way to go. Would she be able to do it? Defeat the Drakoban by shattering the Cloak of Fear? Would she stay true to the magic? And to herself? And use it only for good?

The magic of the Dragon Tail Breath carried within it the possibility of darkness too. Balidova had already demonstrated a desire for revenge—the ability to hate. Some were seduced by the tremendous power of the dragon magic. Would Balidova fall prey to that temptation, like those who had gone before her? Luminora examined the girl in her simple purple shirt and grey pants... her carefree ponytail and brown eyes... her eager expression and calloused hands... and decided to take that risk.

"STEP SEVEN. Breathe purple light into the top of your head. Bring that light straight down from the sky through your entire body, from the top of your head into your neck and shoulders, torso and arms, right down to your fingertips."

The dragon spread its wings wide, raising them to touch the top of the cave. "Bring the light down through your chest, belly, and hips, into your legs and knees, right down into your ankles, feet, and toes. Let that light travel down into the earth's aura, about a foot above the ground."

The dragon lowered its wings and lay them open on the jagged rocky surface, bending its legs as it pressed its body to the cave floor. "Wrap this purple light around the earth as you ground into the earth's energy field."

Balidova stood quiet and still, marinating in an incredible feeling. Ribbons of light danced through her whole body.

After a full minute, she spoke.

"Why not ground straight into the earth itself?"

"The earth has become polluted, but the earth's energy field remains pure," Luminora explained. "If you ground into the earth itself, you will pick up the vibration of chaos. But if you ground into the earth's aura, you will pick up the vibration of *Pure Uncon-*

ditional Love." Luminora stretched one paw out in front and drew it back, as if pulling something toward itself.

"Connect the energy of the heavens, through your body, with the pure unconditional love of Mother Earth. Anchor yourself between these two. Balance yourself between earth and sky. Pull up the loving mother energy from the earth, and pull down the powerful dragon energy from the sky. Allow these energies to form a pair within you. Combine your true passions with your magical ways, and combine your wisdom and communicative power, into one. Speak the words *I AM ME* out loud as you do this."

"I can feel it! As you were talking, I was doing it." Balidova said excitedly.

"I can feel the magic within me! I can feel the power of the earth and the sky coming together inside of me. It feels like an hourglass, with big energy pouring down through my head, spreading through my body like an inverted triangle wave. And this incredible energy is coming up into me from the ground. Both these energies merge right in the center of my heart—a wave coming down and a wave moving up. The colors of the rainbow spreading out in all directions—front, back, left, right, up, down. I *am* me!!"

"Yes, you have this ability, Balidova. You have the power within you to channel the light from the earth and the sky, and spread it around in all directions. Send it out through your powerfully loving heart. Your *lovingly powerful* heart," Luminora declared.

Balidova could barely move. The vibe transfixed her—it was so strong. It pressed on her skin like clay, holding her firmly and molding her into who she wanted to be.

"I feel like I can do anything from this place," she said. "I feel strong, calm, happy. This feels like me."

"The energy is holding space for you, Balidova." The dragon

spread its wings wide, cave light reflecting off its scales in beautiful gold, green, and violet hues. "It's a calm, stable, steady place for you to be YOU."

Balidova closed her eyes, "I can feel it in my body. The energy feels warm and firm, like I'm standing on a solid foundation of peace." She was quiet for a moment, soaking in the feeling.

She opened her eyes. "Thank you. I wish I could hang onto this feeling forever."

"But you can. That's what we're doing here in the crystal cave. That's what I'm showing you. That's what you're doing every time you go back home. Your family is helping you *practice*. Be grateful for the opportunity, Balidova, *grateful* for the opportunity."

Balidova didn't fully understand the dragon's words. "So that's it then? That's the whole seven steps of the Dragon Tail Breath?"

"Yes, Balidova, it is."

"So, that's the end?"

The dragon laughed, a big bellowing laugh, which echoed through the entire cave. "No, dear one. This is just the beginning. Now you know enough to make use of the magic. I have a gift for you, for completing all seven steps."

"What is it?" Balidova asked eagerly.

From behind its wing, Luminora handed her a purple stone. It was slightly larger than a chicken egg, in the rough shape of a triangle. Balidova held the rock, its jagged edges digging into her skin.

"A purple amethyst crystal. It cures nightmares, dispels fears, and enhances intuition. Keep it close to you always."

"Wow. It's beautiful. Thank you." Balidova touched the surface of the stone with her fingertips. She could feel an unusual energy pulsing from it. "So, this rock symbolizes the whole of the Dragon Tail Breath?"

"Do you know why it's called the Dragon Tail Breath?" Luminora asked.

"Why?"

"I will show you. But first, you must demonstrate that you are mastering the elements of yourself—body, mind, and spirit. Solve this riddle and meet me before the full moon passes, before the Cloak of Fear seals over the earth. Before it is too late, Balidova. You have one final task to complete tonight."

Meet me by the oldest cedar tree.
When you stand on its firm ground,
You'll be ready to fly with me.

Balidova turned around to look at the glimmering stones inside the cave. "What does that even mean, anyway?"

When she turned back, the dragon was gone. "Luminora! You can't keep disappearing on me!" she shouted.

All she heard was an echo along the cave walls, *Meet me by the oldest cedar tree.*

She stood alone for a while in the darkness, entranced by the glowing lights, the Dragon Tail Breath, and thoughts of Luminora.

Eventually, she left the underground cavern, blinking her eyes in the evening light. It was 6:00 p.m. now. As daylight waned, a ray of clear silver moonlight illuminated her path. She looked up at the white orb, noticing the shaded spots on its face.

The Crystal Moon.

"I'm naming you after the stone Luminora gave me," she spoke aloud as she held the purple rock up to the sky. She felt the luminescence of the glowing crystal within her—breathing the seven colors of light through the seven energy centers of her body had sparked a chemical reaction within, causing her to light up from the inside out.

Because even in the darkest places, there is light.

CHAPTER 32
THE OLDEST CEDAR

Outside the cave, Balidova held the amethyst carefully in the palm of her hand. The rock glowed, as did the full moon—a sky crystal that became more and more visible as the sun descended.

All at once, the gravity of the situation struck her. Tonight was the seventh full moon of the year. Tonight, she'd learned the seventh and final step of the Dragon Tail Breath. Tonight, she had to shatter the Cloak of Fear. She went over the clues Luminora had given her for the task she was to complete:

Meet me by the oldest cedar tree.
When you stand on its firm ground,
You'll be ready to fly with me.

Inhale.
Exhale.
Looking down, she noticed a caterpillar crawling across the dirt. She watched it for a few seconds, the tiny insect distracting the girl from her negative thoughts. She examined the bug

intently as its many legs moved in unison, making slow but steady progress toward its destination.

At that moment, Balidova thought of how she had made progress too. She'd solved the dragon's riddles in the past. She'd learned the seven steps of the Dragon Tail Breath over the past seven months, despite all the circumstances and people who nearly stopped her. She thought about all the things she once thought she couldn't do, which were now a part of her story—even slowing down to take a deep breath.

"When you're a butterfly, you'll be able to go way faster," she said to the little creature. "This crawling stuff will be a thing of the past because you'll be flying."

Suddenly, an idea popped into her head, and she looked up. *Wait a second, aren't the oldest trees also the tallest? I read that about the giant Sequoias in California. The biggest ones have lived for thousands of years and reach over 300 feet.*

She looked for the caterpillar again, but it had already disappeared. *How am I supposed to tell which is the tallest tree when I can hardly see five feet in front of me? Maybe that's the point,* she wondered. *I need to get up high. I need a better view of the whole area. Where can I do that? I can't climb any of these trees. Their branches start too far up. There's no place to get a good foothold—it's too dangerous.*

She looked around, searching for clues, then remembered.

"The water tower. I can climb up the water tower to get a better view!"

Placing the crystal in her pocket, she jumped on her bike and pedaled through the streets of Cablecar as fast as her legs would take her. She knew the roads well and could easily navigate in the evening light. She cut through her family's backyard and headed straight for the water tower at the far side of the property, past the riding ring. She didn't bother going in the house. It was only

6:00 p.m. and not yet dinner time, so her mom wasn't expecting her to be home.

She made her way up the wooden ladder to the three-foot-wide walkway encircling the entire structure. Thirty feet up, she could see past the treetops. She walked around the tower but felt disappointed. All the trees looked the same. None of them stood out in the sea of green that stretched as far as her eyes could see.

"There are thousands of trees in this forest," she moaned. "And even if I can see the tallest tree, how am I supposed to tell if it's a cedar?"

Balidova sat on the walkway around the water tower, dangling her feet over the edge. She wasn't scared of heights. She loved being right on the edge—between fear and excitement—the same feeling she had when she stepped into the ring for a kumite match.

Swinging her legs back and forth, she heard a cawing sound.

She looked up to see a single black bird staring at her from ten feet away. Its dark feathers blended into the fading evening light. As it flew off, she followed the silhouette with her eyes.

In an instant, she knew what it was trying to tell her. In precisely the same direction the raven was flying, she saw the white flash of a bald-headed bird in the distance.

"Eagle! Eagles nest in the tallest trees. If I find the nest, I'll find what I'm looking for!" Excited, she stood up, nearly losing her balance on the ledge. She scanned the skies again, but no flecks of white were visible, so she sat back down and waited.

Inhale.

Exhale.

Slowly, she calmed down.

A few deep breaths later, everything became more vivid—her senses had turned up a notch. She immediately noticed the silhouette of a lone bird soaring across the horizon, coming closer and closer to her. It circled, then landed on a treetop about a mile away. Soon after, it was joined by another.

That must be a nest. And the tree those birds are sitting on... it seems a bit taller than the others. But it's in a part of the forest I haven't been to before. Is that the tree I'm looking for?

She scanned inside herself. Her body felt good, expansive, warm, and tingly.

That's a yes.

Without giving herself time to question her gut feeling, she took action.

Okay, let's go.

Balidova climbed down from the tower and set off toward the opposite end of the yard that led to the meadow. A short way into the forest, she stopped. *How am I supposed to find the tree? There's no path here. It's just overgrown brush.* She realized she would have to go slowly and follow her intuition.

"Look at where the moon is, Balidova. Keep moving in that direction, with the moon on your right. If you do that, you'll be going in the same direction." She was talking to herself again, as if she were two people: one who knew the way and one who didn't.

She used her sense of smell. Trees grew in groves. A tall cedar would be surrounded by other cedars, with a distinctive woodsy scent, unlike hemlock, spruce, or pine. She could tell it apart because it was her favorite type of evergreen.

She made her way through the woods deliberately, tuning in to how she felt. She paid attention to the moon, the smell, and all her senses—physical, intuitive, and knowing. With each step, she felt an inner pull—subtle yet distinct. When the pull got weaker, she changed directions until it felt stronger again—an inner compass leading her in the right direction.

At one point, she thought she was lost. She got mad at the forest and shouted at Luminora in her mind. Frustrated, she kicked the branches on the forest floor.

THE OLDEST CEDAR

"What am I doing alone in the woods?" she wondered aloud. "There are wolves and bears in here." Afraid, she glanced up at the full moon for guidance and saw clouds beginning to cover it.

She recounted the ancient legend. *'Before seven moons pass in the twelfth year.'*

"I'm running out of time." Balidova looked around the unfamiliar section of forest, unsure of what to do next.

"Focus, girl, focus!" she admonished herself.

"I want to see Luminora again," she announced clearly.

"*'Meet me by the oldest cedar tree,'* that's what Luminora said."

She had to complete the task, for herself and for Luminora. With even more determination, she plunged into the underbrush.

"Show me the tree!" she demanded to the forest, Mother Nature, and whoever would listen. She was deep into the valley now, in the shadow of the mountains which rose around her—a part of the forest she'd not traversed before.

Trudging through the unfamiliar woods, her determination started to wane. She began to feel lost and alone. Her body tensed and seemed to get smaller.

Soon enough, a dark cloud descended upon her mind, sucking out all positive thoughts and sending a chill down her spine. She felt a sinister evil touch her skin as the Cloak of Fear wrapped itself around her. She knew this feeling all too well.

I don't have much time. The Cloak of Fear is sealing.

She felt as if she were trapped in quicksand and could not move. Yet being aware of the dark energy around her, she did not get caught in it. She saw through it. She shook her head vigorously.

This isn't real. It's not my fear.

Specks of light, flickering in the distance, danced in the trees. She continued forward, following the light, until it led her to a familiar, favorite smell—fragrant cedar boughs. She walked to the center of a grove of trees and came upon the largest cedar of them all. A huge conifer, at least twenty feet around, with a small hollow at the bottom. Beside the tree lay a broken mirror. Someone had been here before. *Is that what made the light flicker?*

She stared down at the hole. *I wonder who lives in there?* It looked like a foxhole. A grey squirrel scampered out of it with an acorn in its mouth. The little creature stopped momentarily to look at her, then tore up the tree with its bushy tail twitching.

She eyed the weather-worn, brown ridges of cedar bark, following them up to the top of the tree, where she spotted a clump of sticks and leaves wedged between high branches. She heard the sounds of other birds who called this forest home—blue jays, woodpeckers, and robins. The old cedar stood majestically, shading and protecting them all with its branches.

Balidova planted her feet on the ground and placed her left hand on the tree. She could feel its warmth and wisdom wrap around her like an old friend.

You must've been here for hundreds of years, maybe thousands. What have you seen? What do you know?

She felt a tranquility sweep over her.

She felt her energy shift from fearful and worried to... neutral.

All her fears—from being in an unfamiliar part of the woods—washed away.

In its place, a peaceful feeling trickled down her spine, grounding her to the earth. She felt good and calm, back in her center.

"Wow, you *do* have wisdom, don't you?" She placed her other hand on the cedar, turned around, and stood with the length of her back against the tree, her palms pressed into its bark. Breathing deeply, she felt the solid, steady firmness of the tree trunk, grounding her into the roots of Mother Earth and herself. She sighed with relief, feeling the tree as part of her.

∼

CRASH! A loud sound erupted at the other end of the woods. The ground began to shake, gently at first, and then more strongly, until the entire forest floor was trembling violently.

Earthquake, Balidova thought.

In school, she had learned how this area of the Pacific Rim was on the San Andreas fault line, where two tectonic earth plates joined. Geologists said it wasn't so much a question of whether there would be an earthquake, but more a question of when.

She scrambled frantically to get out of the forest and back into an open area as fast as possible. But as she started to run, she remembered Luminora's words.

If you flee your fears, they will follow you. Turn and face your fears, Balidova.

Plus, she thought ruefully, *there's nowhere to go. I'm in the thick of the woods, and there's no open space nearby.*

"Hold on, girl, stay," she said aloud to herself, stopping in her tracks. "You have something you need to do."

Turning around, Balidova quivered. She was alone in the cedar grove. Or so she thought. She peered into the woods. Alone except for a mammoth black thing in the distance. All the animals had evacuated the area. The air was silent and eerily still. She looked deeper into the trees and saw a beast whose head, body, wings, and tail were of the darkest black—a black that made the night seem bright. Balidova gasped, her breath caught in her throat. That's what Luminora was talking about. The Drakoban!

The beast cast its eyes around, searching for the girl.

Opening its mighty jaw, it spoke in a low growl, "Balidova Forester, show yourself. You will never escape me."

When Balidova didn't respond, the Drakoban spoke again, this time in a more menacing tone. "Girl, I know what you taste like."

Balidova paused for a moment, thinking. *Other than the nurse at the hospital, Mr. Winston's the only one who has a drop of my blood.*

Again, she remained silent, not wanting to give away her location. Again, the Drakoban threatened her.

"My throat is hungry for the taste of a young girl's blood. Like the blood of that moose you saw eons ago!" A creepy laugh erupted from the beast.

How does the Drakoban know about the dead moose in the lagoon? The only person I told was June. Balidova paused, her eyes darting back and forth. *And I told Mr. Winston! Didn't Luminora tell me the Drakoban is a shapeshifter?*

Immediately, Balidova put it together.

The beast is Mr. Winston!

He's not a Drakoban leader.

He's the Drakoban leader.

Balidova's fears were confirmed by the next thing that came from the Drakoban's mouth. "The wind spirit won't save you this time. Show yourself, and I will let you live. Defy me, and I will kill you."

Balidova had told Mr. Winston about the wind spirit that saved her from the wolves many months ago, when they bumped into each other at the hospital. Now she *knew* the dark creature was her science teacher in another shape.

She hung her head down, stunned by her gross misjudgment of his character. Any trust in herself she had built up since Mr. Winston's and Gus's surprise ambush of her at the karate tournament, vanished.

Balidova hesitated at the sound of the Drakoban's words. With nowhere else to turn and her self-confidence wavering, she stepped forward tentatively.

"I am here," she said quietly, pressing her fingertips together nervously.

"Good," the Drakoban replied as its head spun around to find her, tracking the origin of her voice.

Balidova stood perfectly still. The way a frightened squirrel remains motionless when determining what to do next—ready to dart off at any moment.

"You have gone against me enough, Balidova. I warned you to stop learning the Dragon Tail Breath."

The Drakoban continued, breathing heavily. "I only encouraged you to learn the Dragon Tail Breath because I wanted to gain the knowledge of the Dragons of Light for myself. You would only have it for a short time before you lost it, but I would keep it forever. Unfortunately, Gus failed to deliver the *Forget Potion*. So, I had to come in person to take care of you. Well, not in person," he laughed. "In my original form—dragon."

Balidova shuddered at the idea that Mr. Winston was a Drakoban first, a human second. How completely he had deceived her!

She was careful to remain still and quiet. Although the Drakoban knew the direction her original sound had come from, the beast still didn't know her exact location. Dragons could hear and smell exceptionally well, but with their narrow pupils, they could not see well in dim light.

"Come out, girl!" The beast shouted. "If you don't reveal yourself, I'll make you!" The beast stomped its feet, and the ground shook violently.

In that instant, Balidova realized the Drakoban would never let her live. Its entire existence was designed to stomp out the light. And she was a representation of that light.

She decided to take her chances and run.

As she sprinted out from behind the tree where she was hiding, the Drakoban followed the sound of her body moving through the underbrush. The creature unleashed a stream of fire from its jaws, in her direction.

Her lightning-fast, martial arts-honed reflexes saved her life. With an agile leap, she dodged the flames and ran back toward the oldest cedar, hiding inside the foxhole at the base of its trunk. The beast heard her take off and released another burst of flame in that direction. She could feel the heat singe her skin.

Balidova crouched inside the tree, hiding from the Drakoban's fiery blasts. When she realized she was trapped, with no escape, terror rose in her.

She pushed the feeling away.

The dark dragon lumbered near, the ground shaking. Bringing its head near the ground, it sniffed around the tree, catching her scent.

"I found you. There's no escaping now."

The girl could smell the damp darkness of the beast—a mix of earthy and putrid smells that made her nose pucker. She knew this was the end.

As fear overwhelmed her system, she closed her eyes in an attempt to escape the feeling. Then she remembered her dad's words from her karate training—*always look your opponent in the eye.*

With fierce determination, she forced her eyes open, only to see a large red eye staring at her through the hole in the wood. She opened her mouth to scream, but no sound came out. Fear had gripped her throat so tightly that no sound could emerge.

Without warning, something miraculous happened. A little blue bird appeared out of nowhere, flew toward the beast, and pecked the Drakoban in the eye—the same eye that was staring at her. Its white wing tips stood out against the pitch-black eyelid of the dragon.

The beast yanked its head back, shaking its neck violently to rid itself of the pesky intruder. In the chaos, the dark dragon became disoriented and lost track of the girl's location.

Moments later, Balidova heard a high-pitched squawk as the bird fell to the ground, dead.

"Where are you, girl," the creature growled and blinked, with one eye bleeding. It blasted fire in all directions, in a stream of fury.

Balidova crouched in the foxhole. The old cedar protected her from the blast. *This is your second chance. Think, think.*

She struggled to come up with an idea.

Powerless, she cast her eyes down as her body went limp. She was going to die. As soon as the thought entered her mind, all the energy rushed out of her body like a popped balloon.

Unexpectedly, she heard a mosquito buzzing by her ear. But it wasn't a mosquito. It was a bee. She squinted and looked closer—a bee with a bent antenna.

Bumby?

For a split second, she smiled and wondered where Bumby had come from. *Bees don't live alone. They live as part of a hive—something larger than themselves—and each one has a specific role to play.* With that thought, a wave of relief swept over her—a crack in the death grip of the Cloak of Fear.

The bee landed on the ground at her feet, and she looked down at it, along with pieces of bark and pine needles mixed with dirt.

Bumby has a family, just like me.

The bee took off and flew out of the foxhole above her head. She followed its bulky body with her eyes as it rose higher and higher, looking beyond the black and yellow insect to the vast expanse beyond the treetops. The sight of the open sky was just enough for her to remember something she'd felt earlier that same day in the crystal cave. She had the power of the heavens and the earth flowing through her.

I'm Balidova Forester. I am the one.

Immediately, she made a decision.

She would not give up, even if things seemed hopeless. She would summon all the knowledge she'd learned from Luminora.

She would use all that she'd worked so hard for, right now. She would fight till the end.

Inhaling deeply, she drew up the energy of the earth. With another breath, she pulled down the energy of the cosmos. She let the two energies merge within her.

She felt the three main energy centers of her body light up. Between her eyes. At her heart. And in her belly. She felt as though rays of golden light were shooting out of her in all directions.

But the powerful feeling was short-lived. Sounds of the Drakoban sniffing nearby caused fear to rise in her body once again. She tensed. This time she didn't push the feeling away. She didn't try to get rid of it. Instead, she did the opposite. She breathed into it and let it be. She kept sucking in deep lungfuls of air, telling herself to *completely let go and trust.*

Dragon footsteps were very close now, shaking the earth around her.

What do I do? she thought.

She closed her eyes and sucked in a deep breath. *Don't push the feeling away. Let it be. Completely let go and trust.*

She saw the Drakoban's shadow outside the foxhole, yet she felt a trusted sense of calm inside. Something clicked. Instantly, she realized the Drakoban was a reflection of her own fears.

This fear, it's not me. It's not true. I don't have to hang onto it. What did the dragon teach me? Stop. Detach. Remove my commitment to that emotion. Wrap it with love and let it go.

A moment later, her whole body shuddered as she felt fear draining away—like octopus tentacles curling and retracting in the face of waterless air. Amidst her worst fears, she had broken through. She was no longer afraid, even of dying.

Something had shifted within her. Fear had transformed into power.

Not a controlling, dominating power, but a loving power.

It felt warm and strong, expansive and energizing. Her whole body tingled with excitement as if she'd broken through some sort of invisible barrier. She felt as though she were floating in mid-air without a tether or a safety rope—terrifying yet thrilling at the same time.

So this is what it feels like to completely let go and trust.

She felt the Drakoban's presence very near now. She still didn't know what to do, but she was no longer scared. A strange calm overcame her.

She shifted her crouched position, and something dropped out of her pocket. She looked down to see what it was, and an idea entered her mind. Everything became clear.

She knew how she would defeat the beast.

She grinned as she reached down, grabbed the oil bottle, and ran out from the foxhole at top speed, just as the Drakoban unleashed a stream of fire that singed her heels.

CHAPTER 33
TRANSFORMATION CIRCLE

Balidova tore out from the hole in the old cedar tree, diving into the underbrush. Thistles and sharp branches ripped at her skin, but she ignored them as she fought her way through with purpose. The dark dragon heard her movements and followed her deeper into the woods. Its stomping steps made cracking sounds as logs snapped like twigs under sharp claws.

"You cannot defeat me, Balidova. Your only hope is to join me," the beast laughed.

Never, Balidova thought to herself, silently. She did not want to give away her location any more than she already had. She clutched the small glass bottle in her hand and glanced back at the creature gaining ground on her. It seemed almost comical that her only weapon against this massive beast was a 5 ml container of black spruce essential oil. As if answering her thought, the dark dragon released a blast of fire that just missed the girl.

Balidova sucked in a deep breath as a sly grin slid across her face. She looked up and saw the full moon through the trees. Clouds hovered around it, making it only partially visible. She had to shatter the Cloak of Fear before those clouds completely covered the moon. The remaining daylight was fading quickly. All she could see were two glowing red eyes as the Drakoban's black body melted into the dusk.

For a moment, she stood still, being very careful not to make any noise, hoping the beast would lose her again. Then she remembered what Luminora had told her about dragon's excellent sense of smell. She clutched the bottle of oil the dragon had given her even tighter in her palm.

As soon as she opened the lid, the dark dragon immediately spun toward her, sniffing the air. The oil gave off a potent scent. She placed one drop of oil on the ground and ran forward.

A few moments later, the dark dragon came to where the drop was located, just as she wanted. The beast skimmed its nostrils close to the earth, taking in the powerful aroma, but Balidova had already moved further forward, placing another drop on the ground. She kept running, placing drops of spruce oil in a large circle.

As she ran, body movement sparked her memory.

Luminora told me that dragons are incredibly creative creatures. They have the power that creates worlds flowing through them. Isn't that the legend of how the world began—with the dragons of earth, water, air, and fire? If they don't harness that incredible power, it starts to go dormant.

Even though they are gigantic beasts, they have this one weakness—if they retrace their physical steps with the same mental intention, their power is cut in half. That means, if this beast keeps going around and around in a circle with the same intention of killing me, it'll get weaker and weaker.

I wonder if it can happen more than once, and cut its power in half again and again. Balidova liked the sound of that—eventually, the beast would have very little strength left.

Inspired by this revelation, Balidova kept placing little droplets of oil in a large circle in the middle of the woods. She had to trust her instincts now, because that's all she had going for her.

But as she raced through the underbrush, she tripped on a tree root and landed flat on her face. She grabbed her ankle in pain. In one fell swoop, Balidova's inspiration turned to desperation as she realized she would not be able to run away from the beast. She looked around for something, anything, to help her, but saw only the green and brown foliage of the forest.

Woof! Woof!

What's that?

The dragon plodded nearer, almost on top of her now.

Nutmeg? Is that you, Nutmeg? What're you doing out here?

The Drakoban heard the barking too. It spun around in the opposite direction from Balidova. Nutmeg was barking furiously, nipping at the dragon's heels.

What a brave dog. He knows I'm in trouble and came to help me!

Although there was a vast difference in size between dog and dragon, Nutmeg managed to fully distract the beast, the same way a tiny fly can distract a person.

While the dark dragon was preoccupied with Nutmeg, Balidova rubbed a couple drops of spruce oil on her sore ankle and placed the palm of her hand there. She had heard once from the elders of Kitamaat Village that trees had healing powers, as did human hands. She figured she might as well try it. She closed her eyes and breathed into the sore spot, imagining the injury draining away, and her ankle returning to normal.

Nutmeg's barking continued.

Balidova's breathing continued.

She could move her ankle again. She got up and hobbled along, continuing to place droplets of oil in a circle. Her ankle wasn't back to normal, but it was better.

Just as she completed one full revolution, she looked back and witnessed the beast breathe fire down on the dog. The massive beast had finally pinpointed the minuscule dog, who'd been dodging its attacks.

All of a sudden, the barking stopped.

NO!! Not Nutmeg! Balidova screamed in her mind. It took all the self-control she could muster not to utter a sound.

Wait, how did Nutmeg get here anyway? Did one of my sisters follow me and bring him? Someone must have untied him.

Balidova couldn't run fast with her sprained ankle. Any thought she had of simply hiding and saving herself evaporated. The only way to survive was to defeat the beast who had just killed the two animals that led her to Luminora—Nutmeg and the little blue bird.

LUMINORA! Where are you? She screamed in her head.

Meanwhile, the Drakoban followed the scent of the oil, unknowingly completing one full circle. Its power was now cut in half.

AT PRECISELY THAT MOMENT, a dark butterfly appeared out of nowhere and alighted on Balidova's hand. It was black all over except for midnight blue lower wings and white specked wingtips that looked like stars in a night sky.

All of a sudden, she remembered.

Luminora had taught her that she was never alone.

Balidova had learned enough of the magic to know when to ask for help. And now—alone in the woods, with a dark dragon on her tail—was as good a time as any.

As she moved across the dark green, moss-covered earth, tenderly placing her hurt leg on the ground with each step, she grabbed onto tree branches to steady her. Determinedly, she closed her eyes and summoned all the forest creatures to come to her aid. She called upon the strength of the spirit bear to give her courage, the all-around sight of the owl to guide her in the dark, the slipperiness of the fish to dodge blasts of fire, and the bold brightness of the sunflower to face forward and not look back.

As if in answer to her call, the wind picked up and blew across her face. Water began falling lightly from the sky. As the rain hit her body, the sensation distracted her, and the pain in her ankle eased. She let go of the branches and was able to put more weight on her foot, moving faster.

The Drakoban caught a whiff of the newly placed black spruce droplets and kept following her. After reaching one droplet and sniffing the ground, it raised its head and moved forward to the next drop—over and over, around the circle.

The Drakoban was gaining on her.

Balidova continued moving through the trees, but she was no match for its long stride and thick scales, unperturbed by sharp branches. As she brushed thorns and twigs out of her way, she had only one thought in her mind.

I have to get these oil drops in a circle again. I have to complete the second transformation circle.

With owl-like focus and bear-like strength, she slipped through the dense underbrush, carefully placing drops of oil along her path.

The Drakoban followed her.

The rain had picked up now, and was coming down in heavy sheets. Balidova ran like the wind, her wet hair stuck to her face, then felt a gust of air pick her up off the ground. She turned to see the dragon blowing hard. Its fire blasts were being drowned out by the rain, so it was using wind to attack her.

Unexpectedly, Balidova spotted something out of the corner of her eye as she was blown sideways. *What's that at the end of the Drakoban's tail?*

"Come back here, girl!" The Drakoban screeched. "Or I will kill you!"

Balidova ran away from the beast as fast as she could. All those times playing tag with her sisters paid off. To keep her mind off her fears, she imagined her sisters chasing her.

As she placed the last drop around the circle for the second time, she dumped the whole bottle of oil there.

That'll make it stop.

A few seconds later, the Drakoban lumbered up, smelled the intense black spruce aroma, and put its head down to find where the smell was coming from. In doing so, it placed one foot across the threshold of the circle, completing two revolutions. The beast had gone around the same circle, not once but twice! Its power was cut in half not once, but twice! Now it was at one-quarter of its full power.

Suddenly, the Drakoban realized what Balidova was doing. But it was too late. The beast released a shrieking cry into the night as an energy wave emanated from the animal into the circle. It attempted to unleash a fiery blast, but only a small stream of fire emerged from its jaws—a stream of heat extinguished by the rain.

Balidova stopped in her tracks and looked back.

Where do dragons get the energy to make fire anyway?

Spontaneously, she remembered what she'd learned in science class—*energy cannot be created or destroyed, but it can be transformed.*

The Drakoban's power is being transformed—but into what?

CHAPTER 34
THE GIANT SITKA SPRUCE

Balidova had tricked the Drakoban into losing most of its power. But the Drakoban had its own trick to pull on the girl. It screamed as power drained from its body into the circle. Then it lifted its tail. Something was wrapped around the end of it.

Wait. Not something. Someone.

Coiled in the dragon's tail, high in the air was Balidova's sister, May.

"Come here now, or I'll kill your sister," the Drakoban growled. Even with only a quarter of its full power, it was still a formidable creature.

For a moment, Balidova hesitated. Should she risk her safety for her sister? May had saved her from being tied to a pole all night, but they'd been rivals for months, if not years. May had tried to beat her at the team tryouts by playing on her emotions the night before. As Balidova weighed her options, she heard her mom's voice in her head.

Treat others the way you would like to be treated.

She is my sister, after all.

Knowing there was only one right thing to do, Balidova stepped out of the shadows and faced the beast.

"Okay. You win. Just let her go."

"Good girl. You've finally come to your senses." The Drakoban sniggered.

Balidova stepped forward. The beast uncurled its tail and dropped May with a thud. She lay still on the ground.

"You killed her!" Balidova yelled.

"No, she's just in shock." The beast said, unconcerned. "I tend to have that effect on humans."

"Why are you doing this?" Balidova shouted, her voice shaking, her hands on her hips.

"Hasn't your friend Luminora told you, dear girl? The dark and the light forces are battling. And you know which is more powerful," the beast finished with a cackle. "Where is your guardian now? Join me, and I will spare you and your sister!"

For a moment, Balidova was tempted to believe the Drakoban's words. Balidova's energy reserves were very low by now. She had already used up so much of her energy in the battle, and Luminora was nowhere to be found. She did not have the power to resist the dark beast much longer.

On the spur of the moment, she thought of Angel—how much her friend had believed in her on the last day of school, calling her *Balidova Forester, Beater of bullies, Champion of Karate, Destroyer of the Cloak of Fear*. She thought of her mom—how she had supported her at the dinner table with that knowing look when she felt totally unhinged confronting her dad. She thought of Mrs. Marsh—how the principal had not punished her, but winked after she kicked Gus in self-defense. She thought of her sisters—who competed in team kata at her side and respected her kumite abilities enough to not want to face her at the team tryouts. Lastly, she thought of Gus and the word on the dragon poster he'd stuck on her locker, mocking her—Bali-don't-va.

That's not my name. My name's Bali-do-va. I can do this. If not for me, then for everyone who's been there for me, and everyone who believes in me. I can't let them down. I can't let the Drakoban win.

As soon as she made her decision, she heard Luminora's voice in her head, answering her call.

Breathe deep. Bring in the light, and be you.

In that instant, she *knew.* Balidova's eyes glistened with mischief. She wasn't ready to give in yet. She felt into her pocket and pulled out a stone—the plain, grey and white stone the spirit bear had given her. She reached into her other pocket and pulled out her slingshot—one she had fashioned with her own hands. She knelt down slowly, holding both the stone and the slingshot behind her.

The Drakoban, interpreting her kneeling as a pose of submission, said, "Good. Smart girl."

Balidova looked up and saw it. The spot on its neck. The place where Mr. Winston had worn a patch—the weak spot. It carried over when he changed forms. Carefully, feeling her way with her fingers behind her back, Balidova placed the stone in the center of the leather square of the slingshot. As the beast stepped closer, she realized she had one chance.

With lightning-fast reflexes and stone-cold precision, she brought the slingshot in front of her. She held it up, aimed, and fired. The rock hit the beast at the perfect point—right in the weak spot on its throat. Any ordinary object would have bounced off the tough outer covering of dragon skin, but this was no normal object. It contained the magic of the Dragons of Light.

As soon as it touched the dark dragon's scales, the small grey stone burst into a ball of light. Rays of whitish gold flashed under the surface of the creature's skin like lightning bolts as the magic stone coursed its power through the animal. The beast wailed as light penetrated the totality of its skin.

With a deep breath, Balidova turned toward the center of the circle. She had gained some time. The beast was weakened, but not defeated. If she didn't finish it off, it could still destroy her. She needed to do more.

Then she saw it—something that had been there all along without her realizing, something to help her as she channeled the energy of the sky and the earth through her. Distracted by the Drakoban, focused on creating the outer edge of the circle, she hadn't noticed it before—the Giant Sitka Spruce.

THE COLOSSAL TREE stood one hundred and sixty-five feet tall, and nearly forty feet around at the base. Branches protruded from its rugged, weather-hardened trunk like old whiskers off a giant's face.

Balidova stumbled to the center of the circle where the enormous tree stood. She pressed her back upon its trunk. She could feel the uneven ridges of bark bumping up against her spine as the water soaked through the back of her shirt. Rain fell in a torrential downpour now. She stood with her feet planted on the ground, at the base of the tree. Its roots were below her, and although she couldn't see or touch them, she could sense them. They grounded her into a solidity of the earth that gave her strength.

Her arms hung down by her sides, and she placed her splayed-out hands against the wet bark. The tree offered a steadfastness that felt comforting amid the chaos surrounding her. Through her rain-soaked hair, she could see the Drakoban, its black form shuffling around the edge of the circle, white flashes of light rippling through its scales.

The formidable creature raised its head and looked toward the gigantic tree. It sensed the girl as she gathered her power.

Balidova looked up and saw that clouds almost entirely

covered the moon. A jolt of fear entered her heart as she realized she had cut it dangerously close. Was it too late?

The Cloak of Fear is almost complete—it's now or never.

She had severe doubts about whether she could do it—shatter the Cloak of Fear around the entire planet. Her whole body shook as tears welled in her eyes. It seemed impossible. She removed her hands from the tree to wipe her eyes.

She remembered how—many moons ago—the sunflower, describing the various types of fear, had said that *doubt* was the worst of all. Now she knew why. Not because it was the most obvious, but because it was the most subtle.

Doubt is the most dangerous type of fear because it slowly gnaws away at you without you even realizing it's there. After a while, you don't trust yourself and don't even know why. You barely even notice. You just think a feeling of mistrust is normal.

Her self-doubt. It seemed so small and insignificant. Yet everything depended on it. The Cloak of Fear would seal over the earth if she, in this moment, doubted herself.

As these thoughts ran through her mind, she felt her heart rate quicken, her breath shorten, and her body contract in that familiar feeling. The Cloak of Fear was very strong, closing in for the final time, just like the dark clouds enveloping the moon's light. Soon her mind would fall into despair, and all would be over.

The tree... the tree... a voice in her mind whispered.

With only a sliver of hope left, she leaned back and pressed her bare hands onto the trunk of the Giant Sitka Spruce once again. Immediately, she felt a certainty coming from the five-hundred-year-old living being. Her focus shifted to that feeling, and with it, her breath lengthened, her heart rate slowed, and her body relaxed. A calm washed over her as she realized she would not be doing this task alone. The tree was with her.

The rain slowed, and she glanced up, letting raindrops

cascade down her face, melting away her disbelief. Hiding high up in the branches, she spotted the birds and squirrels that called this tree home. She sensed the ants and beetles who crawled through its bark. She knew that the spirit bear and the owl lived somewhere deep in the forest. Over by the river was the fish, and the sunflower stood tall in the meadow. The little blue bird that had guided her from the beginning, and Nutmeg, they had each given their life to save hers. All the creatures of the forest—even the tiniest bees—were with her. They had become her family. They reminded her that *she* was part of the flow of ancient wisdom. She felt a truth rise within her that she had not understood before.

I'm not alone. I'm part of something larger than just me. Not only the tree, but all of Mother Nature is with me.

Balidova felt a blast of fire behind her. The Drakoban was getting closer. Although withering in the light of the stone with every passing second, it could still move and blast flames that would burn her to the ground at close range. She was in danger, and her sister was lying on the ground, helpless.

Balidova flashed back to all the horrible things that had happened over the past seven months. The fear that had gripped her own heart and stopped her in her tracks months ago when her best friend was attacked. Her dad lashing out at her mom and cutting the dishwasher cord. Her sister's jealous behavior, writing on her karate uniform. Gus and Mr. Winston attacking her in the night. Were all these things caused by the Drakoban and the Cloak of Fear?

She immediately *knew* they were related to each other. She wasn't the only one affected by the insidious feeling she had when the darkness overcame her. It happened to everyone.

She could identify the signs now. She knew the Cloak of Fear was upon her when she no longer trusted her feeling, when her thinking became black and white—there seemed only to be two stark options, neither good, with no middle ground. She knew the Cloak of Fear was upon her when she began to have doubts, which grew into worry, overwhelming anxiety, and then all-out terror—a deep-seated, irrational fear that she felt down to her bones. She knew the Cloak of Fear was upon her when she couldn't see a way out of her problems.

No! she shouted inside her head. *This cannot continue. This must be stopped! If the Cloak of Fear seals up, this will be all that I know. This'll be all that anyone will know. Doubt. Worry. Jealousy. Anger. Hatred. Fear. NO!*

As the last bit of moonlight began to disappear behind the clouds, she pressed her back hard against the giant spruce tree, closed her eyes, and took a deep breath. She knew the only way to defeat the beast and the Cloak of Fear in time was to draw upon the ancient wisdom of the Dragon Tail Breath until its full force flowed within her.

WITH HER FEET planted firmly on the ground, she summoned all she had learned in the last seven months.

She breathed the emerald green light in through her heart, letting it travel right through her and pour out her back. Then she watched it morph into golden light, which she breathed in through her solar plexus, from back to front. She breathed sky blue light in through her throat, letting it travel down her backside, breathing orange light in through her sacrum from back to front. All the colors were merging now, weaving into a beautiful, rainbow-colored spiral. She breathed indigo light in through her third eye, letting it penetrate her head and travel down her back to the base of her spine, between her legs. Breathing red light in, from back to front, she created a huge spiral of energy and light, with her body in the center. Lastly, breathing purple light through the top of her head, she let that light extend down and wrap itself around her in a circle, just like a dragon's tail.

Each time she breathed a new color in and out, the spiral got bigger and bigger, expanding exponentially until she was in the center of a massive ball of light. Next, all the colors merged, becoming a glowing orb of rainbow-colored light. She could feel energy pulsing within her, like a heartbeat, waking up her trillions of cells, bringing them alive and activating their life force in a way she had never felt before. At the same time, she felt the tree's energy ignite. Solidity, grounding, and stability backed the explosion of energy within her.

The rain had stopped now, but water droplets that fell from the tree branches tickled her skin as the spiral energy rose outward.

The Drakoban was so close that she could smell it on the other side of the tree. She felt its dark presence envelop her in one last attempt to extinguish her light. All the power of the many forms of fear, amplified through so many people all over the earth... harnessed here and now. It was overwhelming. She felt a heaviness swallow her light field, gradually taking over until only her face was lit.

She stamped her feet as hard as she could, one after the other, to refocus her waning energy, but nothing was left. She was exhausted and spent. She fumbled in her pocket for the purple stone Luminora had given her in the cave. *I need to use everything I've got. I can't do this alone. I'm not alone.*

With a surge of willpower, Balidova wrapped herself with all the love she could think of.

Look for what you want to see.

Although there were positive and negative things about each person in her world, she focused only on the good in her relationships. Her mom's love for her—being there to talk to when she was ready. Her dad's love for her—pushing her to be better. Her sister's love for her—rescuing her in the dark. Her friend's love for her—encouraging her to continue learning the Dragon Tail Breath despite Gus's threats. Her horse's love for her—always waiting patiently for her in the barn, ready for their next adventure.

All this love feels like I'm wearing a Cloak of Love.

It felt so good to encase herself in a blanket of everyone else's love for her. She began to feel more centered and flowing. She felt her light body expand, yet she still felt something was missing. The girl was quiet for a moment.

Ah, I know. Balidova sighed. *I am me. That's the final lesson the dragon taught me in the dark cave. The love of those around me is awesome, but what about my love for myself?*

She spoke out loud, confirming her revelation to herself, wanting to hear it in her own voice. "Love for myself—that's the missing piece." Balidova shifted her weight from one foot to the other and smiled.

When I believe in myself, I can do anything.

She felt a surge of light around her body as tiny particles of light connected and formed a solid energetic shield. She was protected in a bubble of love and light that surrounded her whole body. Negative thoughts and words bounced off the outside of this shield. She imagined them falling like arrows into roses as they touched the invisible boundary that protected her. Only pure unconditional love passed through. She felt a force of life rise from the earth itself, touching and strengthening her heart. The Cloak of Love was complete.

Connecting to the tree's energy, she drew the power of all of nature through its roots and into herself. The power of all the elements—rain, wind, sun, soil—which made the Giant Sitka Spruce as sturdy and significant as it is now—Mother of the forest. With one final burst of determined intention, she squeezed her hands into fists, sucked in as much air as she could, and envisioned a stream of light blasting forth from her heart.

Let the magic do the work. Create from the inside out.

She held the crystal with both hands above her head, allowing it to intensify her powers. A sphere of red, orange, gold, green, blue, and purple light shook the forest as it exploded from Balidova and the tree, and sent a ripple effect outward through the circle. Instantly, she felt like a *Tree of Light*. Calm, strong, and vibrant.

Before the Drakoban realized it, beams of multi-colored light had reached its body, and it started to sizzle on contact like a pile of salt melting in a bucket of warm water. The intense, bright light dissolved its already weakened flesh. The Drakoban let out a haunting cry as it fell, and made one last attempt to plant the seed of doubt in the girl's mind, sending its voice into the girl's mind.

"Where is your precious guardian when you need it most? Luminora has abandoned you in your time of need. Why did it not trust you enough to tell you about me earlier? Does it not think you are capable? I know your ability, Balidova! I have seen your powers for myself."

The dark beast was almost gone now. Only its voice remained, echoing off the wall of trees. *"Do you want to align yourself with a creature who sees you as a peon or a powerful being? Do not forget me, Balidova. We shall meet again."*

Within a matter of seconds, the creature disintegrated into nothingness. Only a single sharp, black talon remained in its place.

As the beast disappeared, the last vestiges of its power were consumed by the rainbow light. Balidova lowered her arms and continued to stand in the center of the circle, riveted in place by the unusual feeling of light coursing through her spine. It was at once the most powerful feeling she had ever experienced, and the most exposed. She felt invincibly strong, and incredibly delicate at the same time, as if she were as solid and magnificent as the Giant Sitka Spruce and as fragile and flexible as a feather blowing in the wind—as if strength and vulnerability were one.

In that moment—her arms splayed out to her sides, one palm clutching the purple rock, her back to the tree—her perspective shifted, and she saw clearly. *Fear is an illusion. Love is the truth. All my fears are a figment of my imagination. The Drakoban feeds off them. The Cloak of Fear amplifies them.*

With only the tiniest sliver of moonlight visible, Balidova planted her feet on the wet ground. All three forces—human, dragon, earth—combined to form a pillar of light that shot through her body and the tree, exploding and extending up through the sky, reaching the clouds, and entering the last hole in the Cloak of Fear, just before it closed forever. She could hear the sound of glass breaking as the dark energy barrier cracked like an eggshell into a million pieces, yet nothing fell from the sky.

SHE COLLAPSED into a crumpled heap at the base of the tree, knowing it was done.

All resistance to the ancient flow of wisdom had been released from her, opening a channel within her for the dragon magic to flow uninhibited. Tremendous energy traveled through her, into the tree, up into the sky, and pierced through the layer of fear surrounding the earth. The illusion had been broken. Like a crack in a block of ice rippling out, this one tiny hole in the Cloak of Fear expanded outward, shattering the entire layer around the planet. And like a hologram, once the illusion was broken in one place, for one human, it was broken everywhere.

Balidova wondered, *Can one person make that much of a difference?* She heard the response come in, through her inner wisdom, not only in words but also in a feeling, a knowing. *Yes—when they channel the power that creates worlds through them and when they wrap themselves with the Cloak of Love.* The slightest curve of a smile traveled across her lips and spread up into her eyes.

By running around the circle and then coming to the center, by breathing the seven colors of light through the seven energy centers of her body, by believing in herself, Balidova had been the movement maker, collecting and channeling energy within her. A catalyst for larger forces. Only by overcoming her own fears could she break the grip of the Cloak of Fear over the planet. Only by completely letting go and trusting could she know what to do. Only by gathering and concentrating on the love around her, wrapping herself with the Cloak of Love, could she channel enough light to become a vessel for three energy realms—human, dragon, earth—to unite.

Yet the cellular system of her body could not sustain that level of energy coursing through it for long. As the light faded, the seed of doubt about Luminora and all the dragon had taught her came to the forefront of her mind.

Why didn't Luminora tell me about the Drakoban before? Why wasn't it here? Did it think I wasn't capable?

Balidova got up and stepped gingerly around the giant spruce tree. She saw the burn mark on the trunk, opposite from where she stood. Blackened bark and singed branches remained as a battle scar to the fear that would have controlled them all. For a moment, she wondered how the darkness could have added to the destruction of the Cloak of Fear, which was itself made of darkness. Then, she shook off the question and left it. She had many things to ask Luminora later.

As water droplets dripped from cedar and spruce branches, she looked up and saw something miraculous. Rays of moonlight pierced through the sky where dark clouds had once been, and the light, mixed with the warm mist, produced an incandescent rainbow. It glowed gently, not too bright, but just enough that she could see it. She placed one hand on her friend, the Giant Sitka Spruce, and smiled.

In that moment, she remembered something Luminora had told her, *"One who is connected to the light is more powerful than millions who are not."*

Months ago, the fish had shown her how to wrap herself with love, but she had no idea there was such a thing as the Cloak of Love or how immensely powerful it was. She had no idea that when you change yourself, you change the world. She had no idea that all matter is connected in an energetic web that binds everything together—toward fear or love—a mysterious matrix of light and dark energy. The Cloak of Fear had gripped her own body, as well as her friends, her family, her neighbors, and people across the world. It had nearly trapped them all.

But not quite. The Cloak of Love was in all those places too.

And now, she could tap into its power.

Because she *chose* to see it.

CHAPTER 35
DANGEROUS DOUBTS

Marinating in the vibe of sweet success, Balidova relaxed and stood by the Giant Sitka Spruce.

Suddenly, she remembered May. The Drakoban had dropped May on the ground with a thud before it disintegrated. She ran over to check on her sister.

"May, are you okay?" Balidova asked, leaning over the girl's crumpled body. "Oh May, why did you come here?"

Balidova started sobbing, thinking her sister was dead. Instinctively, she placed her hands around her sister's head. Her hands began glowing. She could feel the energy moving through them. A few moments later, she saw the same glow in her sister as life force transferred to the girl's body.

May coughed and opened her eyes. "What just happened?"

Balidova leaned down and hugged her tight. "It's done. The Drakoban's dead, and the Cloak of Fear is gone."

"The cloak of what?" May asked groggily, shaking her head.

"The Cloak of Fear." Balidova laughed, sitting up. "I'll tell you all about it later. But hey, why were you in the forest in the first place? Did you follow me?"

May looked a little sheepish. "Yeah. After you beat me at the team tryouts, I wanted to know where you got all your special powers. I wanted some too. I noticed you've been taking off into the woods lately, so I decided to follow you."

"Is that how Nutmeg got here? Did he come with you?" Balidova frowned.

"I guess so, I mean, I didn't bring him on purpose, but I also untied him before I left," May admitted. "I guess he must have followed me?"

Balidova sighed. "Well, that's too bad."

"Why?"

Balidova's eyes welled up. "Because he's dead."

"What?" May said, shocked.

"He died trying to save me." Balidova's head hung down in shame.

There was silence and bonding between the two sisters as they processed that their dog had died, partly due to each of them.

There was nothing either of them could do about it now.

"Well, you'd better get home," Balidova said.

"What about you?" May looked her in the eyes.

"I have some unfinished business," Balidova said, staring off into the distance.

"With who? There's no one here." May seemed confused.

"With Luminora," Balidova said quietly.

"Who's Luminora?"

"Oh, wow, I have a lot to catch you up on." Balidova smiled, looking at May. "But it'll have to wait till later."

Balidova helped her sister up, putting May's arm around her shoulders as they walked through the woods and headed toward the farm. Once she was confident May could make it on her own, Balidova said goodbye.

"Can you cover for me at home? I'll be back soon."

Balidova turned to head back toward the old cedar. That was the place Luminora had said to meet. She remembered the riddle from the crystal cave—*Meet me by the oldest cedar tree.*

She ran toward the outer edge of the circle where the old cedar stood. This tree had led her to the old forest in the first place. Ancient evergreen trees never grew alone. They lived in groves to support and learn from each other, and share nutrients through an underground tapestry of roots—a deeply connected family of trees. Leaning on its soft brown bark, freed from the Cloak of Fear, she noticed a strong, confident feeling within.

Her whole body was pulsing, breathing with the forest.

A halo of forest green light engulfed her, and she felt a deep peace, indescribable by words. A warm, tingling sensation rippled through her body, and a tide of calm, joyful energy washed over her.

So this is what the Cloak of Love feels like.

She pictured her dragon friend with her mind's eye and whispered her name. "Luminora, I made it here. I solved your riddle."

> *Meet me by the oldest cedar tree.*
> *When you stand on its firm ground,*
> *you'll be ready to fly with me.*

All at once, the tree began to move from side to side—the roots shook and pulled up from the ground.

"What's happening? Is this another earthquake?" Balidova shouted. She knelt down, crouching next to the ground, placing her hands over her head to protect herself.

"Have no fear, Balidova. It's me."

She looked up but couldn't believe her eyes. The tree was gone. Luminora was standing in its stead.

~

The dragon's skin was the brown ridged color of cedar bark. Its legs looked like thick branches. But right before Balidova's eyes, Luminora morphed into the array of dazzling colors that Balidova knew well. The dragon's scales glistened in the light of the full moon, hanging in a now cloudless sky.

"But the tree? You...the tree... you're the tree?"

"I have the ability to take any shape—to merge with the trees, the earth, and take any form I please."

"I wish I could do that."

"You can, Balidova. I will teach you in time. Especially now—"

"—that I did it," she said quietly, finishing Luminora's sentence.

"Tell me about it," Luminora encouraged her gently, sensing that the girl needed to process her incredible experience by telling the story in her own words.

Balidova took a deep breath before letting the words pour out of her. "The Drakoban nearly killed me so many times, but all the forest creatures came to my rescue—the blue bird, Bumby, a butterfly, even Nutmeg. I weakened the beast by making it retrace its steps while it held the same intention of killing me, until it was at one-quarter of its full power. Then I nailed it with my slingshot. I used the things you gave me—the grey stone, the oil, and the crystal."

"Very good, Balidova. I had said those things would come in handy. I'm glad you listened. Were they enough? What happened next?"

"With my back to the Giant Sitka Spruce, I channeled the energy. I breathed the Dragon Tail Breath and wove the colors around me until I became a tree of light! The roots of that energy tree—created by the Giant Sitka Spruce and I combined—filled with rainbow light that extended out into the circle of oil droplets. And when they touched the Drakoban, it started to disintegrate."

"Hmm," the dragon purred. "Magnificently done, my dear girl. You must feel very proud of yourself." Luminora paused for a moment. Then the dragon cocked its head sideways. "You have accomplished one of the greatest feats of any human—shattering the Cloak of Fear—and yet you are not satisfied. I read dissatisfaction in your energy field."

Balidova looked up at Luminora intently. She wondered how the creature could tell she was dissatisfied when the dragon couldn't see well enough in the dark to see her eyes.

"You're right. I was terrified. And you weren't there for me. Why? Why didn't you tell me that the dark dragon itself would come after me? Why didn't you warn me?"

Luminora looked at the girl and spoke clearly and steadily. She knew Balidova was on the edge of an emotional precipice and could either fall into a pit of distrust or step back into a meadow of trust and an even stronger relationship with the dragon. "Because then you may not have had the courage to continue. *Everything you need to know is revealed to you. Everything you need comes to you.* You must trust."

Balidova liked those words and mentally tucked them into her back pocket for later use, yet she wondered, *Is there more the dragon isn't telling me?*

"Why didn't you show up when the Drakoban tried to kill me? Did you abandon me?"

"No, I did not abandon you, dear girl. I was watching."

"You were watching!? Watching me get blasted by dragon fire?" Balidova was indignant now, almost in disbelief that Luminora could stand by and do nothing while she was under attack.

The dragon remained steady and serene in its response. "How do you think the blue bird showed up?"

"That was you that pecked the dark dragon's eye when I was

about to be burnt to a crisp? That little blue bird has been you all along?" Balidova said incredulously, thinking of the times the blue bird had guided her.

"Yes. I take on many forms, Balidova. I am all around. In the water and the trees, the sun and the breeze, the birds and the bees." The dragon paused before continuing. "You had to fight the Drakoban yourself, in order to know your true power. You alone could do it. You had to develop confidence and trust—on your own."

"But I could've died!" Balidova shouted.

"Dying is not what it seems. You are returning to spirit form. Living in fear is a much worse fate than death." The dragon spread its wings for emphasis, filling up the entire grove with their expanse, momentarily blocking out the moonlit trees.

"Well, I still don't understand why you weren't there."

"If I had swooped in to rescue you, I would've been saying with my actions, 'I know you're not capable of doing this yourself, so I'll do it for you.' Although tempting, that would not build your confidence; it would destroy it."

"Maybe," Balidova conceded, calming down as she realized her perspective on the situation was not the same as Luminora's, and that Luminora might just have a point. But she wasn't quite ready to shift her viewpoint to see things the way the dragon saw them, yet.

"But the other way almost destroyed me." she finished. The seed of doubt the Drakoban had planted in Balidova's mind about Luminora lingered.

Luminora smiled knowingly, holding a space of love for the girl. "So, how did you do it? How did you defeat the beast instead of getting defeated by it?" Luminora prodded her.

"Okay, okay, I get your point," Balidova conceded. She realized that Luminora was not going to fall for her emotional manipulation tactics.

"In my worst moment, I used the tools you taught me. I've been practicing them for the past seven months, so they'd be available when I needed them. When I asked myself *how do I feel?* The answer was 'terrified!'. Since I didn't like that feeling, and knew from experience that I would be killed if I continued like that, I immediately pivoted and asked myself, *How do I want to feel?* I wanted to feel the opposite of terrified. I wanted to feel strong, capable, and confident." The girl straightened her back on the log as she spoke these words. Just saying them was enough to bring their energy into her body once again.

The dragon nodded its head up and down as Balidova was speaking, acknowledging the girl's story.

"I knew I had to completely let go and trust—to move from how I felt to how I wanted to feel. I used *Accept, Release, Move-on.*" Balidova ran her right hand up her left arm, around her shoulder, and down the same arm. Then repeated the motion using her other hand on the other arm.

"Very nice," the dragon said approvingly.

"It was like a hot air balloon. As soon as I released the weight of my fears, my whole being lifted right on up to feeling powerful. I didn't have to do anything." Balidova shook out her hands and feet. "Once I conquered my fears, the Cloak of Fear no longer had power over me, and I saw through the illusion. I felt the Cloak of Love instead."

"Hmm, good for you, Balidova. That's right. Feeling strong is your natural state of being. You don't have to try to feel that. All you have to do is release the weight holding you down, and you will naturally rise up. *Stop. Detach. Remove your commitment to that emotion. Wrap it with love and let it go.* Each of those words helps you shake off the weight keeping you down—the Cloak of Fear. Thank the emotion for showing up because everything happens for a reason. Keep the love and the lesson, and let everything else go."

The dragon ruffled its wings, then said something that made complete sense to Balidova after all she'd been through. "The Drakoban feed off the fear of others, but the Cloak of Fear only has power over you if you believe it and give it energy. Love, on the other hand, is powerful on its own."

"Wow." Balidova was silent for a while, taking all that in.

Soon enough, her curiosity got the better of her. "When I completely let go and trusted, that broke the hold the Cloak of Fear had over me?"

"Yes. Connecting to a force larger than yourself allowed you to see through the illusion of fear, so it ceased to have power over you. That's why you knew what to do. That's why you could destroy the Drakoban and harness the love energy required to shatter the Cloak of Fear."

"Is that part of the dragon magic?" Balidova asked.

"What?"

"Transforming one feeling into another? Transforming fear into love?" Balidova paused for a moment. "Transforming the Cloak of Fear into the Cloak of Love?"

"Yes. Absolutely. That *is* the dragon magic. You are a powerful creator. You are the one who decides how you experience everything in your world. You get to *choose* how you feel."

"Well, I don't know if I'd take it so far that I get to choose everything. But if I can transform my fear into power? That's pretty cool. I'll settle for that. I don't really get the whole transformation thing yet, but I'm starting to, and I want to." she looked up at the dragon hopefully. "But I don't get why bad things—like Nutmeg dying and May getting hurt—have to happen."

"Let me explain another perspective on the dark to you, Balidova, here in this dark forest." The dragon lowered its head to the ground and looked into the girl's eyes. "The darkness is not bad. It just is. And it's connected to the light. The fertile darkness of the womb is where you came from, and the dark soil of the earth is where you shall return. Do not reject this ground as evil, for it is a part of you. Do not label it as forbidden territory, or it will forbid you from entering the lush landscape of acceptance. Get to know and accept your own darkness and your own fears, Balidova, and know that they carry within them the promise of light. Your fears show you what you do not want. Only then do you truly know what you want. Contrast is your friend. But one thing is required of you—choice. Choose wisely, my dear girl."

When it finished speaking, the dragon lifted its head back up toward the sky.

Balidova replied in a hushed tone, "I've never thought of it like that before."

There was a silence between them for a while, then Balidova spoke up. "Is it really destroyed?"

"What?"

"The Cloak of Fear."

"You have shattered the Drakoban's grip over the earth. All beings are free to choose between fear and love in everything they think, say, and do. They will not automatically come under the influence of the Cloak of Fear. It will be easier for them to choose love and find a balance between these two opposing energies. Fear is not necessarily bad, Balidova—it keeps us safe by notifying us when we are in danger. Too much fear, however, is crippling."

"That's cool." Balidova nodded triumphantly. Then she wrinkled her face. "But what exactly do you mean by 'choose love'? Like when I chose not to get revenge on my sisters when they wrote on my gi?"

"Yes, exactly," Luminora responded. "And when your sister untied you from the lamppost, and when your mother forgave you for not talking to her for many months, and when you and Angel decided to just be there for each other instead of arguing over things, and when your father genuinely congratulated each of his daughters for making it to the finals without preferring one over the other." Luminora paused. "And most importantly, every time you get upset, afraid, lost, or angry and then take a deep breath and calm down. In each of those tiny moments, you are making a decision, choosing not to react with fear, but to respond with love. Even if it's the simple act of loving yourself."

"Hmm," Balidova said, taking it all in. She looked up at the Crystal moon, which was now fully visible. Only a wisp of cloud remained.

"However," Luminora warned, "the Drakoban retain energy cords to earth through those who still choose fear—those who still reside in darkness, inside their hearts."

"You mean, through people like Mr. Winston. And Gus?"

"Yes, and all of us. Fear still exists. We must remain vigilant, not only with others, but also inside ourselves."

"You mean there's still a way the Drakoban can return?" Balidova asked incredulously. "But I saw it shrivel into nothing!"

"The only way the planet can be free of the Drakoban for good is if every human on the planet chooses love over fear, all the time." Luminora looked solemnly at its human friend. "Fear will always exist. And humans will always have to choose."

"Oh, I see," Balidova said quietly.

"Disaster is averted, for now."

"Well, I guess that's better than nothing," Balidova smiled. "Now that the Cloak of Fear is shattered, maybe the Cloak of Love can take its place?"

"Yes. Love gives power structure. It's sustainable. It builds and can last for a long time. As long as human greed, competition and doubt don't get in the way."

"Hmm," Balidova pondered, wondering if this was possible.

The dragon smiled, condensing everything it had told her into four simple words. "Fear destroys. Love creates."

Balidova nodded her head in silent agreement.

The dragon spread its vast, multi-colored wings and spoke one last time. "Come. Climb on my back, and let's go for a ride. I want to show you something. Fly with me."

CHAPTER 36
DRAGON FLIGHT

The dragon touched its wing to the ground, and Balidova climbed on. She straddled the creature's back and ran her hand along its scales in wonder. They felt silky smooth yet superbly strong to the touch—a perfect blend of opposing qualities.

"Hang on tight," Luminora said. Balidova found two thick, rope-like dragon whiskers protruding from the base of Luminora's neck that she grabbed onto. The dragon looked around and caught Balidova's eyes. For a brief moment, they looked at each other—girl and dragon becoming one.

Where two become one.

Balidova chuckled, thinking of Luminora's words long ago—the riddle that had led her to the double tree by the ocean. At that moment, she could talk to the dragon without words. Not only could Luminora hear her, but she could also hear Luminora. They had a silent conversation.

Are you ready? Luminora asked.

Yes, Balidova responded in her mind.

Hang on tight. Here we go. You're about to get the ride of your life.

Was it Luminora's voice in her head or her own? She couldn't quite tell. Again, the words resounded in her head—*where two become one*. At that exact moment, she felt a pulsing sensation in her left eye, the one with a tinge of green.

The dragon spread its magnificent wings outward in full splendor and lifted off the ground with one mighty beat. Its elegant neck stretched in front. A beautiful tail extended behind.

Balidova closed her eyes, scared to look down—until she felt the wind on her face.

When she opened her eyes again, they were already above the treetops, whizzing through the silvery night air. *This must be what it feels like to be a bird*, she thought. *Free. Flowing. This is incredible!* She let out a loud yelp—"Woohoo! I'm flying!!"

Looking down, she could make out her family's entire property in the moonlight—the barn and paddocks, the backyard and woodpile, the garden, the house, and the long semi-circular driveway. As they rose higher and higher, she began to see not only their property but the whole subdivision—the neighbor's houses, the block, the series of blocks extending out from the highway—shadows of houses dotting the landscape like little toy pieces.

Wow, what a different perspective up here.

Right away, she felt Luminora's answer. *Yes, it is, dear one. A completely different perspective. A wider perspective. A higher perspective.*

Luminora soared through the sky, flowing steadily and smoothly, riding the air currents. Balidova felt the exhilaration of being one with the dragon, her dragon. She felt totally safe with her guardian. She felt as though she had merged with both Luminora and the night sky.

As they flew higher and higher, Luminora headed toward town. They glided past Mount Elizabeth Secondary School, the Kitimat General Hospital, and downtown. The night sky's darkness shielded them from view because the dragon had adjusted the color of its scales to blend in with the night.

All of a sudden, Balidova wondered about her own family. *Are they missing me or wondering where I am? I told mom I'd be home for dinner, but it's past dinnertime. Is she going to be mad at me? Was May able to cover for me?* For a moment, worries flooded in.

Balidova leaned forward and pressed her body on the dragon's neck. The thrill of riding on the dragon's back jolted her out of the worries in her head.

They rose higher, far above the treetops, and Balidova saw how the forest stretched for miles down the Kitimat valley. She saw the outline of the aluminum smelter and the home community of the Haisla Nation—Kitamaat Village. She saw how the coastal mountain range rose to snow-capped peaks, touching the clouds like a magical wonderland, and fell again into valleys reaching toward the ocean, extending endlessly toward the horizon. They wove in and out with the birds, playing with eagles and hawks in a roller coaster of joy-filled movement. Although she felt excited, Balidova felt a strange calm within her too—a *calm joy*. Not an exuberant joy, and not a quiet calm, but something in between. She felt good. Balanced. Strong. She felt like she could do *any*thing.

Luminora spoke to her again through its inner voice. *Can you see? Do you see? Look all around Balidova.*

Look all around.

TOGETHER, they passed all the places where she had learned the seven steps of the Dragon Tail Breath.

They flew over the lagoon, where she had been attacked by wolves, saved by the wind spirit, and had first spotted the little blue bird. This was the place where she first became aware that things were not as they seemed.

They passed over the forest where she encountered a tree spirit, startled the hunter who turned out to be Gus's Father, and met the white Kermode bear, who taught her to breathe in the emerald green light through her heart while saying, *All is well.*

They soared above the Kitimat River where she had fallen off Melody and met the water spirit, which transformed into a giant Coho salmon—a fish who taught her to breathe in the golden light through the power center of her body (solar plexus) while saying, *Here now.*

They glided atop the meadow where she'd met the frightening flames of the fire spirit, which morphed into a huge sunflower who taught her to breathe in brilliant blue light through her throat while asking, *What do I want?*

With her eyes fully adjusted to the dark, Balidova could see more than she ever thought possible, even with so little light.

They drifted over the crest of Wolf Mountain, where she had braved the steep climb with Nutmeg, near dark, and finally discovered which creature had the qualities of owl, bear, fish, and flower. She had met the dragon in true form for the first time, and learned the magic of breathing in the fiery orange light through her tanden while acknowledging, *I am a powerful creator.*

They rose high overhead the double tree where she had doubted she would ever solve the riddle—where two become one. This was the place where she had learned the dragon's name. Luminora taught her the magic of breathing indigo light through her third eye while saying, *I know.*

Able to cover many miles in a short time, they rode in silence for a while. The dragon turbo-boosted its speed in the air. Although the town of Prince Rupert was two hours north by car, it was only fifteen minutes by flying distance. Whereas the road traveled inland around a deep fiord, the dragon could fly directly up the coast. Emerging from a cluster of clouds, they sailed past the community fairgrounds of Prince Rupert, where she'd escaped

Mr. Winston and Gus, learned about the Drakoban, and was shown how to breathe in the red light through the base of her spine while saying, *I love and accept myself.*

Later, girl and dragon swooped down near the crystal cave, where Balidova had mustered up the courage to step into the dark, underground world and learn the last step of the Dragon Tail Breath. This was the place where Luminora had taught her to breathe in the purple light through the crown of her head while saying, *I am me.*

Together, they climbed high above the Giant Sitka Spruce, where Balidova had summoned all her powers together, merged with Mother Nature, and become a *tree of light*, sending a column of rainbow light into the sky, collapsing the Cloak of Fear, once and for all.

Each place held conflicting emotions for Balidova— both fear and love. In each location, something bad AND something good had happened. She had encountered terrifying distress and tremendous joy in each place, unlike anything she'd experienced before. She realized what the dragon said was true.

Everything is connected.

All the 'bad things' had some good that had come from them. All the things she hated had revealed a silver lining that led her to a sense of peace and power she didn't know could exist for her.

Everything really is connected. Everything does happen for a reason. It's all happening for me, not to me.

As she looked down at the Dragon's mane between her fingers, Balidova realized that by learning the seven steps of the Dragon Tail Breath and bringing them into her life, she had learned to harness the dragon magic.

A grin spread across her face, from ear to ear, as she felt a deep sense of satisfaction rise within her. She never imagined she would feel grateful for the difficulties she had faced—being an outcast in her own family, not talking to her mom, feeling pressure to be perfect from her dad, getting bullied by Gus and ostracized by Angel, fighting her sister at the competition, trusting Mr. Winston and then having him spectacularly betray her, battling the Drakoban, and blasting through the Cloak of Fear.

Thank you, all those battles made me stronger. They made me who I am today! Now I know what I can do, and things have gotten so much better with my family. Mom and I are talking now. Dad's not on my case that much anymore. And my sisters, well, we help each other out, sometimes.

She also never imagined she would feel grateful for all the difficult people in her life—her sisters, mom, dad, Angel, Gus, and even Mr. Winston.

Thank you, she whispered, *thank you.*

You made me stronger.

You brought me to the place where I am now.

I know who I am—because I know who I'm not.

Slowly, she turned her head to the left and then to the right, surveying the wide, wonderful, expansive sky that filled her vision. She could hear the dragon's voice continue.

See 360 degrees, my dear. When you are standing on the ground, you see only one degree, but there are 359 more perspectives from which to view everything. Find at least one of them.

Balidova looked down at the specks of houses below, then up toward the clouds. She looked forward at the dragon's flowing golden mane, and behind, at the dragon's colorful tail, silhouetted against the sky.

She could hear Luminora speaking to her silently. *There's a silver lining for you in everything, Balidova, just as there is a halo of light behind these clouds.*

Balidova closed her eyes again, breathing in Luminora's

words. She could feel their meaning in her body, as well as in her mind. She could feel their truth.

Everything is happening for you, dear one. Can you see? Can you see? Whether you like it or not, it is still happening FOR you at any given moment. You are learning how to move between worlds, merge the world of dragon and human together—universe and earth—and blend your inner and outer worlds, as one.

Suddenly, Balidova wanted to let go of the dragon's whiskers. In one sweeping motion, she released her tight grip and lifted her arms into the air, hands above her head, as if riding a bike with no hands. Then, Luminora swerved, and the girl's body lurched sideways. Balidova clutched the dragon's whiskers again, feeling her heart in her throat.

Luminora looked around at the girl and smiled. *At first, it feels like you are swinging wildly back and forth between things you like and don't like, and it's uncomfortable—as your life was before we met. But as you slowly gain mastery over yourself—over your actions, your thoughts, your feelings—as you tune in and listen to your inner voice, as you watch and observe, breathe and pause, as you become more accepting of your sisters, your parents, your friends, yourself, those wild swings become less and less, until they transform into the shape of an infinity loop. Now you are moving smoothly and steadily with the flow —of the cosmos.*

Balidova felt such love for this creature. She wanted to hug the dragon forever. She leaned forward and placed her whole upper body on Luminora's neck, her hands holding tight to the dragon's whiskers and her legs gripping firmly to its body.

There is a form and a structure for everything in your life, Balidova. The universe has a plan for you, that you have been carrying out perfectly—even when you think you haven't. From up here, you can see it. From down below, you cannot.

Balidova breathed in the dragon's words. She closed her eyes and felt the wind on her face, the mist in her hair, the dragon whiskers in her hands.

I can feel it now. I feel as expansive as the sky, grounded as the earth, fluid as the waters, and bright as the sun.

I feel like all the elements are within me.

I AM the sun, soil, sea, and sky.

I am ALL of it.

She breathed deeply.

Good, Luminora said silently, *good.*

Slowly, the dragon circled back through the valley, past the Pacific Ocean, toward the town, and back toward the subdivision where she lived. They dropped lower and lower in the sky, behind the house, through the forest, and into the clearing.

Despite Luminora's substantial size and powerful flying force, they landed gently on the ground. The dragon curled its head toward the girl as Balidova jumped down onto the wing and the earth. Standing in front of the dragon's face, she gasped in awe.

For a moment, she was speechless.

"That was incredible. Thank you. Thank you. I don't know what I would do without you." She spoke out loud now.

"Focus on what you want to create, Balidova. Your words and your thoughts have great power. Use them wisely."

Balidova reached out to smack a mosquito that had landed on her arm. She couldn't see it in the dark, but could feel it on her skin. Her senses were extra strong now.

"See through eyes up high, even as you stand here on the ground. See through new eyes. See through my eyes—everything is happening *for* you. When you breathe the seven colors of the rainbow through the seven energy centers of your body, you will see from a higher perspective. You will see the light and step out of the myopic vision of most humans."

"That's amazing," Balidova said. "The best gift ever."

"That is why it's called the Dragon Tail Breath. Because all colors of light, just like the colors in my tail, bring balance to your life. Just as my tail provides balance to me when I'm in flight."

Balidova stood speechless, in awe of the dragon's wisdom. It all made sense. *Balance the two worlds.*

Dad always says, 'the pen and the sword must be in accord.'

Well I say, **the mind and the heart must not be apart.**

Suddenly, her mind flashed to returning home and getting chewed out by her parents for being outside late at night, and her sisters being terribly jealous when they found out she got to ride on a dragon's back.

"Why was I chosen to do this?"

"You displayed the necessary qualities, my dear."

When Balidova looked puzzled, the dragon continued. "You showed *courage* when you dodged the attack of the wolf pack. That is why I first came out of the woods in the form of a mist."

"Really?" I had no idea the wind of peace was you."

"You demonstrated *compassion* when you protected the spirit bear from the hunter, despite the danger to yourself. That is why I taught you Step One," the dragon explained. "You displayed *connection* when you and Melody figured out where to meet the fish, together. Therefore, I taught you Step Two. You showed *consistency* when you returned to the meadow and met the sunflower. I taught you Step Three. You revealed *clarity* of mind when you stood up to your dad as he criticized you for kicking Gus —earning the right to learn Step Four."

Listening intently, Balidova looked at her arm where the mosquito had bitten her. A tingling sensation was building, and a bump was starting to form.

Watching the girl, the dragon carried on with its answer to the girl's question. "You exhibited *curiosity* at the unusually large number of roots of the double tree, solving the riddle and learning Step Five. You expressed *confidence* in yourself and the dragon magic by returning out into the night after being tied up—hence I taught you Step Six. And in the crystal cave, your growing *consciousness* of everything around and within you, earned you the right to learn the final step—seven."

"Wow. I had no idea I was even supposed to do those things," Balidova looked up at the beast in amazement.

"Over the last seven months, you showed courage, confidence, and consistency in your actions. You demonstrated curiosity, consciousness, and clarity of thought. You displayed compassion and connection from your heart. You have completed your task. Now it is time to *celebrate.*" Luminora finished with a flourish.

Despite the dragon's enthusiasm, Balidova couldn't help but ask, "Am I the only one with these qualities?"

"No. Everyone has them, whether they know it or not. They show up in different ways, and at different times. There is a magic that flows through every person."

"Then why am I the one who had to dismantle the Cloak of Fear?" Balidova asked, puzzled. She looked at the dead bug on her arm, remembering how close she came to meeting the same fate.

"Because that is *your* role to play. Everyone has a different role in the hive of humanity, just like the bees. Yet ultimately, *We are all one.*" The dragon looked at the girl gently. "You have come a long way. You are ready to embrace your true nature."

THE DRAGON LOWERED its head until it was at eye level with the girl.

The girl stood up straight, looking deep into the blazing yellow eyes of the beast. All at once, she realized *that* was the common thing between the different ways the dragon had shown up—they all had yellow eyes! She thought of her beloved golden glasses and felt a resolve swell within her. She had the same eyes. She felt a oneness with the dragon.

"Yes, I AM ready to embrace my true nature." She flicked the dead mosquito off her arm.

"There is value and beauty within everyone, including yourself," the dragon continued. "Not because of what you've achieved, but because of who you are. Practice the Dragon Tail Breath often, Balidova, and feel this truth within you! Until next—"

Before Luminora could finish the sentence, the dragon spread its wings wide, lifted up into the air, and blew a plume of fire downward, lighting the whole meadow in one glorious, fiery glow.

CHAPTER 37
I AM ME

Standing in the center of the meadow, the evening moonlight flowing over her, Balidova could still feel the wind on her face, the warm glow of dragon fire on her skin, and the energy of flying within her body. She took a deep breath, shook out her hands, and pinched herself to make sure she was awake. Even after wriggling her whole body, the feeling was still there.

Calm. Steady. Secure.

She still felt like she had detached from all her fears, worries, and doubts and was floating in a cloud.

After taking a deep breath, she rotated her whole torso from side to side, forming a circle of power around herself. A circle that rippled outward, all the way to the tall evergreen trees at the edge of the clearing. *Even when Luminora's not here, I can feel the dragon's energy in me.*

Arms relaxed by her side again, she took a step forward and scanned inside herself to see if the dragon magic was still there. She could feel her whole body buzzing—open and free.

I want to hold onto this forever.

As she walked to the edge of the forest, she noticed something dark fluttering around her. Its midnight black wings made it look like a moving shadow under the moonlight. For a moment, she was reminded of the Drakoban. A pang of fear shot up her spine. But when she realized it was just a bat, the feeling of calm set in again. She turned around and looked at the center of the meadow, where the magic with Luminora had occurred.

Balidova wanted to stay in the forest longer, but she couldn't. It was late, and her family would be waiting for her. She began the trek back, wondering how she would explain her late-night adventure to her family. Balidova knew she couldn't avoid her day-to-day world and stay in the magical world indefinitely.

I have to find a way of bringing the two worlds together.

As she raced back through the forest, she noticed her senses were heightened. She smelled every mushroom, pine needle, cedar branch, and wildflower despite not being able to spot them in the dark. She saw shadows around her clearly and distinctly—silver rays of moonlight through the trees marking leaves, bark, and stones with an otherworldly glow. She heard all the animals of the night—owls hooting, crickets singing, squirrels rustling, even the bees buzzing. She touched the trees lining the path, feeling the smoothness of the papery birch bark, the sticky sap-filled pustules of the pine trees, and the softness of the cedar skin.

I need something to bring back from the magical world into my daily life. Something I can see, smell, touch. Something I can hang onto.

She picked out a small cedar branch and pulled it from the tree, smoothing its edges in her hand. She paused for a moment, and her smile turned to a frown.

Can I hold onto the magic even in my real world? What's my real world anyway? Isn't being with Luminora real?

∾

SHE REACHED the edge of the wood and stepped onto the Forester family property. It was late evening now, past dinnertime, and she saw no signs of life other than the farm animals. Her cat scampered across the yard. She heard horses stomping in their stalls, getting ready to sleep for the night.

As she walked up to the house, she remembered how Nutmeg usually greeted her, wagging his tail. Now he was gone. "Thank you, Nutmeg, for guarding me," she whispered, wiping a tear from her eye.

Entering the house, it was dark, except for a light at the end of the hall. Balidova wondered whether anyone even noticed that she'd been gone for the last several hours since late afternoon. May would have told them she'd been out in the barn tending to the horses or riding. She did have a habit of disappearing—she needed her alone time.

She walked toward the light but found the kitchen empty, except for a plate of food on the counter. Strangely, she wasn't very hungry, so she opened the fridge to get a snack and pulled out an apple. As she did so, she glanced at the dishwasher and saw the broken cord.

She remembered the moment that seemed to have started it all—the secret vow she'd made to herself to never be weak like her mother. How much had changed since then.

Fruit in hand, Balidova headed upstairs but heard the TV in the living room. She peeked in and saw that everyone in the family was fully engrossed in a movie. Her mom gestured with her arms as if to say, "Where were you?" Then she whispered, "Glad you're back. There's food in the kitchen for you."

Balidova gave her mom a thumbs up.

Continuing up the stairs and swinging open the door of her room, she walked over to her desk and looked at all the artifacts she'd collected over the past seven months. One of the rocks on her desk looked just like the grey and white stone the spirit bear had given her. She remembered how she'd startled the hunter—Gus's dad—before he could shoot the bear. Later, the bear taught her the first step of the Dragon Tail Breath.

No wonder Gus was after me and my friends. If I had told the cops about his dad hunting illegally, he could have gone to jail, and then Gus would have had no one to look after him.

All the pieces seemed to be making sense now. She could see how everything was connected. Continuing to scan her room, she saw the medal the Forester sisters had won in team kata. *I guess all that hard training worked,* she smirked. Now she understood why her dad had been so tough on them. The discipline, excellence, and focus he expected from his daughters had challenged them to reach higher. And they did. They had all learned to project their energy into the world.

Well, that worked—a skill that served me well. Balidova smiled, remembering the explosion of energy between her and the tree that finally disintegrated the Drakoban.

She saw the pine cone the fish had left her, and Betsy, her stuffed horse, who had comforted her when she wanted to talk to her mom but didn't yet dare. All these things she had collected had come to her along with lessons from the owl, bear, fish, and sunflower, which had later transformed into a single being—the dragon.

She remembered the moment she first met the dragon on the mountaintop, and later, when she learned its name. She remembered the oil the creature had given her at the fairground a month ago. That oil had been key to defeating the Drakoban. *How could Luminora have known? Everything is connected. Everything does happen for a reason.* Surveying her room, she couldn't help but think, *In this very spot, where I once felt so trapped in my head that I didn't understand the point of life. Now I feel amazing.*

I finally feel like myself.

Balidova thought of the times when she'd shouted at Luminora to come to her, when she'd been so angry she'd punched a hole in her bedroom wall, and when she'd had a fit at the dinner table in front of the whole family. And yet, the dragon was always there for her. All at once, it dawned on her that she didn't have to be perfect to be loved. *I'm strong enough, smart enough, nice enough, calm enough. I'm good enough. And that's all I need to be.*

She pressed her hands together, touched her fingertips to her lips, and looked out the window at the night sky. A warm river of relief washed over her whole body. *I don't have to prove myself anymore. I'm exactly where I'm supposed to be because this is where I am.*

Balidova pulled the purple crystal Luminora had given her in the cave out of her pocket and put it on her desk. She caught her reflection in the mirror. Looking into her own eyes, she saw beautiful almond-shaped ovals and dark hair. Her scruffy t-shirt, dirty face, and pockmarked complexion didn't matter. Her imperfections didn't bother her in the slightest now.

Quietly at first, and then gradually getting louder, she sang...

> I am me,
> just as I am,
> right here, right now,
> completely free
> to be ME.

She stopped moving and stood absolutely still.

What if, by being me, I can bring the dragon magic into this world?

Her body felt strong. Her mind felt calm. Her spirit felt vibrant. Nothing was holding her back. No fears. No pressures. No pleasing others. She was trembling now.

Not with fear. But with joy.

She reached over and grabbed the purple crystal from her desk, remembering the question she'd asked Luminora when they'd first met, "How will I know I'm the one?" Back then, Luminora's answer didn't make sense to her. But it did now—*When you realize you're good enough just as you are.*

Turning the brilliant rock over in her palm, she chuckled. *All this time, I felt like something was missing. And now, I finally found what I was looking for. It's been here all along.*

As she crawled under the covers of her bed, she placed the crystal under her pillow and lay her head on the downy softness. Breathing quietly, she noticed a stream of silvery light entering through the window. She felt a wave of gratitude for her mother and father, for replacing the broken glass from the rock Gus had thrown, and for all the other things they'd helped her with. *You've both been there for me all along, even when I didn't know it. You sure have different styles, but I don't have to choose between you. You're both alright.*

She turned her body around, so her face was fully illuminated in the moonlight. With drowsiness setting in, the moon looked fuzzy, yet she could feel its protective glow surrounding her. She blinked and widened her eyes. All of a sudden, the white ball came into sharp focus. It reminded her of Luminora's eye—as if the dragon were watching over her right then, guarding her, even as she slept through the night.

All this time, since my birthday, the moon's been guiding me, lighting my way, like a friend—the Wolf Moon, Fish Moon, Flower Moon, Mountain Moon, Tree Moon, Fire Moon, and Crystal Moon. What's a full moon anyway? When the sun's light reflects off the moon back to earth. The earth, moon, and sun are lined up, with the earth in the middle.

Jolting upright in her bed, staring directly into the white light, she suddenly had an epiphany. *I've been in the middle of everything* that's happened since the beginning. That's not a coincidence. Things aren't happening randomly, from the outside in.

They're happening from the inside out. From INSIDE of me.

She paused for a moment before the full force of the realization came flooding in—*my thoughts, my feelings, my actions have been affecting everything.*

Stuff's not happening to me. I'm CREATING it.

With that thought, the dragon magic swelled inside her, rising like a tidal wave from her toes all the way up to the crown of her head as she breathed in, and back down to the soles of her feet as she breathed out.

I feel the love within.

I create from the inside out.

I can balance my two worlds.

She looked out her window and noticed how shockingly beautiful the full moon was. It took her breath away. She watched as thin layers of clouds drifted over, dimming its light. Then smiled as it illuminated fully once again, shining with the full force of its brightness when the clouds passed. The moon seemed to be speaking to her. *Come, I am here for you. I will light your way. See, we can have fun together, you and I. Shining bright and bold in the night sky, even with dark all around. All that darkness just enhances our brightness. Let go of all your fears.*

The brilliant moonlight cleansed her of everything she no longer needed. A twinkle spread across her cheeks as she sunk under her covers and gently closed her eyes.

Yeah, I'm 'the one.' And we're all one.

There's magic everywhere.

What if I didn't doubt it anymore?

I mean, the Cloak of Fear is gone.

CHAPTER 38
THE SECRET

The next morning, Balidova flung her bedroom door open and ran downstairs to find her mom. She entered the kitchen, but her mom wasn't there. *Where is she? I need to tell her what I discovered last night.*

She peeked into the dining room and spotted her mom sitting at the end of the long dining room table, pouring over a photo book. Behind her was a large window framed by golden curtains. A green, ornamental rug rested at her feet.

"Mom, guess what!?" Balidova exclaimed excitedly.

"What?" Her mom answered, somewhat surprised at her daughter's early morning exuberance. "Are you going to tell me where you were last night? May said you were out on a long ride, but when I went to the barn to check on the horses after dinner, Melody was there." She raised her eyebrows at her daughter.

"Bike ride. Long bike ride," Balidova grinned. She was way too excited to be tripped up by minor details.

"And you didn't eat the dinner I set out for you," her mom scolded.

"Yeah, I wasn't hungry."

Before her mom could launch another inquiry, Balidova continued. "You'd never believe what happened," she said breathlessly, "last night, when I was out."

Her mom paused, deciding whether to pursue her line of questioning or move on in the face of her daughter's excitement. She stared at Balidova, realizing the girl wanted her full attention. She chuckled at Balidova's unkempt hair and noticed the girl had her t-shirt on backward. The tag was sticking out right below her chin. She must have been in a hurry when she got dressed this morning.

"Really? Well, tell me."

Balidova stepped right up to the edge of the dining table and placed both palms on the flowery vinyl tablecloth, looking straight into her mom's eyes. "I am me," she said, grinning from ear to ear. "I. Am. Me."

BALIDOVA'S MOM put the photo album down and leaned back in her chair, looking intently at her daughter. She still wasn't used to Balidova confiding in her, even though the girl had told her about the dragon. Although they had made up, the months of not communicating with her daughter over the winter had left a scar on her heart. Yet here was Balidova sharing something very deep. Was this for real? Or was this a joke? Balidova *did* like to play tricks, and this wasn't the answer she was expecting.

After studying her for a while, she decided Balidova meant what she was saying. The glint in the girl's eyes and the glow on her cheeks gave it away. Balidova truly was excited about this discovery she'd made.

"Wow, that's exciting. And so true," her mom replied. "But you could have told us where you were going and that you'd be back late, so we didn't worry about you. Why didn't you come home for dinner, as you promised? It was a little thoughtless, don't you think?"

Balidova was taken aback. She wasn't expecting such a response to her incredible revelation. She blinked and scrunched her face, not knowing what to say. Shocked speechless, an uncomfortable pause filled the space between them.

Seeing how her daughter had reacted, her mom took a few deep breaths. Although she wasn't happy, she decided not to question Balidova about her late-night jaunt anymore, since it had led to such a radical discovery. Instead of criticizing her daughter further as she was tempted to do, she decided to let it go and changed her tone. She raised her eyebrows and smiled with her green eyes. Wisps of brown, shoulder-length hair framed her round face.

"Yes. You are you. There isn't a single person in the world exactly like you."

Balidova pulled up a chair and sat down, resting her back against the hardwood. "I know." She continued. "I just realized it. I don't have to be like you, Dad, my sisters, friends, or anybody else. I can just be me. I want to—no, I *need* to be me." Balidova paused for a moment. "And you know what else, Mom?"

"What?" her mom said, smiling with her mouth too now.

"It feels amazing. That idea feels amazing." Balidova sighed with relief, as if finally coming home after a long time away. "I feel like I'm creating what I want, not just reacting to other people's stuff." She leaned back in her chair and crossed her arms to solidify her point, grinning from ear to ear.

Her mom didn't say a word. She just looked at her daughter and pressed her lips together in a knowing smile, nodding her head as if to say, *That's my girl.*

But Balidova wasn't finished. She leaned forward again, placing both forearms on the table, linking her hands. "There's something else I wanna tell you too, Mom."

"What is it? I'm listening," her mom was very curious now. What else could Balidova have to say? What could top the revelation the girl had already shared?

"Remember when the dishwasher cord got chopped at the beginning of the year? Right after I turned twelve? Well, I was so mad about what happened, I made a vow, in secret, to never be like you."

Her mom furrowed her brows. "Really?"

"You just seemed so powerless to me. And dad seemed powerful. So, I vowed never to be weak, like you." Balidova said the words matter-of-factly, as if they were a perfectly logical conclusion any girl would make under similar circumstances.

"Okay," was all her mom could muster. She sat back in her chair with a slightly surprised and confused look.

"But you know what I realized now?" Balidova continued.

"What's that?" her mom replied, unsure if she should brace herself for more shock or be open to receiving something loving. This had been a very unusual conversation already. What else was coming?

Balidova lowered her voice, almost to a whisper, as if the next thing she was about to say was a secret she would share only with her mom—something special between the two of them.

"You were never weak. Not when Dad chopped the dishwasher cord. Not when you kept silent at dinner when I was getting reamed out by Dad for getting in a fight at school. Not when you told me to let go of my anger at my sisters for marking up my karate gi." Balidova looked down at her hands and thought of all she'd learned from the dragon over the last seven months.

"Gentleness isn't weakness. It's just a different kind of power."

BALIDOVA PAUSED, pursing her lips together now, unlinking her fingers and placing the palms of her hands open. She thought of what she'd learned about the power of kindness, especially toward yourself. The kumite match with May at the provincial team tryouts had shown her how important it was to be kind—and honor—not only her sisters, but also herself.

"I get it now."

Her mom sat still, looking at the girl, speechless.

"I don't have to choose one over the other—powerful like Dad or loving like you. I can be both. Loving and powerful."

Her mom sat back in her chair, watching this display of confidence in her daughter and enjoying every moment of it. She'd been waiting for it. She knew Balidova not talking to her for months was just something the girl had to go through—stuff she had to sort out on her own. She didn't probe her daughter too much on purpose. She just gave her space and let her be.

"Well, it sounds like you're figuring some things out, Balidova," Her mom nodded in agreement. "I knew you'd get it... eventually."

Balidova got up from her chair, walked over, and hugged her mom. At age twelve, she was already slightly taller than her. She pressed her lean body next to her mom's stockier build. They held each other tightly for a while.

"Love you, Mom," Balidova said quietly.

"Love you, too," her mom replied softly.

A few moments later, releasing their grip on each other, Balidova announced, "I'm so glad I can talk to you again,"

"Me too," her mom responded, smiling broadly. She paused for a moment, soaking in the closeness. Then her eyes changed, as if she were thinking about something.

Balidova turned to leave when her mom said, "Don't go yet. I want to show you something."

Now it was the girl's turn to be curious. "What is it?"

Balidova didn't know it, but a calculation was happening in her mom's head. The woman knew she had to tell her daughter sometime. Why not now? When their closeness might soften the blow? And when Balidova's confidence was high and could protect her from the shock?

Balidova's Mom gestured for the girl to sit back down. Then she shifted her attention to the photo album she'd been looking at when Balidova first entered the room. She turned one page. Then another. Balidova watched her carefully.

"See these pictures? They're from Indonesia when you were little." She took a deep breath, contemplating whether or not to continue speaking, then blew out the air with a sigh, having made a decision.

She paused a moment longer. "That's where we got you."

"That's where you got me? What do you mean 'got me'?" Balidova said, taken aback.

Her mom put both hands on her face, bracing herself for what was to come. "Oh gosh, well, I decided a long time ago to tell you when you turned twelve, and it's already many months after that. I'll have to tell you sometime, so it might as well be now."

"Are you hiding something?" Balidova sounded worried. "What's going on?"

Her mom exhaled deeply, blowing out a stream of air from her mouth for what seemed like forever, then spoke slowly. "Before I tell you this, I want you to know something. I am your mom. And I love you."

Upon hearing these words, Balidova's eyes grew wide with worry, and her mind started to race. *What could Mom possibly tell me that's worse than what I've already been through?*

Then her mom just said it. "I didn't give birth to you. You're adopted."

"What?" Balidova's whole body tightened and she recoiled in shock. She started blinking rapidly, lost for words. Her voice caught in her throat—she didn't know what to say. Her heart started beating faster and faster. *No wonder I've never felt like I fit into this family.*

"I'm n-not y-your d-daughter?" She said slowly, deliberately, barely able to get the sounds out of her mouth.

"No, no, you are!" her mom insisted.

"Are any of my sisters adopted?" Balidova asked firmly.

"No, only you."

She was full of questions. Her head was reeling. She didn't know where to start first. *No wonder I'm taller than everyone else in the family. No wonder I'm the only one with a green tinge in my eye. No wonder I'm not like my sisters. No wonder I'm 'the one' and not them.*

"Why?" was all she could muster. "Who are my real parents?"

"We are your real parents, Balidova." Her mom sounded a little desperate now.

"I mean, my biological parents."

Her mom looked hurt. She wished she could reel it all in and put the genie back in the bottle. But now that it was out, there was nothing she could do about it. She had to tell her daughter the truth. She couldn't hide it any longer. She took a deep breath in and let the air flow out her mouth loudly.

"Okay, let me explain. When visiting Indonesia twelve years ago, we came across a couple that brought us a baby. We were at a temple, paying our respects. They came up to us slowly, like they'd been watching us for a while. I remember the woman was wearing a purple scarf with a green dragon on it. We had no intentions of adopting anyone, but the circumstances were very unusual. This couple said their child was in grave danger. And they were Scottish and Chinese, just like us! What are the chances of that? Although the nationalities were reversed—Scottish man, Chinese woman. Indonesia has a large Chinese population, and a lot of Europeans because of the Dutch influence."

"My parents didn't want me?" Balidova said hesitantly, stumbling on each word.

"No, no! They wanted to save you, Balidova. They seemed like really nice people. They said you were in extreme danger—that you would be killed if you didn't leave Indonesia at once. You had to be taken far away and raised in a remote location. Otherwise, the Drakoban would get you. I don't even know what that word means. They were so insistent that they begged us, and we couldn't turn them down. It seemed to be the hardest thing for them. The woman took off her purple scarf and wrapped you with it before she left, sobbing."

Balidova was choking back tears. Her head was reeling with a million questions going a mile a minute. "What? The Drakoban? You knew about the Drakoban?"

"That's all I know. They said something about dark dragons—I didn't know what they were speaking of. I just knew that they were so desperate. They said the Drakoban wanted to squash out the light, and that you were a representation of that light. They said you represented an innocence the Drakoban wanted to corrupt... to make you lose trust in yourself. Then you'd have no hope and would be easily controllable. They said if the Drakoban found you, they would kill you. None of it made sense to me. I asked every astrologer and fortune teller I could find about the Drakoban, but nobody could give me any information. Then I started to think the couple might have been crazy. What the heck was the Drakoban? What were they talking about? The circumstances were so unusual, yet there were too many coincidences."

Her mom paused, leaning forward in her chair, placing her forearms on top of the photo album. She hesitated, then lowered her voice. "We couldn't say no. And I was still reeling from having a miscarriage—"

"—Miscarriage? What's that?" Balidova asked.

"I lost a baby I was pregnant with. It died in my belly. The day we met you was exactly one year from when it happened." She looked solemnly at Balidova, who was crying now, and knew she had to finish the story. "So we said yes. We adopted you."

"Because you lost the other baby?"

"No. Because we wanted you." Balidova's mom suddenly realized how much confusion she was causing her daughter. But there was no way out now except forward—by continuing the story. "They insisted that no one find you. So, we took you back to raise you in remote Kitimat. Once we returned to Canada, I was too busy raising all four girls to think much about it. We gave you the name Balidova because of where you were from. We wanted you to have some connection to that place, even if you left when you were only a few months old."

Tears streaming down her face, Balidova closed her eyes. *I've always wondered why my name was so different from all my sisters' names. How will I ever explain what I've been through to my sisters? How am I ever gonna feel loved?*

SHE LIFTED her chin up to the sky, asking for guidance, from her guardian, from herself. She breathed deeply to calm herself down—in through her nose and out through her mouth. Breathing in, and breathing out. In and out. Over and over again.

Slowly, the deep breaths brought her back to neutral.

She thought of the purple scarf in her room. *Well, at least I know why purple's my favorite color.*

Slowly, she wiped the tears from her face and collected herself again. *Just when I feel like I know who I am—when I finally feel good about myself, I realize I don't know anything.*

Balidova gritted her teeth. A small indent appeared on the lower side of her jaw where her facial muscles clenched—just enough for someone looking at her to know that something inside had shifted.

"This changes everything," she said defiantly.

"What do you mean?" her mom said.

"Mom? Do you know what I've been doing for the past seven months? Remember when I told you in the barn that I've been learning something called the Dragon Tail Breath? I have a guardian dragon." Balidova wondered for a moment whether she should tell her mom. Then she decided her mom had been honest with her, so why not. "The dragon's name is Luminora."

"Oh, wow."

"*I* fought the Drakoban. That's what I was doing last night. That's why I was home late. *I'm* the one they're after. They found me. Even here, in remote Kitimat. The Drakoban found me. Luminora's been training me to fight them! I know how dangerous the Drakoban is. They killed Nutmeg and nearly killed me too."

Now her mom looked at the girl in shock. "What? Nutmeg's gone?"

"The Drakoban burnt him to a crisp in the forest last night. Balidova explained. "And hurt May too. But the forest creatures, the tree and I... we banded together and destroyed it in the end."

This was too much for her mom to take in. They both sat there saying nothing, just breathing for a while.

"Are my parents still alive?" Balidova asked quietly.

"I don't know. I haven't received any news that they aren't," her mom answered.

"Then I have to find them. I have to know." Balidova said softly.

"Know what?"

"If they love me."

"But it's too dangerous, Balidova. And they're halfway across the world. You're twelve! How're you going to do that?" Balidova's mom leaned back in her chair and threw her arms up in the air—the idea was ridiculous.

Balidova looked her mom straight in the eyes. "All I know is that I have to find them," she said with a deep resolve in her voice. "I don't know how, but I will."

Balidova glanced at her red winter jacket—sitting in a heap on the floor because her mom had been meaning to repair the ripped sleeve—given to her on her birthday, when it all began. She did not know then, that such an incredible adventure was before her, just as she did not know now what lay ahead.

Balidova touched the emerald green stone hanging on a string around her neck. *Good thing I've got Luminora to help me.*

My guardian dragon.

She will know what to do.

Message from the Trees

Now that you know the tale of how it all began
come and connect with me.
Put your back against my trunk,
open your eyes and you shall truly see
all that is and all that can be.

MESSAGE FROM THE AUTHOR

This book is based on a true story—my story. I was a lot like Balidova when I was young. I also have three sisters, practice karate, and grew up on a farm with horses in remote, northern Canada—in the Great Bear Rainforest. I too sought love and belonging so badly, I would do anything for it—even give up myself. And I did. By age twelve, I didn't know who I was anymore. I was so busy pleasing others. I thought I had to win at everything in order to be worth anything.

I wrote this book because it's the book I wished I had when I was twelve years old; when I was lost and alone, angry and afraid; when I didn't know who I was, only who I was supposed to be. When competing for everything with my sisters was normal and shaped my entire existence.

Like Balidova, I thought the feminine was weak. And I was not going to be weak. So, I rejected it. As a girl, I rejected a big part of myself. I thought I had to choose between being loving and being powerful—I couldn't be both. I thought I had to be different from who I was in order to be accepted in my family, my school, and my society. I learned to value certain parts of myself [the strong, driven, logical, thinking side of me] over other parts [the softer, gentler, intuitive, feeling side]. I always thought of myself as organized, disciplined, rational, systematic, and thorough, but never as creative. I didn't think I had any creativity within me at all.

It felt awful to be trapped inside my own head. It also felt confusing. I didn't know which way was up or down. I didn't trust my gut feelings anymore. I was always rationalizing and justifying everything. I was dependent on others to show me how I *should* feel—except that they were chaotic and volatile too! Yet I handed my heart over to them. In hindsight, I ask myself, *what was I thinking?*

Well, that's the problem. I was thinking too much. I had closed my heart, letting my mind rule. It seemed to make sense that adults, especially the ones that love you, should know what's best for you, right?

Wrong. I lost my genuine feeling as my guide. I lost my sense of knowing what's right for me, and trusting that knowing. It was no longer *how do I feel*, but *how should I feel?* There's a huge gap between those two questions. One small word makes them worlds apart.

How do I feel? is determined by me entirely. When I say it, I look inside myself for an answer. And whatever the answer to that question, whether it's anger, rage, frustration, depression, guilt, shame, blame, or the other end of the emotional scale—hope, calm, peace, joy, gratitude, happiness, or love—none of these emotions are right or wrong. They just are. Let me say that again, none of these emotions are right or wrong. They just are. Asking yourself *how do I feel*, and accepting the honest answer, is a revolutionary act. It brings you closer to yourself.

How should I feel? is the opposite. It's determined by others. The opinion of your father, mother, siblings, teacher, coach, friend, or minister—it cuts you off from acceptance of your own actual feeling and imposes an external measure that outweighs it

— the opinions of others. In essence, replacing your heart with someone else's mind. And guess what happens when you do that? You go off the rails pretty quick. You feel pretty bad, pretty quick. You are no longer in charge of your own life. You no longer have your built-in guidance system—your emotions—to direct you.

Instead, you are completely at the mercy of others. How you feel is determined by how others think and behave. You are in prison—trapped in your own head with societal and family norms as the prison guards. You are no longer yourself. You are who others want you to be.

The mask of success that I put on to survive as a child only came crumbling down when I had my own children. Only they could show me that I had closed my heart, and it was time to reopen it again.

Slowly, I started to re-discover this other part of me that had been hidden for so many years—the feminine, creative, intuitive, softer, gentler, and loving side of myself. At first, I swung to the other end and rejected the masculine energy of willpower in favor of this new concept of surrender.

Then I learned that I need and want them both. This is the ancient wisdom of the yin-yang and many other traditions. Two opposites, together make a whole. Just like breathing in and breathing out are opposite actions. One is not better or worse than the other, they're just different. Together, they form a whole breath. Similarly, masculine drive/power/doing/thinking AND feminine creativity/love/being/feeling make up the whole of me.

I'm not just one energy. I am both, and everything in between. Not just loving or powerful, but *Lovingly Powerful*. For love is the most powerful force that exists.

Two circles going in opposite directions, when joined together, form an infinity loop. Just as the blend of both love and power, feminine and masculine, feeling and thinking, being and doing, fuel my life, moving me forward in an infinite, universal dynamic flow.

What I live now is a balance of both energies, of all energies. Energy is moving in all directions at any given time, and I ride this wave. That's what feels true to me. Sometimes I push forward and do a lot, moving quickly and even forcefully in the world, setting boundaries and making things happen. My teenage son describes me as 'fierce and loving.'

At other times, I surrender, let go, and don't do much at all. Less is more. I am quiet and still. I rest and restore. I watch, listen, observe, and allow things to unfold. I fill my own tank and receive inspiration and ideas from the quiet, fertile void. In this quiet stillness, I get clear about what my intention is in every area of my life. I ask myself over and over again, *what do I want?*

In this way, I avoid a lot of wasted action, going down paths that lead nowhere, or to places I don't truly want to go. I save my energy for *inspired action*, and let it pour out of me to create what I *really* want. I apply my willpower to it and do not stop until I get my wish. I am relentless in moving toward what my heart truly wishes to create, even if it takes decades. Which is what this book took. This book has been brewing in me for many, many years, and now it's time to share this story with you.

My (inner) intention has led to action. My (outer) action has led to results. Together they lead to both achievement and joy. This is a secret formula for life:

INTENTION + ACTION = RESULTS

Willpower and surrender combine to form an infinite flow of energy fueled by LOVE

...of life

...of nature
...of others
and most importantly,
...of yourself.

My worth doesn't come from what I achieve. It doesn't come from anything outside of myself. My self-worth comes from simply being alive—a living, breathing human being on the planet.

Life is not all about training, doing, and achieving external goals such as medals, money or likes. I now *know* that life is about that and so much more. It's about loving and being loved. It's about enjoying nature and adventures and new things you haven't tried before. It's about exploration of the world out there, and the world inside you—your body, mind and spirit. It's about letting those parts of you grow and evolve into who you are meant to be. Those things are way too big to fit into the box of winning and losing, and way too big to be bound by the constraints of competition and comparison. Don't get me wrong, striving for success is a good thing. It's just not the only thing.

Loving yourself, loving others, loving your life and the world around is a love way too big for any box. It must run free. And when it does, you too will be able to really see. Once again, you will come back to... *I AM ME.*

The journey back to myself has been the most deeply satisfying and rewarding journey I have ever undertaken, in the five decades, across the five continents that I've called home. May this book serve as a guidepost, a map, for you on your journey.

~ Lisa MK Ling

MESSAGE FROM THE AUTHOR

P.S. Dragon magic is real. To make it real for you, use the steps Balidova used and watch it come alive in *your* life. Be patient, and have fun!

Dragon magic is true. The core of this whole book, inside and out, is true. Yes, I did go on that inner journey from hating myself to loving myself, from separation to connection. And yes, there is a Cloak of Fear wrapped around the earth. Can you feel it? Yes, you do have a guardian dragon who can teach you the dragon magic —how to connect to yourself, draw light into yourself, master the elements of you (body, mind, spirit) and become the lovingly powerful creator that you are.

When you believe it, when you allow yourself to feel it, you will start to see it. When you allow the magic of a simple smile, or a butterfly, or a leaf blowing in the wind to touch your heart and warm your soul, it will come alive for you. Why wait? Take a deep breath right now, and enter the dragon world.

Better yet, take four deep breaths. Close your eyes. Get quiet and still. Tune inwards.

Breathe in four seconds... 1...2...3...4.

Breathe out four seconds... 1...2...3...4.

Repeat four times...

What do you notice?

This is the beginning. Welcome to a whole new world.

Now that you have the knowledge, what will you do with it?

Dragon Magic

Body time
Earth time
Soul time
Universal time
merge now as one
for Dragon time has come.

FEEL

Don't think, *feel*
=
understanding.

BREATHE

I breathe in.
I breathe out.
I am perfect
just as I am.

∞

Perfection isn't something you do.
It's something you (already) are.

LISTEN

I am listening...
to the rhythm of my heart
to the beat of my breath
to the sound of my voice
to the tingle of my skin
to the feel of the light.
I am listening to myself.

I am willing...
to be attentive
to the sound of the bees
to the whir of the dragonfly
to the flight of the blue bird
to the light of the moon
to the wisdom and wonder of the old cedar
and the power of the Giant Sitka Spruce.
I am willing to be me.

THE DRAGONFLY OATH

Know your power to create,
for love is stronger than hate.

Speak your truth with kindness,
and let go all your blindness.

Be as calm and still as deep waters
and pass this gift to your sons & daughters.

Accept, Release, Move-on from what you no longer need,
so you never are consumed by hatred & greed.

Fill your body and mind with love,
and free your spirit to rise above.

Beware all. Heed this oath of the dragon that flies
or you'll face your worst demise.

Dear Reader

You expect to find me in the meadow,
But will I be there?
Let go your expectations
and be present, here.

Adapt to your environment
and look for a clue
Become a great listener
of mother nature
and you.

The universe has great adventures in store.
Sometimes you'll meet me
and sometimes you won't.
Sometimes things will go as planned
and sometimes—thank goodness—they don't.
If everything had happened as you'd expected,
we never would have met at all.

Leave the door open
to possibilities you have not yet considered,
to outcomes you have not yet dreamed of.
After all, what harm could a little uncertainty and imagination do?
What do you have to lose?
What if the dragon magic could actually come true?

until we meet again...

LUMINORA

COMING SOON
MEET YOUR INNER DRAGON

LOVE.
POWER.
Play

Acknowledgments

Dear
  MJ
  Bodhi
  Pawan
  my sisters
  my parents
  abba and aji
  writing sisters
  flow circle peeps
  family and friends
  girls karate students
  all the kids I've taught
  clients all over the world
  Debora Seidman Soul Writing
  Ross Kerr of Threshold Healing

From the bottom of my heart, I thank you for your presence in my life, for being my teachers, and for providing the beauty, challenge, and contrast from which this book was born.

And thank you to all the readers of this book. Without you, this book would not have been conceived, nor would it be coming alive in the world today. My deepest gratitude for your imagination and openness to new possibilities.

ABOUT THE AUTHOR

JOY SCIENTIST

Lisa MK Ling (JD, LLM, ARCT) is a world class karate fighter (9x Canadian & World Soke Cup Champion), lawyer (Commonwealth Scholar), musician (Royal Conservatory of Music) and mother (of Bodhi and Meijin). In this way, life trained her in the ways of the body, the mind, and the spirit. Over 50 years, across the 5 continents where she's lived she brought all these elements together to learn how to get in the flow (what she discovered as an athlete), stay in the flow (what she wanted as a mother), and live in the flow (what she teaches as a human potential coach).

After years of stressing, struggling, and sacrificing to achieve success, Lisa realized all those outer wins left her feeling hollow inside. During her subsequent search, she stumbled upon a way of balancing inner happiness with outer success through joy, ease and flow. She now shares *the FLoW method* with others through her books, classes, coaching and events. She teaches people of all ages, and organizations of all types, how to *feel the love within* and create *any*thing from the inside out. By being truly who we are, and loving both the dark and the light within us, we can all harness the power of our inner dragon and fly to our highest creative potential.

CONNECT

As you read/work/play through this book, I'd love to hear from you! Let me know how the *Dragon Tail Breath* is impacting your world and helping you become YOU. Tag me **@lisamkling**

I'm also creating a guided journal, app, and teacher's resource to help you absorb the information in this book and apply it to your daily life—if that's your wish. I'd love your input. Stay tuned by signing up at <u>dragonfly.love</u>.

Book two of the DragonFly series builds on book one. Balidova uses the *four steps of manifestation* to create whatever she wants in her life. These are the same four steps I use and share with my family and clients, along with the Dragon Tail Breath, which I practice daily.

This story is set in Kitimat, British Columbia, Canada on the traditional territory of the Haisla Nation. Where the author was born and raised.

In honor of the land, please respect the forests, the oceans and everything in them. Tread lightly on the earth and cultivate health of your body, mind, and spirit.

DRAGON ~ MAGIC

time to show what you're made of

I AM ME productions present

anytime, anyplace, anything, anyone

from me to you
LISA

Look InSide Always

*Feel the love with**in***
*Create from the inside **out***
Balance the two worlds

Made in the USA
Middletown, DE
05 September 2024